Y0-BVO-500

Special Report

‹Bound to Change:›

Consolidating Democracy in East Central Europe

**Edited by
Peter M. E. Volten**

A15045 210275

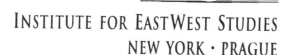

INSTITUTE FOR EASTWEST STUDIES
NEW YORK · PRAGUE

The Institute for EastWest Studies does not take or encourage specific policy positions. It is committed to encouraging and facilitating the discussion of important issues of concern to East and West. The views expressed in this report do not necessarily reflect the opinions of the Board of Directors, the officers, or the staff of the Institute.

Distributed by Westview Press
       5500 Central Ave.
       Boulder, Colorado 80301
       (800) 456-1995

Library of Congress Cataloging-in-Publication Data

Bound to change : consolidating democracy in East Central Europe / ed.
  Peter M.E. Volten
     p. cm. — (Special report)
  Includes bibliographical references.
   ISBN 0-913449-34-2 (IEWS) : $23.85. — ISBN 0-8133-8704-3
(Westview) : $23.85
    1. Europe, Eastern—Politics and government—1989- 2. Post-
communism—Europe, Eastern. 3. Nationalism—Europe, Eastern.
I. Volten, Peter M.E. II. Series: Special report (Institute for EastWest
Studies)
JN96.A2B68 1992
947'.0009'049—dc20   92-26640
                                     CIP

CONTENTS

Vaclav Havel warned euphoric Western observers that the East European revolutions of 1989 would "unleash tidal waves which will continue to disturb the status quo in all parts of the world for years to come." Three years after the revolutions in Eastern Europe, we continue to see those shocks reflected in the post-Cold War environment that has weakened political leadership in the West while contributing to an uncertain political environment in post-communist Europe.

For all practical purposes, communism is dead in Poland, Hungary and the Czech and Slovak Federal Republic. It is nearly dead in the Baltic states, and is in desperate condition in much of the rest of Eastern Europe. Communism and allied authoritarian ideologies are not dead, however, in the former Soviet Union. Moreover, as an ideology challenging open market economies and pluralist democracies, communism and other authoritarian ideologies are alive around the world. Francis Fukuyama was wrong when, in the wake of the collapse of communist regimes in Europe, he wrote his now discredited article in *The National Interest* that "the end of history had arrived." What has ended is the era of Stalinist-inspired communist empire.

This volume presents a much-needed focus on comparative perspectives of the transition from totalitarian rule. George Schöpflin of the London School of Economics deals with the particularly difficult dilemmas of nationalism after communism's demise in Europe. Professor Germaine Hoston, one of the most exciting experts to emerge in comparative politics in recent years, writes a helpful piece about the challenge of democratization in activist states. A useful comparison with the experience in Central and South America is provided by Professors Philippe Schmitter and Terry Karl.

It is necessary that greater attention be devoted to comparative perspectives when analyzing the record and fate of post-communist societies in Europe since 1989. In the spring of 1992, the Institute for EastWest Studies established its fourth major program area to study precisely this issue. The Replication and Transition Program, which captures and replicates the lessons learned from the transition from authoritarian societies in Europe since 1989, is a cross-disciplinary program under the leadership of Professor Yutaka Akino, a member of the IEWS European Studies Center in Prague.

The ultimate test of the power of the revolutions of 1989 will be whether some of the countries of Eastern Europe will successfully complete the transition to pluralist market economies. The Polish, Hungarian, Czech and Slovak states represent the best opportunity for such success. They constitute the case studies in this thoughtful volume edited by IEWS Senior Vice President Peter Volten. The focus on mid-level bureaucracy, the working class, and nationalism present an interesting multi-dimensional view of the complex problems of establishing a functioning democratic political system in post-communist Europe.

This volume resulted from an IEWS special project to test public opinion in Central and Eastern Europe about the obstacles to democratic governance. Special appreciation is due to our colleague Dr. Henryk Szjlafer, a former IEWS staff member now serving as Deputy Director of the Polish Institute of International Affairs in Warsaw, who helped Professor Volten launch this project. In addition, I wish to personally salute Rosalie Morales Kearns, departing IEWS Publications Editor, whose painstaking work is reflected in the high quality of this book and all other Institute publications.

The Institute is grateful to The Ford Foundation for its support of this project and publication. The IEWS also thanks the Rockefeller Brothers Fund, The John D. and Catherine T. MacArthur Foundation, The William and Flora Hewlett Foundation, The McKnight Foundation and The Scherman Foundation for their support of Institute programs.

The Institute for EastWest Studies is pleased to sponsor publication of this volume, the first in a series of works regarding political culture and the striving for democracy. Democracy is no longer an abstract concept for the people of Central Europe. The painful part of the process is how to turn democratic principles and values into concrete political and social decisions which help convince the populace that democracy is indeed a necessity.

John Edwin Mroz
President
Institute for EastWest Studies
Prague
December 2, 1992

Introduction and Assessment
PETER M.E. VOLTEN

> Demagogy is everywhere, and even matters as serious as the
> natural longing of a people for autonomy fuel power plays
> and stimulate deliberate lying to the public.... Many a
> once-feared communist is now an unscrupulous capitalist
> shamelessly and unequivocally laughing in the face of the
> same workers whose interests he once claimed to defend.
> Citizens are becoming more and more clearly disgusted with
> all this, and their disgust is understandably directed against
> the democratic government that they themselves have
> elected.[1]

President Vaclav Havel's somber and discouraging description of the "paradise lost" in Czechoslovakia is not an uncom-
mon tale in the new democracies in East Central Europe. The
smooth transition from communist rule to democracy was soon
followed by scores of problems of unanticipated complexity and
persistence. Above all, the simultaneous change in the political
and economic realm proved beyond the imagination of practitio-
ners and theoreticians alike. Whereas transition in Latin America or Southern Europe concerned merely the change from
authoritarian rule—which appeared more often than not difficult enough—the end of communist rule meant undoing double
totalism and laying the foundations of two buildings in one. The
sequences of the necessary political and economic steps defied
all human experience, and had to be worked out by trial and
error.

Well over two years under way, the new political and
economic systems are taking shape, but the democracies result-

---

1. Vaclav Havel, "Paradise Lost," *New York Review of Books*, April 9, 1992, p.6.

ing from capricious relationships and nebulous interactions between the political community and civil society are uncertain.[2] In which direction are they heading? What kind of democracy will be consolidated in this breathtaking process through a "valley of tears"[3] and agonizing human—individual and group—relations? Worse, will democracy survive or perhaps fall victim to the undemocratic forces looming large on the right and left, and even threatening as an unholy coalition when a desperate society proves ready for these princes of darkness? How real is the disappointment of Havel and other leading democrats or their fear of a "Weimar syndrome"?

In the end, Havel portrays himself, nonetheless, as an optimist: "It is not true that a person of principle does not believe in politics; it is enough for his principles to be leavened with patience, deliberation, a sense of proportion, and an understanding of others. . . . My experience and observations confirm that politics as the practice of morality is possible."[4] *Nil desperandum.* The tremendous efforts of the democratic forces have paid off and will continue to do so. As long as Havel and others crusade against the impulsive parliamentary decision to punish the former communists and high officeholders collectively, i.e., the lustration law, there is hope for reconciliation. In Hungary, President Árpád Göncz opposed a comparable verdict and the Hungarian Supreme Court followed suit, declaring the law unconstitutional. In Poland, revenge against those who were responsible for martial law in 1981, particularly General Jaruzelski, is vehemently opposed by democrats of the first hour like Adam Michnik, the strategist for civil society in "occupied" Poland: "My blackest dream is that we will take all our Communists and send them to Siberia. And then what will we have? Communism without Communists."[5]

Let us remember the extremely short time the transition took. Let us not forget the huge distance travelled from the gruesome, schizophrenic lifestyle under communist rule to the

---

2. See Guillermo O'Donnell and Philippe C. Schmitter, *Transition from Authoritarian Rule* (Baltimore: Johns Hopkins University Press, 1986).
3. Ralf Dahrendorf, "Roads to Freedom: Democratization and its Problems in East Central Europe," in *Uncertain Futures: Eastern Europe and Democracy,* ed. Peter Volten, Institute for East-West Security Studies Occasional Paper, no. 16 (New York, 1990), pp. 10–12.
4. Havel, "Paradise Lost," p. 8.
5. Quoted in *The New York Times,* March 18, 1992.

daunting "opportunities." Let us not forget Havel's famous greengrocer, who acted according to the prescribed "as if" ritual of the system and in doing so himself became a player in the game.[6] Private and official life were opposed yet Siamese twins in "real socialism"—though the official system's life came to dominate personal lifestyle to a mortifying degree. There is no doubt that the fledgling democracies have made a great leap forward under extraordinary conditions. Havel and others are the beacons in treacherous waters, and so far the majority of the population in East Central Europe shares their belief that the new regime is on the right course despite painful setbacks. As a matter of fact, the peoples of East Central Europe have displayed an astonishing patience during the past two years and have proven that belief in democracy is strong enough to offset long economic suffering. Following Huntington's formal criteria, the peoples in East Central Europe have established democracies in their countries.[7] Belief in the best among imperfect political systems, in the promises of liberty, equality, and fraternity, in Western economic success and the Western example of political stability, and in the process of partnership in an interdependent world all foster support for consolidation of democracy. However, belief does not guarantee faith. Even though democracy as a normative model is the point of departure and a powerful weapon against pessimists, disillusioned hopefuls, and old-regime standpatters alike, its rise out of the rubble of "developed socialism" is a Herculean task. The democratic process in East Central Europe is a human struggle for all participants under innumerable threats, even when armed with belief and faith. And all citizens will play their part in the outcome, leaders as well as dispirited, impatient onlookers.

Whether it concerns the silent majority who do not bother to vote or party activists climbing the ladder of political power, a focus on the actors, as individuals and groupings, is essential for observing and evaluating the development of democracies in

---

6. Vaclav Havel et. al., *The Power of the Powerless*, intr. Steven Lukes (Armonk, NY: M.E. Sharpe, 1985), p.16.
7. He defines "a twentieth-century political system as democratic to the extent that its most powerful collective decision makers are selected through fair, honest, and periodic elections in which candidates freely compete for votes and in which virtually all the adult population is eligible to vote." Samuel P. Huntington, *The Third Wave: Democratization in the Late Twentieth Century* (Norman and London: University of Oklahoma Press, 1991), p. 7.

East Central Europe. Democratic institutions are fairly well known, having established themselves remarkably quickly during the transition from communist rule. But they are still shaky and volatile elements in the hands of human players who are learning and internalizing the rules of the democratic game, which Dahl characterizes as participation and contestation in *Polyarchy*.[8] But when are the democratic procedures stabilized and structurized? Can consolidation of the democracies in East Central Europe be seen as achieved when democracy is accepted as the "only game in town,"[9] when political stability, characterized by system maintenance, civil order, legitimacy, and effectiveness exists,[10] or when the "creative chaos of civil society" is working?[11]

In a mature democracy, political and societal actors are mutually and legitimately constrained by written as well as unwritten rules. During the consolidation period, however, actors at all levels of the system are still searching for accepted norms and acceptable habits in their relations with each other. They are acting according to personal interpretations within the bounds of more or less defined fabrics of state and society. The vouchers distributed in the privatization campaign in Czechoslovakia are not meant to fall by the hundreds or thousands in the hands of individuals, but the system allows it and therefore the system itself is to be blamed rather than "smart entrepreneurs." Both President Wałęsa and the Polish government want a strong executive, but they act without a clear constitutional rule to determine the distribution of executive power; the tug-of-war between the two is based on personal views and may be resolved over time only by pressures from a public annoyed by politicking and indecisive government. In Hungary, as Rudolf L. Tőkés argues in this volume, there "is massive disorientation concerning the interpretation and legislative implementation of the government's and opposition's respective electoral mandate."

---

8. Robert A. Dahl, *Polyarchy: Participation and Opposition* (New Haven: Yale University Press, 1971).
9. Juan Linz, "Transition to Democracy," *The Washington Quarterly* (Summer 1990), p. 158.
10. Arend Lijphart, *Democracy in Plural Societies: A Comparative Exploration* (New Haven: Yale University Press, 1977), p. 4.
11. Dahrendorf, "Roads to Freedom," p. 15. See also Ethier's six "principles and categories" favoring consolidation of polyarchic systems. Diane Ethier, ed., *Democratic Transition and Consolidation in Southern Europe, Latin America and Southeast Asia* (London: Macmillan, 1990), pp. 16, 17.

Tamas L. Fellegi points in his contribution to Antall's move to bring the State Property Agency (SPA) for privatization from parliamentary supervision to the realm of the government. While the Antall government extended the powers of the SPA to the management of capital movement, direct parliamentary control was weakened. Worse, "the SPA itself has become a mid-level bureaucracy," with all the potential and real privileges of its new, old, and holdover elites. An example in the economic field is the blurred distinction between civil and uncivil economies during the transition to a market economy. Second and even third jobs, barter, household production, tips, bribes, or foreign currency trade are necessary to survive in present-day East Central Europe, but these disturb a legal economy and civil distribution of wealth and compromise consciousness of correct behavior.[12] In a transition, free interpretations and doubtful, deliberate excuses abound. This is not to say that there should not be a plurality of opinions. The question is whether during the consolidation phase the attitudes, views, and interpretations are becoming more coherent, stable, and more widely accepted and understood. The rule of law is limited when the laws themselves are incomplete and not internalized.

If our understanding of democracy is exclusively one of procedures by which "a state and its relations with society are run,"[13] we would not bother to deal with *what* decision makers and the public think and do. We would merely ask *how* they reach decisions and run state and society. Yet the quality of decisions and the relations between the constituent parts of democratic decision making do matter. They ultimately affect the consolidation of the fledgling democracies. Motyl describes the elements bearing on the quality of democracy as the state, rule of law, civil society, and market economy. He further postulates that they precede democracy in that order of priority (if no state, no law; if no law, no civil society, etc.).[14] The four elements are preconditions for a democracy to work or even to exist. Thus, their development, as well as political and societal views of them, is extremely important for the consolidation process. Due attention to the "substance of regime change"

---

12. Richard Rose, "Toward a Civil Economy," *Journal of Democracy* (April 1992), pp. 18–19.
13. Alexander Motyl, *Dilemma of Independence: Ukraine and the Politics of Post-Totalitarianism* (New York: Council of Foreign Relations, forthcoming).
14. Ibid, chap. 3.

allows for a description of the direction of the consolidation efforts. Moreover, the relationship between the elements and institutional levels of decision making aids in one's understanding of the substance of regime change in terms of "the redistribution of political power, . . . constituency building, . . . and the redefinition of property rights," as Fellegi points out. Finally, attention to the elements of governance may lead to a normative evaluation of the consolidation process, as in the case here of Germaine A. Hoston's conclusion regarding the detrimental impact of Japan's statist ideology on its weak civil society, or Władysław Adamski's advice to coopt the workers' movement in the process of restructuring basic social institutions, or Marek Boguszak's call on the political leadership in the Czech and Slovak Federal Republic to "ensure a civilized, cultured and democratic character of the separation of the common state."[15]

■ *The Legacy of Communism*

After the revolutions of 1989, euphoria and illusions soon gave way to disappointment and the brutally sobering awareness that transformation would be a very long, painful process. Yet hope and belief in the rapidly installed democratic institutions remained overwhelming and led most, if not all, actors to merely look forward, and westward, for a better future that was sure to come. Democratic forces like Solidarity and Civic Forum were all united in the common mission to never permit the return to that dreadful past, to close that chapter once and for all, and to zealously build democracy and a market economy. Marx and Lenin had to be removed from minds, hearts, and memories; their names and those of their followers disappeared quickly from streets and public buildings. Even the word "party," with its negative connotations, disappeared, replaced by "political union," "forum," "alliance," or "movement." Bury the past, forget the evil, let us start with a clean slate, seemed to be the advice. However justified strong resentments against the former communist leaders were, the people had no wish to retaliate in the undemocratic fashion their erstwhile suppressors had shown them, asking, rather, in Tőkés's words, for "symbolic justice and, when warranted by law, financial compensation." "In a fast forward-moving car,"

---

15. For different modes of regime change, see Huntington, "Guidelines for Democratizers," in *The Third Wave*.

Vaclav Klaus once said, "one should not look too much or too long in the mirror."

But the legacy of 40 years of communism has not died so graciously. Ingrained habits, views, even sentiments could not be wished away by looking exclusively forward. The denial of the past, however understandable and in some ways laudable, has its drawbacks. The Olympian jump forward is, after all, an attempt by an injured person, whose landings are not only physically painful, but also mentally disorienting, as progress is not easily forthcoming. In 1992, we are familiar with high inflation, soaring unemployment rates, and drastic losses in real income; these sad experiences need not be addressed here in any detail. They are discouraging enough in and of themselves. But what is often overlooked is that this predicament was forced on a people unprepared. They were not ready for still more deprivation under circumstances theoretically better, not worse, after the revolutions. Consolidating democracy has therefore proved so much more difficult under the burden of the inherited value system. Progress has been impeded by theses and opinions glorified for over 40 years, for instance that

1. Society should not be overly differentiated; people's living standards ought to be as equal as possible.
2. Everyone must work, regardless of whether one's work is meaningful or productive.
3. State institutions know best how to satisfy people's needs; people need not care excessively for themselves.
4. The living standard need not be high, provided it is secure.[16]

■ *Grassroots Views*

Surveys conducted under the auspices of the Institute for EastWest Studies in Poland, Czechoslovakia, and Hungary in October 1991 confirm the ongoing impact of the socialist way of life, as well as the ensuing confusion over the introduction of market principles.[17] Of course, people would like to enjoy the best of both worlds: free health care, free education, subsidized housing, and job security on the one

---

16. Jiri Musil, "Czechoslovakia in the Middle of Transition," *Daedalus* (Spring 1992), p. 191.
17. The surveys were conducted by the Institute for Opinion and Market Research (PENTOR), Warsaw; the Social Research Information Center (TARKI), Budapest; and the Center for Empirical Research Institute for Sociology (STEM), Prague.

hand, and the benefits of equal opportunities for honest entre-preneurs in a limited number of privatized sectors on the other. Economic transition is confusing. Witness, for example, a poll in Hungary in which 69% disagreed with the statement that "it is right that some people earn millions," but 78% agreed that "competent people in our society now have the opportunity to earn a lot of money." Significantly, more than 70% find at the same time that "people get rich here mainly in an illegal way."

State intervention in the economy and the preservation of economic equality are still highly valued, especially in Poland. The government is seen as responsible for supporting agricul-ture (91%), providing jobs for all those wishing to work (83%), keeping prices under control (79%), subsidizing basic foodstuffs (79%), reducing income differences (62%), controlling prices by legislation (74%), subsidizing suffering industries (63%), and passing laws that set limits for maximum and minimum wages (56%).[18]

Reform is definitely perceived as a mixed blessing, depend-ing on where one sits. In his chapter on privatization, Adamski differentiates between various branches and levels of education/ expertise. Although opposition to (limited) privatization is de-creasing in some areas (press and publishing, banking, com-merce, and state farms), Poles are vehemently opposed to commercialization of health services (74% in the survey) and at best lukewarm to the unlimited privatization of large enter-prises. Opposition to any kind of privatization of large industrial enterprises is particularly strong among those who hold posi-tions in the high- and mid-level bureaucracy of the state-controlled sectors. Not surprisingly, farmers, particularly the more vulnerable part-timers, and workers who are less skilled are also skeptical, the former even highly skeptical about the looming expansion of privatization.

The result is a great deal of fear for the future. Fear, however, is a bad counselor. Even though fear apparently applies first and foremost to socioeconomic dissatisfaction, this is easily translated into political disillusionment. In this respect, a striking plurality of 40% of the Hungarian respondents in the survey considered the new regime worse or much worse than the *ancien régime*. Only 31% favored or strongly favored the present regime. While the current economic situation was not

18. PENTOR survey, p.7.

worse, probably better, than in Poland and Czechoslovakia, many Hungarians nonetheless perceived the new regime as unfavorable compared to the "goulash communism" of János Kádár. However, the majority of Hungarians applaud the new developments, and political attitudes toward the old regime were not so favorable. Therefore, it is likely that the major cause of dissatisfaction lies "in economics, rather than in politics."[19] By the same token, the enormous discrepancy between the Czechs and Slovaks as to the positive evaluation of the present regime (71% versus 43%) may be ascribed not only to the political rivalry between the two republics, but also to the both perceived and real economic disadvantages of Slovakia under the new market conditions (15% of the Czechs and 35% of the Slovaks considered the present regime worse or much worse than the past one). In turn, as Boguszak notes, "a natural consequence of the feeling of economic injustice is a tendency toward separatism. Among the inhabitants of the Slovak republic who believe the present system favors the Czech republic, 37% support separation, while only 14% of the others share that opinion." In Poland, appreciation of the new regime relative to its predecessor did not fare much better (41% rated it better or much better while 23% rated it worse or much worse), despite the more severe economic circumstance in the 1980s and the rather successful first phase of the Balcerowicz recovery plan. Indeed, people do look backward when they evaluate the present and they do so in large part looking through "old lenses." To illustrate this from a different perspective: no less than 75% of the Hungarians polled found that "the government undervalues the provision of social security to the population." Only about 20% disagreed with that statement.

Fear is omnipresent, but there are significant differences between the better educated, urban, and young and the blue-collar, rural, and older parts of the population. Fear is divided unequally in another way as well. In Hungary, the most pessimistic answers to questions concerning socioeconomic development refer to the general, nationwide expectations rather than to a respondent's future. The saying "one cannot survive without friends" apparently outlives the old regime, and the prospects for society as a whole under the new regime are viewed with greater fear, possibly even greater skepticism. Aloofness

---

19. TARKI survey, p.8.

and apathy vis-à-vis the state have become longtime companions of the East Central European peoples. Few bothered themselves over who ruled, and few knew their names or were familiar with the decisions proclaimed, for so often they proved to be non-decisions taken by anonymous collectives. This mood persists under the new regimes, as Mason, Nelson, and Szklarski observed in 1991 in the case of Poland:

> The post-Communist fledgling democracy in Warsaw today is burdened with attitudes of social disintegration which undermine all kinds of authority, not only Communist. What the government needs now is help from society. This help should come in the form of altruism, cooperation and trust.[20]

Altruism, cooperation, and trust are in very short supply in a society where individualism and materialism are the standard bearers, by necessity or even by virtue. "The only well-articulated interests in Poland today, ironically," writes Krzysztof Jasiewicz elsewhere, "are the residua of the *ancien régime*: the interests of the workers employed in the mammoth, uncompetitive state enterprises, and the interest of socialist private farmers."[21] Support or opposition to change is "determined by existential and statutory group interests rather than by these groups' fundamental ideals and guiding values," adds Adamski in his chapter here. In an environment where economic change is increasingly perceived as a threat rather than an opportunity, relations are likely to be seen in zero-sum perspectives, if not directly between individuals, then between small and narrowly defined parochial entities. "We the People" of 1989 was followed by Garton Ash's aptly captured hopeful outburst "Après le déluge, nous."[22] It now seems to be degenerating into a desperate "Après le déluge, moi."

■ Civil Society

A fragmented society, thriving on a great deal of egoism, conflict, and mistrust, is not conducive to the establish-

---

20. David S. Mason, Daniel N. Nelson, and Bohdan M. Szklarski, "Apathy and the Birth of Democracy: The Polish Struggle," *East European Politics and Societies* (Spring 1991), p. 233.
21. Krzysztof Jasiewicz, "From Solidarity to Fragmentation," *Journal of Democracy* (April 1992), p. 67.
22. Timothy Garton Ash, "Eastern Europe: Après le Déluge, Nous," *New York Review of Books*, Aug. 16, 1990.

ment of a market economy. As long as civil society is defunct, the "rules of the game," including those of the market, are tenuous and lacking in direction. Laws can be written, but without institution building through civil society, the legal system either remains abstract or turns into a repressive device. Furthermore, institution building must take place in the nonmaterial sphere as much as in the economic one. Civil society must develop healthy cross-cutting identities throughout all segments of the nation. A civil society is not an arithmetic accumulation of individual and group interests,[23] but an interrelated, non-zero sum set of transactions.

The problem is not that there is no plural society in East Central Europe today. Institutional plurality has developed rapidly, as seen in the numerous societies, clubs, local and regional unions, and political movements. But they still seem to be the product of the reaction against the former centralist mammoth. Their identities are almost one-dimensional, and they appear as thousands of separate islands, an archipelago, but one without connections. Their whole is not more than the sum of their total. The shock of the liberation from the yoke of communism has produced a fragmented, imbalanced social fabric rather than a plural society with overlapping and cross-cutting segments.

There may be one focus of overarching loyalty that survived communist rule and, as George Schöpflin describes in this volume, is resurfacing as a source of identity: nationalism. But, as he explains, nationalism may not revive the "moral-cultural universe" of the peoples in East Central Europe and thus positively contribute to a new identity of an open society. Instead, its origins in culture and its affective, uncompromising nature may be confused and abused in the political realm as a means in the struggle for power. The interests of nationalism supersede all others. "Social atomization, conflicting interest, and group and individual egotism,"[24] as Geremek remembers

---

23. "Civil society can be conceived as an aggregate of institutions whose members are engaged primarily in a complex of non-state activities—economic and cultural production, household life and voluntary associations—and who in this way preserve and transform their identity by exercising all sorts of pressures or controls upon state institutions." John Keane, *Democracy and Civil Society* (London: Verso, 1988), p. 14.
24. Bronisław Geremek, "Civil Society Then and Now," *Journal of Democracy* (April 1992), p. 10.

from his struggle in Poland, may be suppressed but not healed. Domestic identities will again be locked up in a closed society, at least for those with a minority view. Many Slovaks view the federal government, Prague, or indeed the Czechs, as the new interventionists, who to their own advantage replace communist centralism as the root of the economic problems in Slovakia. At the same time, Boguszak adds, "among those inhabitants of the Slovak republic who consider the Czech republic to have the advantage in the present system, 66% disagree that Hungarians living in Czechoslovakia [i.e., Slovakia] should have the same right to use their own language as Czechs and Slovaks, while among others it is 46%." Nationalism and separatism are tested vehicles to use in blaming others for the current difficulties. "Among those who are in favor of the separation of Czechoslovakia into two independent states, 21% in the Czech republic and 80% in Slovakia think that Jews have too much influence on political or economic life." Nationalism in this sense reduces civil society, hampers its autonomous institutions, and curtails its input in the democratic reflections of government. Nationalism must be "secularized and subject to other influences." If not, Schöpflin asserts "the propensity to see all matters as involving nationhood, whether properly related to nationhood or not, [remains] one of the key characteristics of the contemporary Central and East European scene."

Whatever the intensity of nationalism and other nonmaterial interests are, the conflict with the primacy of material interest will continue for a long time and by its nature will never be completely resolved. As a matter of fact, there is no answer to the question of what comes first: bread or political freedom? Communism collapsed once the rulers conceded that "if you cannot give them more bread, give them more freedom," but there is no solution now by changing the latter clause into "give them more nationalism." On the contrary, democracy is a precondition for containing overly nationalistic policies and balancing material and nonmaterial interests.

During the consolidation of democracy, economic and political reforms are both necessary, but neither one is sufficient. They are related, yet require separate treatment, and the time frames for achieving political and economic reform may differ considerably, as Hoston so clearly demonstrates for the Japanese road to modernity.

Given these complexities, Dahrendorf has concluded elsewhere: "This is not exactly an encouraging story. Political transition leads to economic frustration, resulting in instability and unrest. Economic transition leads to political frustration, resulting in instability and unrest. Either way, liberty is the victim." Freedom is a prerequisite for civil society—the key to any successful transition—and economic transition "needs free and empowered citizens as much as a political community that is moving from one-party rule to democracy."[25]

But can we expect enough energy and power from the shattered "We the People" to build more than the fledgling, fragmented civil society we have seen emerging in East Central Europe? Or do they have to rely more on "the political community"—the elites in and out of government—in building the "vibrant 'public sphere' between the state and civil society," as Hoston implies? She also refers to Easton's central concept of the state's role in the "authoritative allocation of values for a society," acknowledging the influence of the activist state as much as the need for an independent sphere of social life that influences that allocation. Hoston clearly sets out the threats that Japan's statist ideology and the interpenetration of the public and private spheres by patronal cliques and political "corporations" pose to civil society and democracy. However successful its industrial development, the Japanese activist state at the same time assumed a damaging influence in the allocation of values, as in the cases of regime-biased education, suppressive laws, or the impediments to organization and association of public dissent and opposition.

■ *Political Community*

An activist state need not be the same as an activist political community, comprised of a wide variety of elite groups and political parties; the key is the distribution of power. Whereas the former as a single actor may wield too much power in the political process and use it to the detriment of civil society and against opposition, the participants of a political community are power contestants by definition. In modern societies, the distribution of political power largely rests in the hands of parties. Political parties play a pivotal role in *power politics* between government and opposition, as *power brokers* between

---

25. Ralf Dahrendorf, "Transitions: Politics, Economics, and Liberty," *The Washington Quarterly* (Summer 1990), pp. 139 40 and 142.

government and interest groups, and as *power mobilizers* among interest groups and in society at large. Parties are the most prominent means for furthering horizontal and vertical integration, while at the same time allowing a mechanism of checks and balances in the power structure. As the leading parties can be called upon to take part in government, they are both power holders and mobilizers, and in that sense they can provide the "vibrant 'public sphere' between state and civil society." Then, they will also actively allocate values for society. Such a political community is called upon to be an important thread of the social fabric as the mass of free citizens proves unable to sort out the many issues at stake in a modern state. The highly fragmented and segmented societies in East Central Europe badly need the binding and organizing power of parties for the consolidation of democracy. "Organization is the road to political power, but it is also the foundation of political stability and thus the precondition of political liberty. The vacuum of power and authority which exists in so many modernizing countries may be filled temporarily by charismatic leadership or by military force. But it can be filled permanently only by political organization."[26]

In order to avoid the unstable or undesired military leadership mentioned by Huntington, parties need by implication structured leadership among and between themselves. In that regard, an enormous responsibility rests in the hands of the political elites in East Central Europe. Because fragmentation there is so great (and thus interest articulation weak), and because political participation is low (and thus the dependence on the elites so high), the social fabric has to be woven to a very large extent from the top.

What inevitably comes to mind from these observations is the desirability of embarking on a consociational course in consolidating democracy. As Schöpflin argues, "consociational systems seek to draw all the different segments into the decision-making process through elite representation, a kind of grand coalition." For this to happen, Lijphart's consociational model requires that the elites show "coalescent behavior." Adversarial behavior would lead to or reinforce the unstable situation of "centrifugal democracy."[27] To be sure, there is no guarantee that

---

26. Samuel P. Huntington, *Political Order in Changing Societies* (New Haven: Yale University Press, 1968), p. 461.
27. Lijphart, *Democracy in Plural Societies*, p. 106.

in a plural society consociationalism will bring about political stability. Moreover, it is sometimes argued that the compromises between the dominant actors among coalitions during the consolidating phase are dependent on the prior existence of social consensus. The latter precedes compromise but rarely survives it, as we have indeed seen during the transition in the common opposition against the communist regime that evaporated after the transition.[28] The breakup of Solidarity and Civic Forum and the multiplication of parties and party elites attest to that fact in Poland and Czechoslovakia and to a lesser extent in Hungary. Finally, the considerable lack of articulation of interests in party programs and the diffuse aggregation of elite views complicate the delineation of coalescent or adversarial attitudes. For example, it will take time before the four major dimensions of the differentiation of political opinion and beliefs Jasiewicz describes here can be identified with certain political elites and parties in Poland. He concludes that there is practically no correlation between these dimensions: "knowing a given party constituency's position on one [issue] hardly helps us predict its location on another. To reduce this complex picture to a single-dimensional one (left-right, or along any other lines) would be an oversimplification. For the present fragmentation of the Polish Parliament, neither a bad electoral law (which could have been better) nor inexperienced party leaders (who could have acted more wisely) should be blamed. This fragmentation reflects the state of mind of the public; lost and confused, facing so many choices and so few constants."

One can only hope that party organization, elite education, and dialogue will enable the Polish political community to get out of this vicious circle. If not, the dangers of a centrifugal democracy are becoming very real, and consociationalism will be precluded. But if the elites assume real leadership and show coalescent behavior, then the stabilization and consolidation of the uncertain democracy are feasible, for "under the unfavorable circumstances of segmental cleavages, consociational democracy, though far from the abstract ideal, is the best kind of democracy that can realistically be expected."[29]

---

28. Ethier, *Democratic Transition*, p. 13.
29. Lijphart, *Democracy in Plural Societies*, p. 48.

■ Three Different Countries— Three Different Democracies?

The three countries under discussion differ in important ways from each other, particularly regarding the degree to which they now resemble or are likely in the future to resemble a consociational or other form of democracy. Consociational characteristics are present in all three countries, though. It is fair to say they will be plural societies and be governed by coalition governments. The fragmentation of civil society is apparent in all three countries as well. Furthermore, the role of the Roman Catholic Church in Poland, the strong and politically powerful banking and business elite in Hungary (as both Tőkés and Fellegi point out), the general differentiation of social classes in all three countries, or ethnic cleavages (above all in Czechoslovakia) already reflect or carry the seeds of segmented cleavages. In their diagram in their chapter in this volume, Philippe C. Schmitter and Terry Karl place Czechoslovakia closest to the consociational model. However, they put Hungary halfway between their consociational and corporatist labels and Poland close to the populist type of regime, which is also characterized by a powerful state and weak societal input in the democratic system. They observe that "one kind of democracy may gradually evolve into a qualitatively different kind." Indeed, the question is: in what direction are these democracies moving during the consolidation process?

Huntington has characterized Poland's transition as "transplacement,"[30] a gradual change of power from the communists to the opposition via vibrant societal resistance, roundtable negotiations, and a mixed communist-democratic Parliament. Poland's freely elected Parliament in the fall of 1991 was to be the final blow to the communists, who were pushed back into a minority in opposition. Significant for the Polish liberation was that the opposition under communist rule turned to society and introduced an "evolutionist strategy" (Michnik) based on the autonomy of society outside the state. One premise of that strategy was "that Polish society should muster enough courage, determination and faith in itself to keep up pressure long

---

30. Huntington, *The Third Wave*, chap. 3.

enough to realize those aims."[31] The reinvigorated civil society proved, if not always vigorous, tenacious and—in the end—successful. National identity was vindicated, slowly but decisively.

Under the new circumstances, however, populism rather than popular appeal may affect the nature of the regime. The sixty-odd percent that does not cast its ballot is a troublesome majority that may push Schmitter's present classification towards the upper right in his diagram. If Wałęsa wins his battle with the government and Parliament about a strong presidency, or if another Tymiński stands up in new presidential elections, the distribution of power in favor of the state under populist rule may become reality. The fragmented society and segmented polity would continue to exist, but would become surrogate participants in the democratic process. If, as Jasiewicz asserts on the other hand, the *pospolite ruszenie* is finished and the present pattern of numerous parties continues, Poland could become an "electoralist" democracy, with a weak multiparty government and the instability of centrifugal democracy. While avoiding a populist, strong state regime, the consolidation of plural society and the creation of a stable government would largely depend on the ability of the elites to articulate plural views and to behave in a coalescent way. An essential and most immediate step for Wałęsa and the new government should be agreement on an electoral law reducing the number of parties and a constitutional arrangement prescribing the powers of the president, government, and Parliament. That is, Poland could build democracy through consociationalism.

In Czechoslovakia, transition took the form of "replacement" of the old regime rather than transplacement. The spark of the student revolt and the collapse of the regimes in the neighboring countries allowed the formation of a new government in a matter of days, not months.[32] The contrast between old and new elites is the strongest in Czechoslovakia. Consociational democracy seems the best one can get, given the Czech-Slovak strife on top of all the other divisions the new democracy is experiencing.

---

31. Z.A. Pelczynski, "Solidarity and The Rebirth of Civil Society in Poland, 1976–81," in *Civil Society and the State*, ed. John Keane (London: Verso, 1988), p. 362.
32. I differ here with Huntington, who classifies the Czechoslovak transition as transplacement.

The suffering in both parts of the country is uneven, or is at least perceived as such. Moreover, whereas the Slovaks see themselves as the underdogs or a Czech "colony" in their history until Husak elevated Slovakia to at least an equal status after 1968, the Czechs lived through the "destruction of the Bohemian tradition"[33] and the brutal disconnection from "their attachment to Western culture," a distinct feature of this country in the region.[34] For the Czechs, their historically ingrained impulse for freedom and social progress was freed in 1989, and the transition is seen as a promising second chance in this century. If the federation in one form or another is to survive, there is little else than consociational democracy the elites can pursue in consolidating and stabilizing the political order in the Czech and Slovak Federal Republic. No doubt, the federal state and government will be weakened as a result of the June 1992 elections. The two major parties and their leaders, Klaus and Meciar, are too far apart both in national-ethnic and political-economic terms to form a strong government backed by a homogeneous majority in Parliament. Even so, prospects for a consociational democracy in Czechoslovakia are dim; centrifugal forces are likely to continue to confirm the de facto split of the polity and society.

In the event of a formal division into two states, democracy may fare better in the Czech republic than in Slovakia, where populism, nationalism, the Hungarian minority question, and economic deprivation are likely to complicate the democratic process. Meciar and his nationalist colleagues, possibly even coalition partners, will have to explain a great many things to a population that to date never has counted a majority in favor of secession. As Boguszak observes, "In Slovakia, the clear victors [in the June 1992 elections] were the parties that advocated fundamental change not only in economic reform but also in the federative arrangement." And, he concludes, "the confederative principle is the most strongly advocated." However, Meciar and the victorious parties have pushed their nationalistic views quite far and have antagonized their Czech counterparts, perhaps too much for them to consider a confederation of sorts. Meciar's campaign is an example of how harmful elite behavior can be by

---

33. Mihaly Vajda, "East-Central European Perspectives," in *Civil Society and the State*, ed. Keane, pp. 354–55.
34. Jacques Rupnik, "Totalitarianism Revisited," in *Civil Society and the State*, ed. Keane, p. 287.

turning a smoldering issue of the people into a heated debate and by confusing an ethnic-cultural question with a political power struggle. Pushing sensitive issues unnecessarily far in a segmented society can only hurt the consolidation of democracy, and Meciar's and others' records do not look promising for democracy in an independent Slovakia. Whereas a democratic coalition may be found in the Czech lands, the danger of a populist government with possible authoritarian tendencies looms in Slovakia.

In Hungary, the transition was first a "transformation" of the economic order into "goulash communism" and then the more sudden attempts since 1988 to reform the political system from within. Characteristically, this was an elitist affair, and has endured as such. Even during the pathbreaking roundtable negotiations in 1989 between the communists and the opposition, the public at large was hardly involved. The "pact" between the Hungarian Democratic Forum and the Alliance of Free Democrats half a year later was another expression of elitist, even paternalistic politics, reminiscent of precommunist times. Yet the pact was a brave act rendering a service to a workable parliamentary democracy. From the point of view of party interests, the future opposition party—the Alliance of Free Democrats—surrendered its power to block legislation, a seemingly naive decision; from the point of view of democratic consolidation, however, it helped to clearly delineate government and opposition, and paved the way for constructive legislative work. Just as important was the agreement about the powerful position of the prime minister, which was to ensure a strong government. This agreement also proved an altruistic gesture rather than power play, as the opposition soon felt Antall's performance to be exceedingly centralist and individualist. Antall's coalition government, and in particular his own party, acts as if it were the single power, almost as in a majoritarian system. Party allegiance is crucial for the—rather frequent—hiring and firing of ministers and even senior "nonpolitical" nominees. This style has led to an increasing polarization between government and opposition, a strong perception of "us versus them." This was illustrated when Jeszenszky "declared dissent in general, but social democracy and liberal politics in particular, un-Hungarian, and defined the notion of 'Hungarian' in only Christian terms," as Fellegi reminds us. It is doubtful whether this quasi-majoritarian style will disappear after the next elections and another coalition takes office. Rather, Hungary seems to be moving in the Schmitter/Karl diagram towards the upper left corner, establishing what could be called a "corporatist-coalition" democracy. In a way, one can even speak of continuity as regards the style of the previous regime. "The frustrated electorate," concludes Tőkés, "remained unconvinced that what transpired in Hungary was a change of the political system rather than a mere shuffle of the ruling elites."

The corporatist label also implies a powerful state and its bureaucracy, and Hungary is no exception. Although the transformation process before 1989 allowed the movement from party to state and private positions, the new elites did not purge the holdovers, but largely maintained "a marriage of convenience." Regionally and locally, old elites were reelected in great numbers, state officials found their way to state enterprises, and the most competent among them survived in private business. In other words, the former party-state network that penetrated the society and economy so deeply was not replaced or disrupted, but was rather transformed and complemented with the new elites. As pointed out earlier, the Antall government used its power to control the redistribution of massive state assets, but the role of "corporatist" networks of all three elites should not be discarded. According to Tőkés, "It will be this new bourgeoisie that will determine the shape of Hungary's politics in the years to come. . . . It is the short-term outcome of the inter-elite competition for shares from the economic carcass of the old party-state that will decide the future balance of political power in Hungary."

The consolidation of democracy in Hungary has come a long way, in large part because of the strength and energy of the political community. It is clearly an example of democratization from the top. Hungary knows an activist "'public sphere' between the state and civil society," although one should add that the political community's identity, particularly that of the government, tends to coincide with the state itself. The parties and political elites are only remotely connected with society at large. The bridge to civil society is unfinished, and it is likely to take considerable time before parties have planted their roots firmly among a stable, responsive electorate.

The consolidation of democracy in the three East Central European countries is taking place in different ways and is producing different political orders. They all face serious and often similar difficulties, particularly in economic reconstruction. Yet the legacy of communism rests on different cultures and is different in itself in each country. Thus, the harsh communist rule after 1968 produced a spiritual void in Czechoslovakia, and its special treatment in the industrial development of Slovakia accounts for specific problems that Hungary and Poland do not face. A civil society has to be built from scratch, the intelligentsia is sparse and aloof, the state is in danger, and the federal government weak and divided. In Poland, fragmentation has taken place at all levels, ruining the *pospolite ruszenie* and splintering the political leadership. The remnants of the state may still be relatively robust enough to support populist, centralist rulers, but will not satisfy a quarreling, electoralist regime for too long. Civil society has evaporated as a political force. The crucial question in both countries is whether the elites are able and willing to embark on the road to a consociational democracy, admitting or even encouraging diversity and pluralism between their constituencies but simultaneously seeking compromise in governance. Political organization and party formation are the key to the consolidation of democracy and all the elements bearing on its quality. In Hungary, the economic choices may not be less painful and the political stakes not lower, but the political and social fabric has withstood the pressures from below so far. A traditional inclination towards elitism and centralism resurfaced and seems to be accepted, though grudgingly by the opposition, as a trusted means to regime consolidation.

■ *The International Community*

The domestic developments described in this volume, no doubt, were in the past two years and will be in the future influenced by the international community. If Gorbachev had not decided to let East Central Europe go, the threat of military intervention would have prevented even the beginning of the revolutionary changes we have witnessed. The collapse of the Warsaw Pact and CMEA has had a dramatic impact on the political and economic orientation of East Central Europe. Association with the European Community opens new avenues, notwithstanding the fact that the real benefits will trail behind aspirations for some time to come. All the same, Hungary, Poland, and the CSFR are back in Europe, with which their future is intimately linked.

This is perceived as a success of foreign policy and a

blessing for these countries, but it may also in certain ways be a curse. The industrialization and modernization in East Central Europe on the "periphery" will also include drawbacks vis-à-vis the "core" industrialized world. These countries might find "that economic processes are interdependent and that while the progress of one sector may become the source of a beneficial 'spread' effect, it can also cause a more deleterious backwash, creating stagnation and decay, even as it reproduces and magnifies existing patterns of international income inequality."[35] It has already become increasingly clear to many observers that Western assistance may lead to dependence rather than to domestic strength and viability. Markets are likely to remain closed, except for a brain drain, and the economic policies of the East Central European countries may have to be shaped too much according to Western interests.[36] Arbatov has warned about the "Neo-Bolsheviks of the IMF" and concludes that "far more than the personal reputation of Mr. Gaidar, Jeffrey Sachs . . . and a bunch of anonymous IMF experts are at stake. More important are the reputations of the market as an institution, Russia's leadership and, finally, the West, for it has taken on itself a great responsibility."[37] By the same token, in the longer run disappointment and remorse rather than rejoicing will overshadow East Central Europe's relations with the West. The consolidation of democracy will be supported only to some extent, while the perception of an international partnership will be damaged. A perceived failure of this spectacular chance to join the community of democratic and free nations could have detrimental domestic effects, especially where nationalistic sentiments are an easy prey for the mobilizers of forces of discontent. This is not to say that the West should do more in economic and financial terms, which is not the subject of this study.[38] The point is that

35. Andrew C. Janos, "Social Science, Communism, and the Dynamics of Political Change," *World Politics* (October 1991), p. 104.
36. See Peter Gowan, "Old Medicine, New Bottles: Western Policy toward East Central Europe," *World Policy Journal* (Winter 1991-1992), pp. 1–33.
37. *The New York Times*, May 7, 1992. See also "Critics Accuse IMF of Being Inflexible in Seeking Changes in New Democracies," *The Wall Street Journal*, April 13, 1992.
38. For an assessment of the Western effort to assist Central Europe, see *Moving Beyond Assistance: Final Report of the IEWS Task Force on Western Assistance to Transition in the Czech and Slovak Federal Republic, Hungary and Poland* (New York and Prague: Institute for EastWest Studies, New York, 1992).

Western countries should do their utmost to prevent raising false expectations and to foster the appreciation of a reasonable Western commitment.

In this respect as well as in the light of this study, Western institutions like the IMF and the World Bank should not focus almost exclusively on economic reform and impose conditionalities of Western assistance as if one is dealing with developing countries, particularly in Latin America. Democratic consolidation, political change, and the establishment of the rule of law should not be subordinated to stringent Western interpretations of the "laws" of a market economy. As argued before, regime change and economic reform go hand in hand, failure of one threatens the other, and there is no recipe for sequencing the undoing of double authoritarian rule. Economic reform in East Central Europe should not take place primarily according to Western images and business interests. The democratizers should be left room for policy choices vis-à-vis their electorate. They are the ones who deserve and need full support in their struggle against undemocratic forces, injustice, and creeping capitalist inequalities. They are the ones who will face the ultimate verdict of society.

Economic change cannot be left to economists in either the East or the West. The name of the game is the politics of transition, of which economics is only one, admittedly essential, part. The multifaceted process of democratic consolidation in East Central Europe is a normative-emotional as much as a rational-material challenge to democratizers in East and West. Belief in the best among imperfect political systems must be strengthened in an East-West democratic—not just economic—partnership. Democrats in East Central Europe need all the support they can get in their neverending struggle for the consolidation of a democracy that, for better or for worse, is bound to change.

PART I

COMPARATIVE PERSPECTIVES

1

The Problem of Nationalism in the Postcommunist Order
GEORGE SCHÖPFLIN

In this chapter, I shall concentrate on the problem of nationalism in Europe, with specific reference to Central and Eastern Europe, and the role played by nationalism in the process of constructing democracies in the aftermath of the collapse of communism. The European dimension is important in this connection for several reasons. European nationalism has deep cultural roots; indeed, I would argue that the doctrine of nationalism was derived from the European experience to fit a particular set of circumstances in which the cultural rootedness of communities was politicized in order to meet the requirements of the new political conditions that obtained with the fading of dynastic, religious, and feudal loyalties at the end of the 18th century.[1] This was followed by the corresponding rise of the new politics, which were informed by a claim to far wider access to political power than before and involved the new dynamic social and economic conditions of modernity.

Nations infused by the new doctrine of nationalism came into being at this time, though they did have well-established ethnic bases stretching back centuries.[2] This cultural rootedness is much less a feature of nationalism in less developed countries, for example, where on the whole nations tend to be political constructs, in the sense of being created as an act of will by post-colonialist rulers. In these nations, identity is determined far more by political than by cultural factors.

---

1. Elie Kedourie, *Nationalism* (London: Hutchinson, 1960); Olwen Hufton, *Europe: Privilege and Protest 1730–1789* (London: Fontana, 1980).
2. John Armstrong, *Nations Before Nationalism* (Chapel Hill, NC: University of North Carolina Press, 1982).

A number of specifics relating to West and Central and East European nationalism must be mentioned here. In Western Europe, the slow emergence of state formations with a set of shared political, economic, social, and other habits received the idea of nationhood as the dominant legitimating principle in what was a well-established institutional framework. France, England, Holland, and Sweden illustrated this process most obviously.[3] Hence on the Western fringes of Europe, there emerged what might be termed "nations by accident," in that various steps were taken over the centuries that had the unintended consequence of producing what turned out to be nation-states, communities with a shared cultural order and political cohesiveness.

These states were not yet legitimated by the emerging doctrine of nationalism, i.e., that the world was divided into nations and only into nations, that each individual belonged to a nation and only to one nation, that nations corresponded to some specific territory, and that certain important consequences flowed from this, notably that members of a nation should be ruled only by other members of that nation. This made the redistribution of power implicit in popular sovereignty feasible, in that there was no danger that newly empowered groups would seek to establish a separate nation-state of their own. The link between nationhood and political power was clearly spelled out and has not been broken since.

In Central and Eastern Europe, on the other hand, the process was different. The political order that preceded the reception of nationalism was based on the four a-national empires, legitimated by dynastic and/or religious claims, that had failed to promote culturally cohesive communities. Indeed, what was striking about them was their internally diverse and disparate nature in most respects. These ruling empires—Russia, Austria-Hungary, Prussia, and the Ottoman Empire—found themselves in a contradictory situation. When they attempted to modernize themselves, which inevitably implied the loss of power for some groups, they triggered off a resistance from among the potential losers, which then fought back by using the

---

3. Charles Tilly, ed., *The Formation of National States in Western Europe* (Princeton: Princeton University Press, 1975); Andrew Orridge, "Varieties of Nationalism," in *The Nation State: The Formation of Modern Politics*, ed. Leonard Tivey (Oxford: Martin Robertson, 1981), pp. 39–58.

newly defined doctrines of nationalism to secure their power. The contest for power between the empires and these sub-elites marked the development of nationalism in Central and Eastern Europe in the 19th century.[4] The result was the formation of new elites, not the elimination of elites. But the sub-elites were not strong enough to validate their claims against the empires, except in the Ottoman Empire, where they had the backing of the West.

There was, however, a further factor that complicated matters. In Western Europe, the protagonists of the new doctrine of nationalism, the intellectuals, defined and proclaimed their ideas in relatively complex societies, in which the contest for power took place among various social groups, notably the representatives of the declining old order, the rising entrepreneurs, and the emerging working class, with the result that power was diffused and the intellectuals could not establish a preeminent position for themselves. Indeed, much of the 19th century was characterized by an ever more desperate critique of the bourgeois order on the part of intellectuals.[5] In Central and Eastern Europe, however, the older order was stronger and societies were far weaker, so that intellectuals came to dominate the scene and acquired an authority that they deployed vigorously in the definition of nationhood.

Because the political challenge to intellectuals was weaker, their claims were less contested and, indeed, to a certain extent they could define their terms independently of society and impose their concept of nationhood on it. The drive for intellectual purity was thus added to the various nationalist ideologies that were formulated and, as a result, nationalism in Central and Eastern Europe acquired an exclusive, messianic quality that it did not have in the West.[6] This high-profile role of intellectuals and the particular expression of nationalism associated with them have proved to be an enduring part of Central and East European politics. In this respect, the nations that came into being in the area can be termed "nations by design," and many of their characteristics differ from those of the West. In particular, there is a long tradition of using or rather abusing national-

---

4. Anthony Smith, *The Ethnic Origin of Nations* (Oxford: Blackwell, 1986).
5. George Steiner, *In Bluebeard's Castle* (London: Faber, 1971).
6. Zygmunt Bauman, "Intellectuals in East-Central Europe: Continuity and Change," *Eastern European Politics and Society* 1, no. 2 (Spring 1987), pp. 162–86.

ism for political purposes not connected with the definition of nationhood, for example, delegitimating political opponents by calling them "alien" or resisting the redistribution of power on similar grounds.[7]

■ *The Functions of Nationhood*

So much for the historical antecedents of nationalism in Central and Eastern Europe, which help to explain some of its more intractable features in the contemporary period. What this historical sketch does not answer, however, is the question of why nationalism survives at all. Its Marxist and liberal opponents have written it off countless times, yet it lives on, despite having been dismissed as "irrational" or "dysfunctional" or "atavistic." This implies that nationalism must have a function that no other system of values has been able to supplement, and, contrary to the claims of its detractors, that it remains a living and authentic experience, unlike, say feudalism, and operates by rules that are rational in their own context.

These functions must be sought in the cultural origins of nationalism, rather than in its political expression.[8] The starting proposition is that every community looks for its moral precepts —the definitions of right and wrong, pure and impure—in its storehouse of cultural values and seeks to defend this from challenges, whether real or perceived. In this way, communities construct the rules of a moral-cultural universe, by which they are then defined. If this corpus of values were to disintegrate, the community itself would be threatened. Crucially, it is by reference to the moral-cultural universe that communities define the bonds of loyalty and cohesiveness that hold it together. These bonds, in turn, create the bases of identity that are at the center of a community. Reference is made to these, in addition, whenever questions of communal existence and belonging are on the agenda. Furthermore, communities also use this moral-cultural resource to articulate the affective dimension of politics. This is not in itself a pathology; all groups possess emotional as

---

7. My own views are set out in George Schöpflin, "Nationalism, Politics and the European Experience," *Survey* 28, no. 4, pp. 67-86.
8. I have explored some of these themes in greater detail in George Schöpflin, "Nationalism and National Minorities in Central and Eastern Europe," *Journal of International Affairs* 45, no. 1 (Summer 1991), pp. 51–65.

well as rational expression in their collective activities. Finally, it is through these cultural traits that the boundaries of a community are constructed, whether these are external boundaries or internal ones. External boundaries define the community in question against other communities. Internal boundaries refer to the acceptability or unacceptability of certain patterns of action or thought.[9]

The problems raised by nationalism in the political realm can be derived from the foregoing. Thus, although in politics nationalism has universalistic claims, in reality these cannot be substantiated. Nationalism can define the identities of members against nonmembers of collectivities, but it says nothing about the distribution of power within a community or the allocation of resources. But because nationhood taps into the emotions underlying collective existence, it is easy enough to confuse the codes relating to political power and those governing political identity, something that has happened repeatedly in the last 200 years.

In this sense, nationalism can be used as an instrument to legitimate political demands that are entirely unconnected with, say, the distribution of power, but this lack of a logical and causal nexus is muddled by the reference to the affective dimension that nationhood conjures up. For example, in concrete terms, Slobodan Milosevic has (for the time being) successfully convinced the Serbs that the reason for their economic plight is not that the Serbian economy is run badly but rather because various aliens (the Kosovo Albanians, the Croats, etc.) are threatening the integrity of the Serbian nation, although in fact the two factors have nothing to do with each other.

■ *Nationalism Encounters Communism*

The problem of nationalism has been further exacerbated by its encounter with communism over the last 40 years. At the level of theory, communism and nationalism are incompatible. Communism insists that an individual's fundamental identity is derived from class positions; nationalism, that it derives from culture. In practice, however, the relationship between the two doctrines, both of which were partial responses to the challenge of modernity, was much more ambiguous.

---

9. On boundaries, see Fredrik Barth, ed., *Ethnic Groups and Boundaries: The Social Organization of Culture Difference* (London: Allen & Unwin, 1969).

Communist rulers, especially after the second de-Stalinization of 1961, found themselves impelled to come to terms with the national identities of their subjects, and they made a variety of compromises with it even though this diluted and undermined the authenticity of their communist credentials. There are countless examples of communist parties using nationalism in this way.

For societies, communist parties could never be authentic agents of the nation, given the parties' ostensible anti-national ideology, but this did not preclude their taking advantage of the new post-1961 dispensation to express national aspirations in the space provided. It was this meeting of the two agendas, that of the rulers and ruled, that helped to explain the initial success of, say, the Ceauşescu regime's mobilization in the 1960s and 1970s, when there was a coincidence between the aims of communists and Romanian society.

Where there was no direct overlap, nationalism could function as the expression of social autonomy and the hope that society would gain greater access to power. This raised a problem, however. As argued already, nationalism is an excellent instrument for determining identity, but it has little or nothing to say about political participation. In this sense, these demands for autonomy expressed through nationalism—"we should have the right to decide for ourselves because we are members of the Ruritanian nation"—were another illustration of the confusion of codes to which this area is subject. Theoretically the demand for, say, freedom of the press or assembly cannot be derived from nationhood, although in practice this may not be at all clear. In this respect, nationalism came to be entrusted with a function that it could not really discharge, and tended to point societies towards confusion and frustration and unrealizable expectations.

The communist period had another legacy of major relevance to the current period. By sweeping away all other competing ideas, programs, and values, which the communists insisted on in order to sustain their monopoly, they made it much easier for some of the core values of nationalism to survive more or less intact, more or less conserved in their original premodern or semi-modern state despite far-reaching social transformation. This meant that some, though not all, of the national disputes and problems of the precommunist period were simply pushed under the carpet, so that with the end of communism these have automatically reappeared.

In addition, the reflexivity of modernity, that "social practices are constantly examined and reformed in the light of incoming information about those very practices, thus constitutively altering their character,"[10] was much impeded by communism, which claimed to be guided by absolute standards. Thus, the kind of relativization that has made nationalism a manageable problem in Western Europe, where the demands for power on the basis of nationhood compete for demands based on other identities and interests (class, economic interests, gender, religion, status, etc.), has not really taken place or is only now beginning to emerge. The propensity to see all matters as involving nationhood, whether properly related to nationhood or not, is one of the key characteristics of the contemporary Central and East European scene and will not change until nationalism is secularized and subject to other influences. In effect, what is essential is that postcommunist politics develop cross-cutting identities, rather than cumulative ones.[11] This will take time.

■ *One-Sided Modernization*

Communist rule forced these countries through a one-sided modernizing revolution, which has had a considerable impact on two areas affecting nationalism. In the first place, the particular virulence of nationalism in the precommunist period can be attributed at least partly to the fact that large sections of the population were backward and were subjected to the initial impact of modernization, whether through the market or the state, in being brought into a new kind of community. This is always a traumatic process as traditional communities are swept away, and Central and Eastern Europe was no exception. The communist transformation effectively liquidated the region's peasantry, traditionally bound by the village, illiterate, and suspicious of the city and urban life.

Inevitably, those who were forced to leave the land looked for answers to their newfound existential problems and gener-

---

10. Anthony Giddens, *The Consequences of Modernity* (Cambridge: Polity Press, 1990), p. 38.

11. See the argument in Patrick Dunleavy and Brendan O'Leary, *Theories of the State: The Politics of Liberal Democracy* (London: Macmillan, 1987).

ally discovered these in nationalism, although for some sections of society the communist answer of promised utopia, hierarchy, and authoritarianism was quite acceptable. The failure of the communist system to integrate these societies meant that nationalism continued to provide answers, especially after communism was manifestly seen to have failed. However, this factor is not entirely negative. If the extremes of nationalism are to be associated with the trauma of modernization, the gradual assimilation of the Central and East European peasantry into urban ways should see the long-term abatement of the kind of nationalistic excesses that are potentially so damaging.

Second, even though the communist revolution was a partial one, it did very effectively extend the power of the state over society, constructing a modern communications network that has allowed the state to reach virtually the whole of the population, in a way that was not true of the prewar era. The use of electronic media to spread a message, whether communist or nationalist, is far more effective than what was available before electrification. To this extent, Central and Eastern Europe has been globalized, making the reception of the global message of material aspirations easier to transmit, though its reception will be slow. The absolute claims of nationalism will only be relativized when the processes of reflexivity and globalization are advanced. No national community can be secure in its nationalistic claims if these are constantly examined and redefined under the impact of ever more information. A modern system of communications can only accelerate this process.

■ *Nationalism and Postcommunism*

A particularly intractable problem raised by Central and East European nationalism is its territorial aspect. Given the history of nationalism in the region and the strong emphasis on territory in nations by design, it is to be expected that the codes of nationhood will carry particularly strong emphases of this kind, in that nationalists tend to insist on linking nation with territory, to demand ethnic purity, and to define the political and cultural roles of this unit very strictly. An example of this is the debate in Hungary over whether Jews are or are not members of the Hungarian nation and whether or not Jews are the bearers of values alien to Hungarians. The claim that they are not members of the Hungarian nation is proclaimed by some of the radical nationalist populists in the Hungarian Democratic Forum.[12]

The fact is that despite the ethnic purification of the wartime and immediate postwar periods, the idea of a territory being inhabited solely and exclusively by one national group is untenable and, for that matter, always has been. Central and Eastern Europe has been characterized by ethnic intermingling to a far greater extent than Western Europe, making the nationalist imperative that much more difficult to implement in the past or in the present.

However, there is an added factor to note here. The conditions of modernity in the late 20th century assume a high degree of urbanization and mobility, both domestically and internationally, and this will inevitably give rise to large-scale non-native populations akin to the Fourth World of the West. There is no sign that the countries of Central and Eastern Europe are aware of this in any way; indeed their thinking remains locked into past patterns.

Yet both this coming problem of migrant minorities and the already extant problem of autochthonous minorities require new thinking in this field. There is, in fact, considerable evidence of the contrary happening. Throughout the area, minorities are becoming the focus of tension and conflict, with the attendant danger of new forms of political mobilization taking place along these cleavage lines. Thus, sections of both ethnic majorities and minorities are consciously using the political situation to bid for political power, to secure their positions as far as the new conditions permit. The position of the Hungarian minority in Romania or the Serbs of Croatia illustrates this clearly. In these and other cases, new elites have come into being and are in the process of generating power as spokespersons for their national group. Potentially, this raises the risk of major and insoluble conflicts of a zero-sum nature.

■ *Consociationalism*

In fact, West European practice suggests that majority-minority conflicts do not have to become the new battleground for power, provided that certain conditions are

---

12. For more details, see George Schöpflin, "Der unterentwickelte Konservativismus in Ungarn" (Underdeveloped conservatism in Hungary), *Europaische Rundschau* 19, no. 1 (Winter 1991), pp. 51-58.

observed. In particular, the system of consociationalism has proved its worth in a number of states riven by deep cleavages.

Consociationalism, then, is a way of governing deeply segmented polities. In states where there are major and strongly persistent cleavages (ethno-national, religious, racial, social, linguistic), majoritarian politics will clearly be a recipe for disruption, as each group looks to maximize its advantage to the detriment of others. Indeed, if relations between two ethno-national communities deteriorate and reductionist mobilization takes place, separation and possibly territorial realignment will be the only solution. But short of that, the techniques of consociationalism are worth discussing, especially as they have been fairly successful in several multinational states in sustaining a democratic order.

The key aspect of consociationalism is that it is anti-majoritarian and thus completely alien to the Anglo-Saxon tradition of political organization. Notably, it recognizes the collective rights of groups, both as against other groups and as against their members. This may certainly derogate from individual rights and seem contrary to the principle of the equality of all before the law, but is nevertheless desirable if the alternative is disruption or low-level civil war (in Northern Ireland, for example, where the consociational solution was attempted too late, after reductionist mobilization made its chances of success futile). In fact, of course, European political systems generally recognize that rights of diverse groups are a part of modern social and political life; extending these to ethnic or religious groups, subject to certain safeguards, can hardly be termed undemocratic.

The adoption of consociationalism, however, imposes a major burden on the majority. By and large, nation-states are regulated by the moral-cultural codes of the majority, and it is precisely this that makes the position of the minority so difficult—it has to compromise its own codes in too many respects. When this happens, the minority will look to alternative ways to put its aspirations into effect, conceivably looking as far as secession. Consequently, the majority must accept that its own codes will have to be compromised for the sake of maintaining the state. This is very much what has been put into effect in Switzerland, the ultimate consociational success story.

Consociational systems seek to draw all the different segments into the decision-making process through elite representation, a kind of grand coalition, although other institutional forms can also be envisaged, such as regular consultation with all groups by the president. The basic elements of consociational systems include consultation with all groups in order to build support for constitutional change; a veto by all groups over major issues affecting them; a proportionate sharing of state expenditure and patronage; and substantial autonomy for each group to regulate and control its supporters. The bureaucracy should develop an ethos of ensuring that policies are implemented accordingly; for its part, the government should keep much of its negotiation behind closed doors in order to prevent popular mobilization around a particular issue that can be related to group identity. A set of tacit rules of the game should be adopted.[13]

Consociationalism, however, imposes two essential conditions in order for it to work. In the first place, all the groups concerned must be willing to work towards accommodation and be ready to bargain; that, in turn, means the creative use of both substantive and procedural solutions that will help all the parties. In other words, all groups must work to avoid zero-sum game situations, even at the risk of ambiguity. Above all, there must be no major winners or losers. Second, the leaders of a group must be able to secure the support of their followers, otherwise the consociational bargains will fall apart; the success of this will depend on the confidence of the members of the group in the system as a whole—a recognition that their interests will be taken into consideration in the bargaining. Thus, the leadership of the group must be able to see solutions for the membership. Society, as well as leaderships, must be sophisticated for consociational solutions to work well.

Other factors important to the success of consociationalism include a readiness to delegate as much as possible to the groups themselves, i.e., extensive self-government. This is complicated in modern societies by the erosion of the territorial principle; on the whole, in dynamic societies, members of different segments will tend to be dispersed throughout the entire area of the state, and it would be fatal to consociationalism to base devolution of

---

13. The classic exposition of consociationalism is Arend Lijphart, *Democracy in Plural Societies: A Comparative Exploration* (New Haven: Yale University Press, 1977). See also G. Bingham Powell, Jr., *Contemporary Democracies: Participation, Stability and Violence* (Cambridge, MA: Harvard University Press, 1982), pp. 212–18.

power solely on territory. Next, the principle of proportionality should be observed rigorously, with if anything an overrepresentation of smaller groups; the minority veto is, of course, the ultimate resource for the protection of small segments. Overrepresentation, however, should not be confused with affirmative action strategies, which have the different objective of promoting the equality, not the stability, of minorities.

There are various helpful, though not essential, preconditions for the success of consociationalism. These include the relative equality of the segments, the absence of a group with an absolute majority, and a relatively small total population, for this means a smallish elite, in which there is a strong chance that members of that elite will share values through similar or identical educational and other experiences. There should also be the overarching loyalty to a legitimating ideology of the state and a corresponding moral-cultural external boundary towards other states. In addition, a tradition of political accommodation can be very useful indeed. It should be noted that these preconditions are neither necessary nor sufficient for the success of consociationalism, but they are helpful.

■ Federal vs. Consociational Arrangements

Finally, a word is needed here about federal versus consociational solutions. It should be clear from the foregoing that territorial solutions are much less likely to be successful in resolving national conflicts than nonterritorial ones. Territorial arrangements have the weight of tradition behind them, both communist and noncommunist, but are less and less effective under modern circumstances of high mobility. Furthermore, given the impossibility of drawing ethnically "just" frontiers, the territorial approach is likely to leave the parties to it dissatisfied. There is, of course, a superficial attractiveness in the seeming simplicity of setting apart a particular territory for a particular ethnic group, but it does nothing to tackle the problem of the minority-within-the-minority. Territorial arrangements tend to involve complex problems of overlapping competencies (e.g., the difficulty of negotiating a Czech-Slovak agreement) and can promote a siege mentality in the minority. Without very rigid controls, for example, of a kind that would certainly infringe on the democratic right of free movement within a polity, the minority will always fear dilution through immigration by members of the majority.

■ *Consociationalism and Postcommunism*

What, then, are the chances of introducing consociational practices into postcommunist systems? The countries that would be involved include the Czech and Slovak Federal Republic, Yugoslavia, Romania, and Bulgaria; recognition of some of these practices would be valuable in Poland and Hungary as well. For the moment, Romania and Bulgaria can be effectively ruled out, though for different reasons: Romania cannot be considered a democracy and the problem of relations with the national minorities is particularly acute; in Bulgaria, the grounding of anything resembling a stable democratic order has so far eluded the elites, and representation of the Turkish and Pomak minorities has been contested.[14]

In Yugoslavia, the centrifugal tendencies of the past year bear testimony to the rather pallid attempt at communist consociationalism. Accommodation of the different segments was overridden in favor of the majority principle, with the result that the smaller segments have looked toward opting out of the state entirely. Essentially, the South Slav lands have seen two attempts to construct a Yugoslav state, and both have failed. Royal Yugoslavia was flawed by the absence of any clear agreement between Serbs and Croats as to the distribution of power, both real and symbolic, and the impossibility of reconciling the centralizing Serbian tradition with the legalistic-federalist tradition of the Croats. That experiment ended in the disastrous bloodbath of World War II.

The communist attempt to remake Yugoslavia was based on a different legitimating ideology, that of Titoism, and worked up to a point for four decades, though it did so as much by sidestepping the national issue as by seeking to resolve it. But this solution, too, was flawed, principally because the existence of Yugoslavia as a single state was too closely linked to the success of Titoism. Once the communist experiment failed, the existence of Yugoslavia as a single state was also called into question. The events of 1989–1991 can be regarded as a failed

---

14. See Duncan Perry, "The New Prime Minister and the Moslems," *RFE/RL Report on Eastern Europe* 2, no. 3 (Jan. 18, 1991), p. 9.

debate, albeit one involving high levels of force, about the terms of restructuring the state.

■ *Has History Returned?*

There is a fashionable line of Western analysis to the effect that postcommunism has been accompanied by a revival of all the old, interwar and pre-World War I ethno-national conflicts. Underlying this pattern of thinking is a barely concealed acquiescence in the suggestion that, while communism may have had many negative points, at least it kept the peace among these warring tribes of Central and Eastern Europe, and, further, that in a sense they do not deserve democracy, because all they do with it is slide into nationalistic squabbling.[15]

This line of analysis largely misses the point, and does so on a number of counts. It misunderstands the nature of Central and East European history, makes glib and superficial comparisons with Western Europe, assumes that Western practices can be translated overnight, if not indeed imposed in near colonialist fashion, to Central and Eastern Europe, and takes no account of the destruction of values and bonds of solidarity wrought by communism over the last 40 years. In effect, this line of argument concentrates on the surface phenomena of postcommunist politics and sidesteps the complex realities with which these countries have to cope.

■ *In Lieu of a Conclusion*

It has already been argued that the maintenance of a democratic order is an essential condition for the resolution of ethnic conflicts, so some assessment must be made of the problems and prospects of the relationship between democracy and nationhood. Given the ease with which the codes and rhetoric appropriate to nationhood are transposed to other political issues, there will always be a danger that sections of the population will become vulnerable to demagogic manipulation, when the affective dimension of nationhood is deployed to mobilize support for causes that require other, often more difficult, solutions. Economic difficulties are the most obvious.

---

15. Misha Glenny, *The Return of History* (London: Penguin, 1990) is a good example.

There is clearly a real possibility that if the economies of the postcommunist states remain in a state of crisis and the populations are subjected to deprivation over a period of time, they will lend a ready ear to nationalist agitation. The Milosevic phenomenon illustrates this quite unmistakably. This would seem to imply that economic stabilization should be a high priority for these states. But there is more to it than that. These political systems are still untried and in an early stage of development under postcommunism, and the creation of an institutional order that will function smoothly enough to attract popular loyalty will take some time. Here the legacy of depoliticization, the impatience with politics as such, the propensity to look for easy, radical solutions (as expressed in the extraordinary vote for Tymiński in Poland or the readiness of the Jiru valley miners to be manipulated by Iliescu against the Bucharest demonstrators) are negative factors.[16] Politically untried populations, lacking the range of cross-cutting interests and not yet experienced in relativizing nationhood, are much more prone to the kind of reductionist thinking that can lead them to take refuge in nationalism. This can potentially be used to legitimate authoritarian systems. However, as this chapter has sought to argue, there is no question of a predetermined slide into authoritarianism in Central and Eastern Europe, and political instruments for avoiding this course are available. In this sense, nationalism is not an irrational, unmanageable force, but is dependent in part on other processes and is subject to skills of political management.

---

16. I have looked at some of the problems of postcommunism in George Schöpflin, "Postcommunism: Constructing New Democracies in Central Europe," *International Affairs* 67, no. 2 (April 1991), pp. 235–50.

2

The Types of Democracy Emerging in Southern and Eastern Europe and South and Central America

PHILIPPE C. SCHMITTER
TERRY KARL

On April 25, 1974, a conspiracy of young military officers overthrew the longstanding Salazar/Caetano authoritarian regime in Portugal. At the time, no one imagined that this seemingly isolated and definitely idiosyncratic event would be followed in relatively short order by the demise of over 40 other autocracies—first, in the neighboring, semi-peripheral, Southern European countries of the First World; later, in the Third World periphery of Latin America and Asia; and, more recently, in Africa. Surprising as these regime changes were to most of the actors involved and to all the academics observing them, they pale in comparison to the shock produced by the sudden collapse of Soviet-style regimes in the Second World during 1989 and 1990.

Mainstream experts on Soviet and East European politics had literally staked their reputations on the stability, nay, the immutability of the systems they were studying. While those working on Third World autocracies were aware of persistent problems with legitimation and rising difficulties in economic performance,[1] the most that sovietologists could imagine in terms of change was some gradual evolution within "Leninist institutional settings" towards more pragmatic policies and lead-

---

1. Although, in all fairness, it should be stressed that very few of these analysts (the two of us included) predicted such a massive shift toward democratization in Latin America, Asia, or Africa. Pressed for an answer about the likely future, they would probably have responded: "More of the same, with some alteration in the type or extent of authoritarian rule." Needless to say, this prediction might still come true, although only *after* a substantial and protracted experiment with open, competitive, and account-able politics.

ership styles. Jeane Kirkpatrick popularized this perception and exploited it to justify US support for allegedly more malleable authoritarian regimes.[2]

Eppur si muove! Dramatic and irreversible transformations in regime type have occurred—not just in those East European countries that had already undergone the greatest evolutionary changes away from the Leninist or Stalinist "matrix," but also in places like Albania, Romania, Bulgaria, and Mongolia, where that matrix was still relatively intact. Even the Soviet Union, where one might have thought that "great power status" (and responsibilities) would have impeded such destabilizing change, has been affected—not just in its political-ideological institutions, but also in its national identity and borders.

■ Can Transitions in Eastern Europe Be Compared to Those in Other World Areas?

Political scientists with expertise in other parts of the world tend to look upon these events in Eastern Europe with "imperial intent," i.e., as an opportunity to incorporate (at long last) the study of these countries into the general corpus of comparative analysis. Indeed, by adding postcommunist regimes to our already greatly expanded case base, one could even imagine bringing the powerful instrument of social statistics to bear on the study of contemporary democratization. Scholars of democratization were initially inhibited by the small number of

---

2. On the limited, evolutionary conception of possible change under totalitarianism, the *locus classicus* seems to be the work of Robert C. Tucker on "revolutionary mass-movement regimes": *The Soviet Political Mind* (New York: Praeger, 1963), pp. 3–19; and idem, *The Marxian Revolutionary Idea* (Princeton: Princeton University Press, 1970), pp. 172–214. Also see Ken Jowitt, "Soviet Neotraditionalism: The Political Corruption of a Leninist Regime," *Soviet Studies* (July 1983), pp. 275–97; or idem, "The Concepts of Liberalization, Integration and Rationalization in the Context of Eastern European Development," *Studies in Comparative Communism* 4 (1971), pp. 79–92. Jeane Kirkpatrick's earlier views can be found in "Dictatorships and Double Standards," *Commentary* (November 1979), pp. 34–45. For a critique, see Giuseppe di Palma, "Legitimation from the Top to Civil Society: Politico-Cultural Change in Eastern Europe," *World Politics* (October 1991), pp. 49–80. Interestingly, both Jowitt and Kirkpatrick have recently sought exculpation: Ken Jowitt, "Weber, Trotsky and Holmes on the Study of Leninist Regimes," *Journal of International Affairs* 45, no. 1 (Summer 1991), pp. 31–50; Jeane Kirkpatrick, *The Withering Away of the Totalitarian State . . . and Other Surprises* (Washington, DC: American Enterprise Press, 1990).

instances and their geographic concentration to case studies in Southern Europe and Latin America; we were hesitant to advance "tentative conclusions" about highly uncertain and contingent outcomes.[3] Now, we can test these observations in contexts quite different from those that generated them in the first place.

Specialists on the area, not surprisingly, have tended to react differently by stressing the cultural, ideological, and national peculiarities of these cases—especially the distinctive historical legacy bequeathed by totalitarian as opposed to authoritarian *anciens régimes*. In their resistance to "acultural extrapolation," some former sovietologists would bar outsiders from reducing their countries (now more numerous, diverse, and autonomous in their behavior) to mere pinpoints on a scatterplot or frequencies in a cross-tabulation. The lessons or generalizations already drawn from previous transitional experiences and now being made about the difficulties of regime consolidation should *ex hypothesi* be rejected. Presumably, some (as yet unspecified) "new science" of regime change must be invented and applied if one is to make any sense about the eventual political trajectory of ex-Leninist or ex-Stalinist systems.[4]

This brief chapter is not the place to thoroughly debate such a contentious issue. Our working assumption is that, provided

---

3. See Guillermo O'Donnell and Philippe C. Schmitter, *Transitions from Authoritarian Rule: Tentative Conclusions about Uncertain Democracies* (Baltimore: Johns Hopkins University Press, 1986).
4. See Ken Jowitt, "Weber, Trotsky and Holmes," cited above, and "The Leninist Extinction," in *The Crisis of Leninism and the Decline of the Left*, ed. D. Chirot (Seattle: University of Washington Press, 1991), pp. 74–99.

    For a more constructive attempt to suggest the "new analytical categories needed to account for the different dimensions of the current transition process (in East Central Europe)," see Grzegorz Ekiert, "Democratization Processes in East Central Europe: A Theoretical Reconsideration," *British Journal of Political Science* (July 1991), pp. 285–313. Ekiert, while noting the differences, is not so categoric about the need to reject all work on other areas. See also Russell Bova, "Political Dynamics of the Post-Communist Transition: A Comparative Perspective," *World Politics* (October 1991), pp. 113–38.

    Our impression from conversations and meetings with scholars from the postcommunist societies is that they are much less inclined to reject the relevance of democratization experiences in Southern Europe and Latin America than are North American area specialists. This does not obviate the possibility that their fascination with the Spanish or Chilean "model" may be misguided or misleading.

the events or processes satisfy certain definitional require-ments,[5] their occurrence in Eastern Europe or the former Soviet Union should be considered, at least initially, analogous to events or processes happening elsewhere. More than that, they should be treated as part of the same "wave of democratization" that began in 1974 in Portugal and has yet to dissipate its energy completely or to ebb back to autocracy.[6] Hence, all these cases of regime change—regardless of their geopolitical location or cul-tural context—should (at least hypothetically) be regarded as parts of a common process of diffusion and causal interaction. Only *after* (and not *before*) this effort at incorporation, mapping, and analysis has been made, will it become possible to conclude whether concepts and hypotheses generated from the experi-ences of early-comers should be regarded as "overstretched" or "underverified" when applied to latecomers. Only then will we know whether the basins containing different world regions are really so interconnected and moved by such similar forces. The particularity of any one region's cultural, historical, or institu-tional matrix—if it is relevant to understanding the outcome of regime change—should emerge from systematic comparison, rather than be used as an excuse for not applying it.

■ Distinctive Aspects of Regime Change in Eastern Europe

This is not to say that one should deliberately ignore possible sources of contextual variation across world regions. To the contrary, sensitivity to what is different about

---

5. For example, in some cases such as Romania, Bulgaria, and Albania, it was at first unclear as to whether the *ancien régime* had indeed been deposed and whether the ensuing elections were conducted under fair enough conditions to consider that the winners were attempting to establish a different form of political domination. Subsequent events, especially in the process of government formation, have made it clear that a genuine regime change has taken place.

6. Several authors seem to have independently picked up this notion of "waves." Schmitter has explored in it an essay entitled "The Consolidation of Democracy and the Choice of Institutions" (Paper presented at the East-South Systems Transformation [ESST] Conference, Toledo, Spain, January 4–7, 1992). See also Sidney Tarrow, "'Aiming at a Moving Target': Social Science and the Recent Rebellions in Eastern Europe," *P.S.* (March 1991), pp. 12-20; and Samuel B. Huntington, *The Third Wave: Democratiza-tion in the Late Twentieth Century* (Norman, OK: University of Oklahoma Press, 1991).

Eastern Europe[7] may provide a useful corrective to the contemporary literature that is so centered on Southern Europe and Latin America. Most importantly, it may encourage comparativists to pay more attention to variables we have either taken for granted (e.g., the existence of relatively established national identities or of relatively well-functioning market mechanisms) or examined and rejected as less important. For the record, we propose to list without further elaboration the parametric conditions that seem most likely to affect differentially the outcome of regime change in the East as opposed to the South.[8]

Condensing and simplifying, four contrasts stand out: (1) in the point of departure; (2) in the extent of collapse of the *ancien régime*; (3) in the role of external actors; and (4) in the sequence of transformative processes. Needless to say, these are all somewhat interconnected and could well be assembled under other rubrics.

Point of Departure

In an analysis of the point of departure of regime changes, the primary issue is not the "classical" one of differences in level of development, literacy, urbanization, and so forth. Nor, strictly speaking, is it the type of autocracy, i.e., totalitarian, "Leninist," or "Stalinist," that has collapsed. In the first category, the East European countries and most of the republics of the former Soviet Union seem to overlap considerably with the previous cases in Southern Europe and Latin

---

7. For obvious reasons, the case of the former German Democratic Republic should be excluded. It was equivalent only to the point at which the dynamics of reunification took over.

8. It should be noted that these parametric conditions do not radically juxtapose the Eastern and Southern cases, but overlap to some degree. For example, the Soviet Union, Yugoslavia, and Czechoslovakia are not alone in having problems of national identity and borders that complicate the democratization process. Spain, and, to a much lesser extent, Portugal, had to deal with demands for greater regional autonomy, even secession. Similarly, countries in Latin America have had to cope with over-bloated state apparatuses and unproductive public enterprises, even if the issue did not approach the magnitude of the problem of privatization in former command economies. In this respect, the Central American cases of Nicaragua and El Salvador, in particular, may have more in common generically with those of Eastern Europe than with their regional neighbors to the south.

America—certainly as far as human skills, social mobilization, and productive capacity are concerned.[9] In the second, most of these political systems had degenerated already into some form of "partialitarian" or authoritarian regime, not entirely removed from the ways in which the Southern European and Latin American cases were governed. Romania and Albania were obvious exceptions, although their high degree of personalization of power suggests a possible analogy with such cases of "sultanism" as Somoza's Nicaragua, Trujillo's Dominican Republic, and Stroessner's Paraguay. Nonetheless, we would readily concede that the peculiar monopolistic fusion of political and economic power into a party-state apparatus remained a distinctive attribute of the East.

But what is most striking are the differences in point of departure in socio-occupational structure as the result of so many years of policy measures designed to compress class and sectoral distinctions, equalize material rewards, and, of course, eliminate the diversity of property relations. Except where a "second economy" had emerged earlier and prospered commercially (namely, Hungary), East European social systems seem very "amorphous" in their structure, and it is difficult to imagine how the parties and interest associations that are so characteristic of all types of "Western" democracy could emerge, stabilize their respective publics, and contribute to the general consolidation of the regime. At least until the twin shocks of marketization and privatization produce more substantial and more stable class and sectoral differences, the politics of these neo-democracies are likely to be driven by other, much less tractable, cleavages (e.g., ethnicity, locality, personality).[10]

---

9. Although we would agree that there are important qualitative differences in development levels, especially with regard to production and distribution systems, that may make it much more difficult for the Eastern countries to exploit these aggregate assets in a more open context of political or economic competition.

10. Our thinking on this matter has been influenced by the work of David Ost, "Shaping the New Politics in Poland" (Paper presented at the conference on "Dilemmas of Transition from State Socialism in East Central Europe," Harvard University Center for European Studies, Cambridge, March 15–17, 1991). We would also like to thank David Ost for his particularly thoughtful criticism of an earlier draft of this paper.

The Extent of Collapse of the
Previous Regime

When we examine the extent of collapse of the previous regime, here, too, the contrast is striking. Not only were the regime changes less foreseen and the opposition forces less prepared to rule than in the south,[11] but once new governments were formed the role of previous power-holders declined precipitously and significantly. There were a few exceptions where rebaptized (and possibly reformed) communists managed to do well in the initial "founding elections" and to hold on as a group to key executive positions, but even then they often proved incapable of governing effectively and were displaced in relatively short order, as in Albania and Bulgaria. By our calculation, only in Romania, Mongolia, Ukraine, Azerbaijan, Estonia, and Serbia are former communists continuing to play a significant role either as a party governing alone or in alliance with others.[12] This contrasts with Southern Europe and Latin America, where neo-democracies were often governed initially by centrist or rightist parties that included important elements (and persons) from the previous regime in their ranks, and where de facto powers such as the armed forces, the police, or the state apparatus retained very significant power to intervene in policy making and to affect the choice of institutions. Spain, Brazil, and Chile may be the most extreme cases, but almost everywhere (except Portugal and perhaps Argentina) the transition takes place in the shadow—if not under the auspices—of the *ancien régime*. Given the virtual abdication of their previous rulers, East Europeans could harbor the (momentary) illusion of a tabula rasa upon which to build new rules and practices.

---

11. Although it is hard to beat the initial Portuguese case for sheer surprise and unpreparedness to rule! Elsewhere in Southern Europe and Latin America—except, most notably in Nicaragua—opposition groups had much more time to anticipate coming to power and even to prepare elaborate contingency arrangements. On the importance of surprise for the East European transitions, see Timur Kuran, "Now Out of Never: The Element of Surprise in the East European Revolution of 1989," *World Politics* (October 1991), pp. 7–48.

12. No doubt, this generalization overlooks the possibility, even the likelihood, that forces from the *ancien régime* are still well entrenched in local units of governance and production and can, therefore, pose much more of an obstacle to democratic consolidation than would be apparent from the parties and persons governing at the national level. We are indebted to Steve Fish and his forthcoming dissertation for this point.

The Role of External Actors

One of the more confident generalizations of the previous literature emphasized the much greater importance of domestic forces and calculations as opposed to foreign influences and intromissions in determining the nature and timing of regime transition—hinting, however, at the likelihood that the latter would play a more significant role subsequently in the consolidation phase.[13] There seems to be virtual unanimity that this generalization does not apply in the case of Eastern Europe. Without a previously announced and credible shift in the foreign and security policies of the Soviet Union, neither the timing nor the occurrence of regime change would be explicable. In a few cases, e.g., Romania and East Germany, even active intromission by Gorbachev seems to have been necessary. Moreover, there is much more evidence of "contagion" within the region, i.e., events in one country triggered and accelerated a response in its neighbors. Unlike in Southern Europe and Latin America, where democratization did not substantially alter long-standing commercial relations or international alliances,[14] regime changes in Eastern Europe triggered a major collapse in intraregional trade and the dissolution of the Warsaw Pact. Into this vacuum moved an extraordinary variety of Western advisors and promoters—binational and multilateral. To a far greater extent than elsewhere, these external actors have imposed political "conditionality" upon the process of consolidation, linking

---

13. For the initial observation, see O'Donnell and Schmitter, *Transitions From Authoritarian Rule*, pp. 17–21. It should be noted that the cases on which this generalization was based did not include those of Central America. In that subregion, external influences and intromission have been (and continue to be) much more significant. For a criticism with regard to Southern Europe, see Geoffrey Pridham, ed., *Encouraging Democracy: The International Context of Regime Transition in Southern Europe* (Leicester: Leicester University Press, 1991).

14. Greece's (temporary) withdrawal from NATO is a minor exception—counterbalanced by Spain's (contested) entry into NATO. The decision by all of the Southern European countries to become full members of the EC did not so much alter existing patterns of economic dependence as intensify them. For an assessment of the impact of democratization on regional security, cooperation, and integration in the Southern Cone of Latin America, see Philippe C. Schmitter, "Change in Regime Type and Progress in International Relations," in *Progress in Postwar International Relations*, ed. E. Adler and B. Crawford (New York: Columbia University Press, 1991), pp. 89–127.

specific rewards explicitly to the meeting of specific norms, or even to the selection of specific institutions.[15]

The Sequence of Transformation

All of the above differences pale before the significance of the sequence of transformation, in our opinion. In none of the Southern European or Latin American cases did the regime change from autocracy to democracy occur alone, in complete isolation from other needed social, economic, military, and administrative transformations. However, except for Central America, it was usually possible to deal with these variegated demands sequentially. In some specially favored cases, major structural changes were accomplished under previous authoritarian auspices. For example, most of these transitions "inherited" acceptable national identities and boundaries— even if the degree of local or regional autonomy remained contested. In a few, the military had already been largely subordinated to civilian control, or the economy had undergone substantial restructuring to make it more internationally competitive.

---

15. This issue is discussed at greater length in Philippe C. Schmitter, "The International Context for Contemporary Democratization: Constraints and Opportunities Upon the Choice of National Institutions and Policies" (Paper presented at the East-South Systems Transformation [ESST] Conference, Toledo, January 4–7, 1992). To the above general observations about the external context in Eastern Europe, one could add another, more specific, condition: namely, the sheer fact that it is located in such close geographic proximity to centers in Western Europe of much greater prosperity and security. This makes the "exit option" much easier, especially for relatively skilled persons. On the one hand, this threatens to deprive these emergent democracies of some of their most highly motivated actors and to leave their consolidation in the hands of less talented ones; on the other hand, the very prospect of such a mass exodus increases the prospects for their extracting external resources intended, precisely, to prevent that from happening.

Again, the parallel with Central America emerges. Here, too, the indirect influence and direct intromission of foreign agents have been of considerable importance, both in determining the timing and nature of their transitions from authoritarian rule and in "conditioning" the consolidation of their respective democracies. These actions by the United States, in particular, are not unrelated to the region's geographical location and the threat that sizable flows of refugees could pose to its security. The present case of Haiti well illustrates the problem—and the difficulty of bringing effective external power to bear on an issue as complex and uncertain as regime change.

In Eastern Europe, however, not only are such major trans-formations all on the agenda for collective action and choice, but very little authoritative capacity exists for selecting priorities among them. There is a great deal more to do than in the South, and it seems as if it must all be done at once. The code words are *simultaneity* and *asynchrony*. Many decisions have to be made in the same time frame, and their uncontrolled interactions tend to produce unanticipated (and usually unwanted) effects. Even within a given issue area, the absence of historical precedents makes it difficult to assert theoretically what should come first: holding elections or forming a provisional government; drafting a national constitution or encouraging local autonomy; releasing prices or controlling budget deficits; privatizing state industries or allowing collective bargaining; creating a capital market or sustaining a realistic exchange rate; the list could continue ad infinitum. Even if "transition theory" can offer a few generic insights strictly within the political domain, these risk being quite irrelevant given simultaneous—rather than sequential—demands for changes in major economic, social, cultural/national, and military institutions. For example, one knows in the abstract that the formation of provisional governments can be a bad thing, especially before the configuration of national party systems is evident, but what if (as seems to have been the case in the Czech and Slovak Federal Republic) it is necessary to head off a polarized conflict among nationalities? In retrospect, it seems to have been a crucial error for Gorbachev to have convoked (or tolerated) elections at the republican level *before* holding a national election that would have legitimated his own position and, with it, the all-union framework of territorial authority, but presumably this choice with regard to timing reflected a correlation of forces within the CPSU and the military at the time.

One thing is becoming abundantly clear—and this was observed already in the classic article of Dankwert Rustow that lies at the origin of much of today's work on transition—that without some prior consensus on overarching national identity and boundaries, little or nothing can be accomplished to move the system out of the protracted uncertainty of transition into the relative calm (and boredom) of consolidation.[16] This places the former Soviet Union and Yugoslavia in a radically different

16. "Transitions to Democracy," *Comparative Politics* 2 (1970), pp. 337–63.

sequence, and it is not inconceivable that all of their "inheritor republics" will be paralyzed by a similar imperative.

Even with this last observation, and accepting that the above four clusters of variables do, indeed, make a strong possible case for "a change to change" as one shifts attention from the South to the East, we would still stick to our operating assumption that these cases of regime change should be treated conceptually and theoretically as analogous and, therefore, that it is to be expected that they face the same range of alternative outcomes as their predecessors.

■ *The Range of Alternative Outcomes to the Demise of Autocracy*

Political democracy can be defined in most generic terms as "a system of governance in which rulers are held accountable for their actions in the public realm by citizens, acting indirectly through the competition and cooperation of their representatives."[17] In order for this arrangement to work, certain procedural norms must be met.[18] However, even where there are (1) control over decisions by elected officials; (2) frequent and fair elections; (3) adult suffrage; (4) widespread eligibility to run for office; (5) rights to free expression, speech, and petition; (6) access to alternative sources of information; and (7) rights to form/join associations and parties, actors may not be successful in producing a stable and legitimate form of governance, i.e., in establishing a type of democracy that is appropriate for and accepted by a given population.

Another way of putting the point would be that *political democracy in its most generic sense may persist, but may not be consolidated into a specific and reliable set of rules or institutions.* Some countries may be "condemned" for the foreseeable future to remain democratic only because no feasible alternative mode of domination is (presently) available. Elections are held, associations are tolerated, rights are respected, and the procedural minima are met with some degree of regularity, but the *ensemble*

---

17. For a more detailed explication of this definition, see Philippe C. Schmitter and Terry Karl, "What Democracy Is . . . and Is Not," *Journal of Democracy* (Summer 1991), pp. 75–88.
18. These have been explored most thoroughly in the work of Robert Dahl, especially, in his *Dilemmas of Pluralist Democracy* (New Haven: Yale University Press, 1982). In Schmitter and Karl, "What Democracy Is . . . and Is Not," two additional items have been added to the original seven.

of rules and institutions does not jell into regular, acceptable, and predictable patterns that can reproduce themselves over time and command the allegiance of citizens. "Democracy" is not replaced by something else—say, some form of autocratic rule—it just persists by acting in ad hoc and ad hominem ways in response to successive problems.

To repeat, not all polities in transition will make it to some stable type of democracy. Some will be overthrown by force and replaced by authoritarian regimes. Some will never make it across the minimal threshold and will persist in a variety of intermediary statuses.[19] Still others will become democracies and yet not succeed in consolidating themselves into a particular, stable institutional configuration. Finally, the fortunate ones will settle into some recognizable and reproducible type of democracy—often, as we have said, not the one they originally intended.

Taking into consideration the four differences outlined above, our hunch is that the East European cases may be faced with the following paradox: their transitions have been (astonishingly) rapid, nonviolent and definitive, i.e., new actors have come to power without using physical force to eject their predecessors, and they have effectively eliminated the prospect of a return to the status quo, in a relatively short period of time,[20] but their consolidations promise to be lengthy, contorted, and inconclusive, i.e., compared to most (but not all) of the regime changes in Southern Europe and Latin America, they will have more difficulty in selecting and settling into an "appropriate" type of democracy. While it is by no means foreclosed that some of these countries will revert to some other form of autocracy than was previously practiced or that they will attempt to

---

19. In their *Tentative Conclusions about Uncertain Democracies*, p. 9, O'Donnell and Schmitter suggest two such intermediary types: (1) the *dictablanda*, where authoritarian rule is tempered by some respect for the rule of law and the rights of individual contestation, but political power is not subjected to uncertain and free electoral competition; and (2) the *democradura*, where civil rights and partisan competition are permitted, but restrictions are placed on which persons may vote or hold office, which parties may compete, how votes are counted or aggregated into districts, what sources of information are available, how independent elected officials may be from the control of self-appointed ones, etc.

20. Romania and, more recently, Georgia are obvious exceptions to the generalization about nonviolence; the former Soviet Union and former Yugoslavia are exceptions to the generalization on the relatively short transitional period.

establish hybrid forms of *dictablanda* and *democradura*, our hunch is that the most probable outcome will be protractedly "unconsolidated democracy"—if only because some degree of continual obedience to the procedural minimum will be imposed by their dependence on the European Community and other Western countries.

■ The Types of Democracy That Might Emerge

The literature on "kinds or types of democracy" is abundant, varied, and inconclusive. None of the well-worked distinctions would seem to serve our purposes. The typologies based on cultural or geographic attributes are inappropriate and methodologically deficient.[21] The classical reliance on the structure of executive institutions, presidential vs. parliamentary, seems excessively formalistic, even when supplemented by the new category of "semi-presidential."[22] Nor does the number of parties, even when supplemented as in the case of Giovanni Sartori with information on the nature of their competitive relationship (centripetal vs. centrifugal),[23] seem to provide an adequate handle on the problem. Contemporary democracies are more "pluri-dimensional," especially due to the develop-

---

21. For example, Gabriel Almond, "Comparative Political Systems," *Journal of Politics* 18, no. 3 (1956), pp. 391–409.

22. Juan Linz has devoted a great deal of learned attention to the issue of the effects of presidentialism and parliamentarism on the consolidation of democracy. See his "Democracy: Presidential or Parliamentary: Does it Make a Difference?" (Paper presented at the Latin American Regional Institute of the American Council of Learned Societies, Comparative Constitutionalism Project, Punta del Este, Uruguay, October 31-November 4, 1988); also idem, "The Perils of Presidentialism," *The Journal of Democracy* (Winter 1990), pp. 51–69. Linz's argument has been subsequently discussed by Donald Horowitz, Seymour Martin Lipset, and Linz himself in *The Journal of Democracy* (Fall 1990), pp. 73–91. For an interesting application to the case of Chile, see Oscar Godoy Arcaya, ed., *Hacia una democracia moderna: La opción parlamentaria* (Towards a modern democracy: The parliamentary option) (Santiago: Ediciones Universidad de Chile, 1990). On semi-presidentialism, see Maurice Duverger, "A New Political System Model: Semi-Presidentialism," *European Journal of Political Research* (1980), pp. 163–83; also idem, ed., *Les regimes semi-presidentiels* (Semi-presidential regimes) (Paris: PUF, 1986).

23. Giovanni Sartori, *Parties and Party Systems: A Framework for Analysis* (Cambridge: Cambridge University Press, 1976); also Jean Blondel, "Party Systems and Patterns of Government," in *An Introduction to Comparative Government* (London: Weidenfeld and Nicolson, 1969).

ment of elaborate systems of functional interest representation that complement and occasionally replace the territorial, partisan nexus.[24] The work of Arend Lijphart, first, on the delineation of an alternative "consociational" model to the dominant "pluralist" one and, more recently, on a complex, multivariate distinction between "majoritarian" and "consensus" patterns of democracy, is potentially more relevant, but it too leaves out the critical dimension of associability and interest politics.[25]

In figure 1 (at the end of this chapter), Philippe Schmitter has proposed a means for delimiting different kinds or types of democracy that is neither dependent on formal institutional criteria (although it is not difficult to fit presidentialism-parliamentarism, federalism-unitarism, and differing legislative systems in it), nor restricted to the public, territorial, and electoral aspect of politics (although it should be possible to measure differences in party systems and coalitional arrangements according to its coordinates). Admittedly, the scheme is rather abstract and specifies not so much a limited number of nominal or ordinal types as an extensive property space within which individual cases can be plotted.

The horizontal axis is defined in terms of *the dominant principle of aggregation*. Is the democracy organized predominantly according to the principle of counting equally the sheer number of its citizens that support a given candidacy or policy? Or is it ordered in such a way that it tends to weigh the intensity of its citizens' preferences, whether aggregated according to class, religion, region, ethnicity, or nationality? Both principles can claim validation in democratic theory, although they lead to quite different institutional expressions. This dimension captures in slightly altered language the basic underlying distinction stressed by Lijphart in his book *Democracies*. At the one end are the majoritarian democracies where decisions are made and justified in terms of the equal aggregation of preferences across

24. Peter Lange and Hudson Meadwell, "Typologies of Democratic Systems: From Political Inputs to Political Economy," in *New Directions in Comparative Politics*, ed. H. Wiarda (Boulder/London: Westview Press, 1985), pp. 80–111.
25. Arend Lijphart, "Typologies of Democratic Systems," *Comparative Political Studies* (April 1968), pp. 3–44; idem, *Democracies: Patterns of Majoritarian and Consensus Government in Twenty-One Countries* (New Haven: Yale University Press, 1984).

the unit as a whole—broken down in some federalist cases by multiple levels of governance. At the other are those in which authoritative allocations depend on the formation of a much broader consensus by extensive deliberation and compromise among subunits of unequal size and intensities of preference.

The vertical axis represents the scheme's greater novelty. It is an effort to capture a "classic" distinction within democratic political theory between *the mix of public authority and private activity*. This controversial issue was well exemplified historically by the struggle between the Jacobins and the Girondins during the French Revolution over whether democracy is better served by an active and capable state that intervenes to rectify inequalities generated by other social and economic institutions and to ensure that the formal rights of citizenship will be effectively exercised, or whether democracy is better assured by relying on the competitive interactions between individuals and institutions in civil society and by restricting the role of the state to policing contracts made voluntarily and spontaneously by these private actors.

The former, a "statist" and "activist" conception of democracy, may be presently on the ideological defensive, but it has by no means disappeared. For example, severe economic depression, war, or even a significant increase in the level of international threat perception could bring it back very quickly. The latter, the "societal," "passive," or just plain "liberal" conception of democracy, may have become virtually hegemonic in recent decades, establishing a presumption favorable to private activity over public authority, but there is every reason to believe that this could also change rapidly if, for example, the spontaneous interaction between social groups starts to produce increased awareness of ethnic differences and eventually violence, or the unequal bargaining between capitalists and workers begins to generate greater and greater inequity and class conflict. Hence, while there is every reason to suspect that in the contemporary context more actors would choose societal forms of democracy than during previous "waves" of democratization such as the ones that succeeded World Wars I and II, the crisis conditions surrounding present transitions may eventually compel them to opt for more "statist" solutions.

Figure 1 leaves room for "impure" cases. Only the four extreme corners are given specific labels: *corporatist, consociational, populist,* and *electoralist*. The rest, especially the space located right in the middle of the figure, should be characterized as "mixed type" democracies. The literature from Polybius through Montesquieu to the US founding fathers consistently stresses the desirable features of such "mixed polities." It is arguable that the contrasting qualities of different ruling formulas—concentrated and dispersed, territorial and functional, popular and elitist, accountable and autonomous, federal and unitary, compulsory and voluntary—can complement each other's virtues and countermand each other's vices. Now, let us attempt to place some recent (and not so recent) democracies in the property space of figure 2 and see whether these assumptions are borne out.

Bearing in mind the tentativeness of the scoring and the substantial number of cases that have yet to cross the minimal threshold (*) or become consolidated (?), figure 2 does suggest that many of the new democracies are based on a mixture of principles of aggregation and centers of power. Relatively few of the recent experiences could be confidently placed in one or another of the extreme corner cells. It is not clear whether this grouping of cases around the middle of the plot is the product of genuine collective choice by the actors involved or whether it is the artefact of a measurement device that fails to discriminate accurately between cases.

Clustering along one diagonal that runs from corporatist (with Austria [A] as the archetype) to electoralist democracy (with the United States [USA] as the closest well-established approximation) are a number of relatively successful cases of recent regime transition: from Spain (E), Uruguay (UGY), and Venezuela (VEN) in the upper left to Chile (RCH) and Colombia (COL*) in the lower right—with Guatemala (GUA*), El Salvador (ELS*), and Paraguay (PGY?) as *democraduras* that could become extreme examples of electoralism. What this axis seems to pick up are *differences in the basis of group representation*, i.e., between those democracies rooted more in the functional categories of class, sector, and profession and those in which territorial constituencies of region, community, or locality tend to predominate.

A second diagonal runs from the lower left (with Switzerland [CH] as the most consociational case), picks up the as yet unconsolidated cases of Yugoslavia (YU???) and Czechoslovakia (CZ?), and then moves toward the populist type of democracy in the upper right—with Brazil (BR) and Ecuador (ECU) as relatively well established cases and Costa Rica (COS), Portugal

(P), Poland (PL?), and Turkey (TU) as near approximations. Very speculatively, we have placed Romania (ROM?), Bulgaria (BUL*), and the Soviet Union/Russia (SU*) in the populist cell, although it is obviously too early to judge where these highly transitional regimes are heading. This axis seems to select democracies according to *the principle of organization of executive power*. It stretches from the lower left corner with the multiple executive of Switzerland through a series of coalitional arrangements characteristic of parliamentary regimes and culminates in "personalistic" concentrations of presidential power in the upper right corner.

The Federal Republic of Germany [D] occupies a strategic location at the epicenter of the plot. It has important corporatist and consociational practices, a form of "chancellor democracy" that combines elements of presidentialism and parliamentarism, and a mix of state and societal elements in its "social market economy" policies—not to mention an electoral system that has both proportional and majoritarian aspects. Perhaps it is this balanced eclecticism that has made the institutions of the Federal Republic such a model for today's nascent democracies— and not just its spectacular economic and political success when compared to its predecessor regime.

Italy [I] since fascism is an outlier, with its almost pure form of parliamentarism, although recent discussions about constitutional reform have hinted (so far without effect) at moving it toward a more mixed configuration. France [F] under the Fourth Republic would have occupied a spot nearby, but under the Gaullist constitution of the Fifth Republic it moved toward a populist system based on more majoritarian principles and statist practices.

The last remaining cluster in figure 2 contains three countries that are strongly majoritarian with a focus on a highly visible presidency or prime minister, but have less dominant state capacities than the populist type they otherwise resemble: Argentina (RA), Peru (PER*), and Greece (GR).

■ Correlation Between Modes of Transition and Types of Democracy

Terry Karl, in her comparative analysis of regime changes in South and Central America, has advanced a major hypothesis, namely, that the mode of transition from autocracy has a significant impact on the possibility of a democratic outcome and, where that was possible, on the kind of democracy that would subsequently emerge. This argument rests on the assumption that the conditions under which the previous regime collapsed, was overthrown, or consented to step aside, and whether or not this involved mass mobilization and elite loss of control, would determine the initial distribution of resources among actors, and that these temporary disparities in power would be converted—through rules, guarantees, and roles—into enduring structures that discriminate against some and favor others. Despite considerable variation in constitutional traditions, cultural norms, levels of development, geostrategic location, role in the international system, length and type of autocratic rule, and previous economic order among the cases, this suggests that those polities undergoing a generically similar experience during the transition would end up with generically similar types of democracy—if and when they succeeded in consolidating themselves.[26]

An impressionistic juxtaposition of four distinctive "modes of transition"—by *imposition* (coercive, elite dominant), by *pact* (negotiative, elite dominant), by *reform* (negotiative, mass ascendant), or by *revolution* (coercive, mass ascendant)—with the distribution of kinds of democracy in figure 2 produces some suggestive, if inconclusive, correspondences. The tightness of the eventual fit will depend on whether those cases presently marked with (*) manage to cross the minimal procedural threshold and whether those now cursed with a (?) succeed in consolidating the precarious democratic institutions they have initially chosen.

The first pattern is relatively well known: all those countries that followed the route of *revolution* in ridding themselves of autocracy failed to consolidate any type of democracy within ten or more years of having made the transition. They all became "noncompetitive, single party dominant" regimes with-

---

26. For the original argument, see Terry Karl, "Dilemmas of Democratization in Latin America," *Comparative Politics* (October 1990), pp. 1–21; also Terry Karl and Philippe C. Schmitter, "Modes of Transition in Southern and Eastern Europe, Southern and Central America," *International Social Science Journal* (May 1991), pp. 269–84. For an application of this argument specifically to Eastern Europe, see Laszlo Bruszt and David Stark, "Paths of Extrication and Possibilities of Transformation," and Laszlo Bruszt, "Transformative Politics in East Central Europe" (Working Papers on Transitions from State Socialism, Center for International Studies, Cornell University, no. 91–5, July 1991).

out autonomous institutions in civil society. The one clear exception is Nicaragua, where external actors played a significant role in producing a different outcome. Another partial exception could be Romania, although its recent "revolution" may have actually been more imposed from above than achieved from below.

Those countries that chose the path of *pacts* ended up arrayed along the diagonal that runs from the upper left corner of corporatist democracy to the lower right one of electoralist democracy. Venezuela, Spain, Uruguay, and Chile are closer to the former; Colombia to the latter. Hungary is a case of a spuriously pacted transition (some of its key agreements were subsequently rejected by the electorate), and its location is a bit eccentric with regard to the diagonal, as is that of Poland, the other Eastern case of an unsuccessful (if protracted) effort at pacting.

The transitions by *imposition* have generally remained in the upper right corner as different versions of populist democracy. Brazil, Ecuador, Portugal, and Turkey seem to fit the generalization well; Bulgaria and the Soviet Union are presumptive confirmations. Paraguay may have "descended" into the status of an electoralist democracy, although the absence of information makes it difficult to classify with any confidence. El Salvador and Guatemala seem to have taken a similar route from an unsuccessfully imposed transition to purely electoralist (and, so far, unconsolidated) democracy.

The *reformist* transitions either failed to make it to consolidated democracy in Latin America in the past (Argentina [1946–1955], Chile [1970–1973], and Guatemala [1946–1954]), or are so recent in Eastern Europe that it is not yet clear how to classify them as types of democracy. The CSFR, Poland (where there was also an important pacted component), Slovenia, Croatia, and the Baltic republics are cases in point. The German Democratic Republic began in this mode, but its subsequent trajectory was determined by the intromission of external forces from the FRG. Our hypothesis would be that transitions driven by reform impulses from below and resolved by nonviolent means will eventually array themselves along the diagonal running from consociational to populist democracy.[27]

---

27. The recent Polish presidential elections demonstrate how tempting this populist alternative may be, especially in the face of rising economic insecurity.

Finally, there is that group of relatively unfortunate polities that have had *ambivalent transitions* that combined simultaneously elements of elite continuity and mass mobilization, threats of violence and reluctant acceptance of compromise. Argentina, Peru, and perhaps Romania and Georgia (as well as the Philippines) seem to fit this description. All of these moved—admittedly, to differing degrees and with differing success—toward an intermediary zone between populist and electoralist democracy where the emphasis is clearly on assembling numbers of individuals rather than weighing intensities among social groups, but the weakness of state authority and the fragmentation of the institutions of civil society leave the regimes suspended in a sort of unconsolidated "no-man's-land."

Before reacting too triumphantly to these findings, we would hasten to observe that the scorings on both the modes of transition and types of democracy are tentative (and, of course, may be displaced by subsequent events in several cases). Alternative ways of conceptualizing both the independent and dependent variables could produce quite different patterns of association. Other conditions such as economic development, social structure, or historical tradition may do a better job of predicting outcomes, or conjunctural conditions such as the performance of the economy or pressures from outside powers might have an overriding influence. Nevertheless, the "interocular impact test" does seem to support the initial hypothesis: the way a given polity goes through its transition from autocracy conditions both whether democracy is consolidated and, if so, what type of democracy will emerge.

■ Tentative Conclusions on the Prospects for Democracy

First, political democracy in the contemporary period may be rooted in a fundamental paradox: the modes of transition that appear to enhance initial survivability by limiting uncertainty may preclude the democratic self-transformation of the economy or polity further down the road. Cruelly, the conditions that permit democracies to persist in the short run may constrain their potential for resolving the problems of poverty and inequality that continue to plague them. Indeed, it is reasonable to hypothesize that what occurs in the phase of transition or early consolidation may involve a significant trade-off between some form of political democracy on the one hand

and equity on the other. Thus, even as these democracies guarantee a greater respect for law and human dignity when compared to their authoritarian predecessors, they may be unable to carry out substantive reforms that address the lot of their poorest citizens. If so, the "successful" democratic transitions of the 1980s and early 1990s could prove to be the "frozen" democracies of the next century.

Second, while this may be the central dilemma of elite-dominated processes of democratization, there may be important and lasting differences between countries like Spain, Uruguay, Hungary, Poland, and, most recently, Chile, with their relatively pacted transitions, and Portugal, Brazil, Ecuador, Turkey, and the Soviet Union, with more unilaterally imposed ones. Pacted democracies, whatever their defects, have been honed through compromise between at least two powerful contending elites. Thus, their institutions should be more flexible and malleable when faced with the need to bargain over substantive issues and/or demands for the revision of existing rules. In Uruguay, for example, while the agreed-upon rules made it very difficult to challenge agreements between the military and the parties on the issue of amnesty for crimes committed during authoritarian rule, the left opposition, excluded from this agreement, was nevertheless able to force the convocation of a plebiscite on this major issue—which it subsequently lost. It is difficult to imagine that anything similar could occur in Brazil. Because the armed forces there exerted almost complete control over the timing and content of the transition, they never curtailed their own prerogatives nor fully agreed to the principle of civilian control, and they have not been compelled to adopt institutional rules reflecting the need for compromise. The contrast between the cases of Uruguay and Brazil raises a hypothesis that merits investigation: to the extent that transitions are unilaterally imposed by armed forces who are not compelled to enter into compromises, they threaten to evolve into civilian governments controlled by authoritarian elements who are unlikely to push for greater participation, accountability, or equity for the majority of their citizens. Paradoxically, in other words, the heritage left by "successful" authoritarian experiences, that is, those characterized by relatively moderate levels of repression and economic success that have left the military establishment relatively intact, may prove to be the major obstacle to future democratic self-transformation.[28] This same danger exists, albeit to a lesser extent, in civilian-directed unilateral transitions, e.g., Mexico under Salinas, because the institutional rules that are imposed are likely to be systematically rigged to favor incumbents and to permit less scope for contestation.

Third, the attempt to assess possible consequences of various modes of transition is most problematic where strong elements of imposition, compromise, and reform are simultaneously present, that is to say, where neither incumbent elites nor newly ascendant power contenders are clearly in control, the armed forces are relatively intact, and no clear sequences of modes can be worked out. This is currently the case for Argentina, Peru, Romania, Bulgaria, and Georgia. The Argentine change of regime, for example, given the military's defeat in the Falklands/Malvinas War, the high level of mass mobilization at early stages of the transition, and the absence of pacts between civilian authorities and the armed forces, on the one hand, and between trade unions and employers, on the other, has combined elements from several modes of transition. Such a mixed scenario, while perhaps holding out the greatest hope for political democracy and socioeconomic equity in the long run, may render a consistent strategy of any type ineffectual in the short and medium run and, thus, lead to the repetition of Argentina's persistent failure to consolidate any type of regime. The prospects for failure are even greater in Peru. Given the absence of explicit agreements between the leading political parties, the possibility of mass mobilizations in the midst of economic depression, the presence of an armed insurgency, and a unified military, Peru is currently the most fragile democracy in South America. Romania and Bulgaria occupy similarly precarious positions in Eastern Europe, even if the actors and lines of cleavage are quite different.

Such predictions are discouraging, but they may be offset by more hopeful observations stemming from recent trends that could affect the contingent choices of contemporary democratizers in a positive fashion.

---

28. The notion that especially "successful" authoritarian regimes paradoxically may pose important obstacles for democratization can be found in Anita Isaacs, "Dancing with the People: The Politics of Military Rule in Ecuador, 1972–1979" (Ph.D. diss., Oxford University, 1986); and Guillermo O'Donnell, "Challenges to Democratization in Brazil," *World Policy Journal* 5, no. 2 (Spring 1988), pp. 281–300.

On the one hand, the Cold War features of the international system have changed remarkably, and this may offer new opportunities for the reformist mode of transition in Latin America and Eastern Europe.[29] The failure of two of the three cases cited in this category, Guatemala (1946–1954) and Chile (1970–1973), was profoundly affected by US intervention, motivated in large part by the ideological identification of mass-based reforms with the spread of Soviet influence on the continent. US intervention against peasant-based movements in Central America has been justified in the same manner. Similar calculations about their impact on the relations between the superpowers seem to have encouraged armed intervention by the Soviet Union to suppress reformist-type transitions in Hungary in 1956 and Czechoslovakia in 1968. To the extent that the global state system loses its "bipolarity," the credibility of such accusations becomes increasingly difficult to sustain, thus potentially creating more space for mass ascendant political movements. The fact that this mode of transition failed in the past, especially in Latin America, does not mean that it will not succeed in the future.[30]

On the other hand, this discussion of modes of transition and varying probabilities for survival has not presumed that democracies will benefit from superior economic performance, which is fortunate, given the state of contemporary Latin American and East European economies. Most observers assume that crises in, for example, growth, employment, foreign exchange earnings, and debt repayment necessarily bode ill for the consolidation of democratic rule, and few would question the long-term value of an increasing resource base for political stability. But austerity may have some perverse advantages—at least, for initial survivability. In the context of the terrible economic conditions of the 1980s, the exhaustion of utopian ideologies and even of rival policy prescriptions has become painfully evident. Neither the extreme right nor the extreme left has a

29. This possibility is explored in Terry Lynn Karl, "Central America at the End of the Cold War," in *Beyond the Cold War: Conflict and Cooperation in the Third World*, ed. George W. Breslauer, Harry Kreisler, and Benjamin Ward (Berkeley: Institute of International Studies, University of California, Berkeley, 1991), pp. 222–54.
30. There are important differences here, however, between South America and the Caribbean Basin. Military interventions, which have been confined to the latter region in the past, predated the Cold War and are likely to continue after its demise. As the case of Panama shows, the rationale may simply change to other bases of threat or insecurity.

plausible alternative system to offer—to themselves or to mass publics. Although populism, driven by diffuse popular expectations and disenchantment with the rewards of compromised democracy, is always a possibility—witness the experience of Peru and the recent elections in Argentina, Brazil, and Poland—it cannot deliver the immediate rewards that have been its sustenance in the past.

To the extent that this situation diminishes both the benefits expected from working within the system and the rewards from engaging in antisystem behavior, it enhances the likelihood that some form of democracy will endure. This suggests a possible hypothesis for future exploration, namely, that the relationship between democratization and economic performance, rather than rising or falling in tandem, may be parabolic. Conditions to strike bargains may be most favorable in the midst of protracted austerity, as well as in the midst of sustained plenty. They may be worse when the economy is going through stop-and-go cycles or being hit with sudden windfalls or scarcities. If true, this could provide a ray of hope for the otherwise unpromising decade ahead.

Finally, there is no a priori reason why one type of democracy cannot be gradually and voluntarily transformed into another. Electoralist regimes may evolve into populist or mixed-type democracies; corporatist democracies may become increasingly pluralist or competitive. While pacted transitions do establish an improvised framework for governance that can become an institutionalized barrier to change in the future, this "freezing" scenario is subject to modification. This may be brought about preemptively when some ruling groups, having experienced the advantages of democratic rule, become more inclined over time to seek accommodation to potential pressures from below, or it may occur through the direct pressure from below of organized social groups exercising their new rights and capabilities for collective action.[31] Democracies are never fully and definitively consolidated; moreover, whether from above or

---

31. Paul Cammack has argued that a ruling coalition might make strategic concessions in its own long-term interest to help sustain democracy, especially after having experienced the failure of militaries to act as reliable allies. See his "Democratization: A Review of the Issues," *Bulletin of Latin American Research* 4, no. 2 (1985), pp. 39–46. There seems to be little evidence for this predicted behavior in the current period, however, and further democratization through mass pressure seems to be more likely.

below the process of democratization can be continual and may even be irrepressible.

The notion that one kind of democracy may gradually evolve into a qualitatively different kind suggests that the dynamics of democratic consolidation must differ in important ways from the transition in order to avoid "freezing." Because the overriding goal of the transition is to reach some broad political consensus about acceptable means for reducing uncertainty and preventing a recurrence of autocracy, successful transitions are necessarily characterized by accommodation and compromise. But if this emphasis on caution becomes an *overriding* political norm during consolidation, democracies may find it difficult to demonstrate that they are better than their predecessors at resolving fundamental social and economic problems. Thus, consolidation, if it is to be successful, should require skills and commitments from leading actors that are qualitatively different from those exhibited during the transition. During this later phase, they must demonstrate their ability to differentiate political forces rather than to draw them all into a grand coalition, the capacity to channel competing projects toward the political arena rather than to keep potentially divisive issues off the agenda, and the willingness to tackle incremental reforms, especially in the domains of income distribution and civil-military relations, rather than defer them indefinitely. If the patterns of protracted autocracy that have afflicted Southern and Eastern Europe and the cycles of regime change that have plagued South and Central America are to be broken and to be replaced by an era of lasting democracy, democratizers must learn to divide as well as to unite and to raise hopes as well as to dampen expectations.

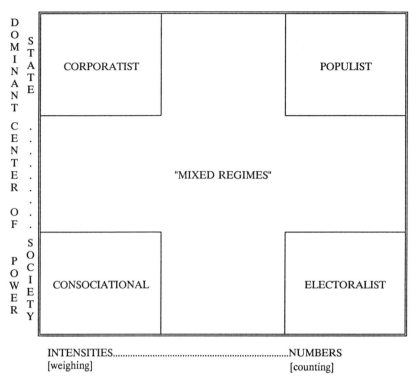

FIGURE 1. KINDS OF DEMOCRACY: THE PROPERTY SPACE

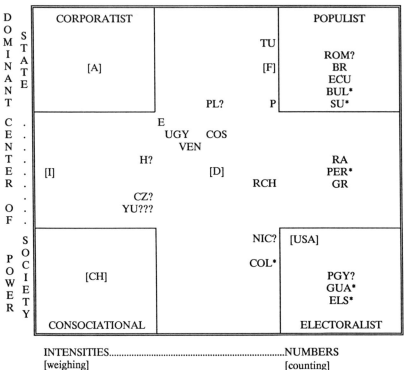

FIGURE 2. KINDS OF DEMOCRACY: SOME RECENT [AND NOT SO RECENT] CASES

* These cases have not yet crossed the minimal democratic threshold.

? These cases have crossed that threshold, but are not yet consolidated into a recognizable type of democracy.

3

The Activist State and the Challenge of Democratization: A Comparative Historical Perspective
GERMAINE A. HOSTON

■ *Political Development, Democratization, and the Problem of the State*

The revolutions in Eastern and Central Europe, coupled with the dramatic failure of the democracy movement in China in the year of the 200th anniversary of the French Revolution, have reinvigorated scholarly interest in the determinants and characteristics of transitions from authoritarian rule to democracy. To be sure, interest in democratization among Western comparativists had already entered a new phase with the transitions in Spain and Portugal and the wave of democratization that occurred in Latin America during the 1980s. Efforts to identify patterns in transitions from military authoritarian rule to democracy gave rise to a distinguished set of new studies.[1] Nevertheless, with a few notable exceptions,[2] this new scholar-

The author wishes to express appreciation to the Institute for EastWest Studies and to other participants in the IEWS democratization workshops at the Hague and in New York for the opportunity to obtain valuable comments and suggestions on this paper. The author is also indebted to Sharon F. Schwartz, J. Richard Iton, and Kim E. Bettcher for their research assistance.

1. See Guillermo O'Donnell, Philippe C. Schmitter, and Laurence White-head, eds., *Transitions from Authoritarian Rule*, 4 vols. (Baltimore: Johns Hopkins University Press, 1986); Larry Diamond, Juan J. Linz, and Seymour Martin Lipset, eds., *Democracy in Developing Countries*, 4 vols. (Boulder: Lynne Rienner, 1988-1990); Robert A. Pastor, *Democracy in the Americas* (New York: Holmes & Meier, 1989); Enrique Baloyra, *Comparing New Democracies: Transition and Consolidation in Mediterranean Europe and the Southern Cone* (Boulder: Westview, 1987); Paul W. Drake and Eduardo Silva, eds., *Elections and Democratization in Latin America, 1980–1985* (San Diego: Center for Iberian and Latin American Studies, University of

ship in comparative politics did not share with the field of political theory a renewed interest in the notion of civil society, its relationship to the state, and its role in democratization that was sparked, at least in part, by the resistance of the Solidarity movement in Poland.[3] By contrast, as other chapters in this volume illustrate,[4] the analysis of the democratization process in Eastern and Central Europe appeals instinctively to an appreciation of the concept of civil society. It is clear that a nascent civil society supported by the Roman Catholic Church and the Solidarity movement nurtured the revolutionary process in Poland, as it did in Brazil, Chile, and Spain.[5] It is equally evident that an urgent challenge of the continuing democratization effort in Eastern and Central Europe lies in constructing strong and

---

California, 1986); and Carlos Huneeus, *Para Vivir La Democracia* (Santiago: Editorial Andante, 1987).

2. See, for example, Susan Eckstein, ed., *Power and Popular Protest: Latin American Social Movements* (Berkeley: University of California Press, 1989). On the treatment of the role of the Church, see Alfred Stepan, ed., *Democratizing Brazil: Problems of Transition and Consolidation* (New York: Oxford University Press, 1989); Scott Mainwaring, *The Catholic Church and Politics in Brazil, 1916–1985* (Stanford: Stanford University Press, 1986); Scott Mainwaring and Alexander Wilde, eds., *The Progressive Church in Latin America* (Notre Dame, Ind.: University of Notre Dame Press, 1989); and Joe Foweraker, *Making Democracy in Spain: Grass-Roots Struggle in the South, 1955–1975* (New York: Cambridge University Press, 1989). Also see the assessment of the literature on Latin America on this point in Geraldo L. Munck, "Identity and Ambiguity in Democratic Struggles," in *Popular Movements and Political Change in Mexico*, ed. Joe Foweraker and Anne L. Craig (Boulder and London: Lynne Rienner, in association with the Center for US-Mexican Studies, University of California, San Diego, 1990), pp. 41–42, n. 16.

3. See, for example, John Keane, ed., *Civil Society and the State: New European Perspectives* (London: Verso, 1988); idem, ed., *The Media and Democracy* (Cambridge, MA: Blackwell, 1991); idem, *Democracy and Civil Society* (London: Verso, 1988); J. Cohen, *Class and Civil Society: The Limits of Marxian Critical Theory* (Amherst: University of Massachusetts Press, 1982); Christopher Pierson, "New Theories of State and Civil Society: Recent Developments in Post-Marxist Analysis of the State," *Sociology* 18, no. 4 (1984), pp. 563–71; B. Frankel, *Beyond the State* (London: Macmillan, 1983); and J. Cohen and A. Arato, *Social Theory and Civil Society*, forthcoming.

4. See also the studies collected in *Uncertain Futures: Eastern Europe and Democracy*, ed. Peter Volten, Institute for East-West Security Studies Occasional Paper, no. 16 (New York, 1990); *Eastern Europe and Democracy: The Case of Poland*, Institute for East-West Security Studies Special Report (New York, 1990); and Vaclav Havel et al., *The Power of the Powerless*, ed. John Keane (London: Hutchinson, 1985).

5. See the brief discussion in Alfred Stepan's Introduction to *Democratizing Brazil*, pp. xii-xiii; and Beate Kohler, *Political Forces in Spain, Greece and Portugal* (London: Butterworth Scientific, 1982).

vibrant civil societies among the ruins of repressive Stalinist regimes that left no room for the emergence of the free associations of autonomous individuals that characterize civil society.[6]

It was the totalistic character of those *anciens régimes* that focused our attention on civil society, as it was so often conceived in opposition to the state. Yet this totalism has also bred profound ambiguities concerning the state and its role in democratizing postrevolutionary societies. It is a poignant irony in Eastern and Central Europe that the legacy of the old regime is such that it is the government, the organs of state power, to which men and women now turn to take the lead in both resolving major economic difficulties and cultivating the civil societies that are viewed as essential for democratization. At the same time, a profound antipathy to the state is reflected in the conviction among many that the key to democratization lies in the negation of the state, in the removal of the state from the economic arena, in the creation of a "free market." These antinomies became quickly evident in Poland, where the leader of the anticommunist Solidarity movement sought almost immediately upon assuming leadership of the country extraordinary governing powers to address urgent economic difficulties.[7] Not surprisingly, similar tensions have also emerged in Hungary and the Czech and Slovak Federal Republic.[8]

The focus on the state as the locus of the problem is consonant with the endeavors of some Western scholars to "bring the state back in" to the study of comparative politics.[9]

---

6. See Charles S. Maier, ed., *Changing Boundaries of the Political: Essays on the Evolving Balance between the State and Society, Public and Private in Europe* (Cambridge: Cambridge University Press, 1987), p. 11; G. W. F. Hegel, *Hegel's Philosophy of Right*, trans. T.M. Knox (Oxford: Oxford University Press, 1970), addendum to §182; and Reinhard Bendix, John Bendix, and Norman Furniss, "Reflections on Political States and Civil Societies," *Research in Political Sociology: A Research Annual*, vol. 3 (1987), p. 19.

7. In his chapter in this volume, Krzysztof Jasiewicz has noted that there is significant popular support for a "new authoritarianism" in the democratization era.

8. See the chapter by Rudolf L. Tőkés in this volume; and Ivan Gabal, "Contradictions and Inconsistencies in the Czechoslovak Situation," p. 10 (Paper presented at the IEWS and Netherlands Institute of International Relations conference on "Overcoming Obstacles to Democratization and Institution Building in Europe," The Hague, November 9–11, 1990).

9. See Peter B. Evans, Dietrich Rueschemeyer, and Theda Skocpol, eds., *Bringing the State Back In* (Cambridge and New York: Cambridge University Press, 1985).

Nevertheless, inasmuch as this trend may issue in a project that seeks primarily to negate the past, it may slight key elements of the democratization process that rely on a more complex understanding of the relationship between the state and civil society than the extremes of anti-state economic liberalism would suggest. Charles Taylor has suggested that, by relying on a "model of a self-regulating social life" that does not adequately recognize a need for political activism among citizens within and beyond the bounds of state institutions, laissez-faire liberalism threatens to "depreciate political freedom altogether." The danger here is that the "civil society notion [c]ould be sidetracked and drained of much of its force," Taylor argues, "[and] its weight as a counter-thrust to bureaucratic power would be neutralized."[10]

An examination of democratization in historical and comparative perspective—in such diverse settings as Japan, Latin American societies, and the recently democratizing Portugal and Spain[11]— supports an appreciation of how important the construction of civil society is to the task of democratization. It is argued in this chapter that the solution to the problem of democratization lies as much in the cultivation of a vigorous civil society and what Habermas refers to as a vibrant "public sphere" between the state and civil society as in the introduction of the constitutional and representative state institutions that are commonly associated with political democracy.[12] Historically, in Habermas's analysis, the liberal public sphere "devel-

---

10. Charles Taylor, "Modes of Civil Society," *Public Culture* 3, no. 1 (Fall 1990), pp. 116–17.
11. I am indebted to Peter Gourevitch for pointing out to me the importance of the notion of civil society in studies of the democratization of Spain and Portugal. See, for example, the role of labor organizations in José Maravall's description of *The Transition of Democracy in Spain* (New York: St. Martin's, 1982), pp. 10ff; and Foweraker, *Making Democracy in Spain*, pp. 231ff.
12. There are at least two conceptions of civil society in Western thought, with the Teutonic one incorporating the family in a manner that the Anglo-Saxon version does not. See Antony Black, *Guilds and Civil Society in European Political Thought from the Twelfth Century to the Present* (Ithaca: Cornell University Press, 1984), especially chapter 3. Space does not permit an extended theoretical treatment of continental versus Anglo-Saxon approaches to the notion of civil society. Here "civil society" is used with reference to Black's characterization of it in contradistinction to the "corporate organization and mentality of guild life" as "a set of practices and beliefs centered upon a market economy, social mobility, individual self-determination and private property" (p. 30).

oped to the extent to which the public concern regarding the private sphere of civil society was no longer confined to the authorities, but was considered by the subjects as one that was properly theirs." The judgments of private individuals that were inhibited by the state came to assume the status of public opinion, as the public sphere "was now casting itself loose as a forum in which the private people, come together to form a public, readied themselves to compel public authority to legitimate itself before public opinion."[13] Habermas stressed the emergence of a private world of letters and an independent press where political judgments were made outside the structures of state authority.[14] The key point here, however, lies in the emergence of a sphere of social life—one that is much larger than merely a capitalist economy, as it was treated by Marx[15]— that is potentially outside the purview of the political yet insists on the right to make political judgments that influence the "authoritative allocation of values for a society."[16] In Habermas's account, in Western Europe this assertion of a claim to power in the form of "rational-critical public debate" historically challenged the legitimacy of the claims to rule of existing authorities and provided a basis for self-government. It established what Taylor refers to as a notion of "subjective rights," in which the ruled claimed the accountability of the ruler to contractual obligations that were the basis of the relationship, while it authenticated the notion of the existence of society as an independent source of authority. It is the flourishing of civil society in this broader conception that is crucial to the democratization process in Eastern and Central Europe today.

---

13. See Jürgen Habermas, *The Structural Transformation of the Public Sphere: An Inquiry into a Category of Bourgeois Society*, trans. Thomas Burger (Cambridge: MIT Press, 1989), pp. 23–28. There are some ambiguities in Habermas's presentation. Although he refers to "the public sphere of civil society" (p. 23), his graphical representation of his conception posits the "public sphere" between civil society and the state (p. 30). Habermas is not alone in this ambiguity, which runs throughout Antonio Gramsci's work on the subject.
14. Cf. Taylor, "Modes of Civil Society," pp. 108–9.
15. It is curious that the identification of civil society with a self-regulating capitalist economy, which is common in popular discourse concerning the need to build civil societies in Eastern and Central Europe, should have emerged from Marx's truncation of Hegel's original conception. See ibid., p. 108.
16. David Easton, *The Political System* (New York: Knopf, 1953), p. 129.

This assertion implies a broader conceptualization of democracy than those offered by many. The case of Japan illustrates emphatically that there is a distinction to be drawn between a "modest meaning of democracy" as proffered by Samuel Huntington, on the one hand, and a performance-oriented conception of democracy that incorporates an appreciation of outcomes, on the other. Put differently, it is possible to have the institutional accoutrements of democracy, without a healthy and autonomous civil society, but the result may not be a working democratic system that in fact allows for the alternation of those in power. A key element of democratic politics is accountability, and the existence of both a viable opposition contending for power and political parties that articulate competing values or interests of different constituencies is essential to a system that is democratic in practice.[17] Since the Meiji Restoration of the late 1860s and 1870s, Japan has been endowed with the institutional arrangements for choosing its leaders that are commonly identified with political democracy. These arrangements did not at first permit the "entire adult population" to participate in elections as citizens as they would after World War II, two decades after universal manhood suffrage was passed.[18] Yet, at the beginning of this century, Western democracies themselves inspired criticisms of elitism by Joseph Schumpeter, Vilfredo Pareto, C. Wright Mills, Gaetano Mosca, and others; and in the view of Japanese liberals and Marxists themselves, the Japanese political system fell short not only of the ideal of "bourgeois democracy" but also of these imperfect approximations.[19] It is important to note that the same institu-

---

17. Cf. Gerald Curtis, *The Japanese Way of Politics* (New York: Columbia University Press, 1988), p. 242.
18. See this stipulation in Terry Lynn Karl, "Dilemmas of Democratization in Latin America," *Comparative Politics* 23, no. 1 (October 1990), p. 2; and Donald Share and Scott Mainwaring, "Transitions through Transaction: Democratization in Brazil and Spain," in *Political Liberalization in Brazil*, ed. Wayne A. Selcher (Boulder: Westview, 1986), p. 177; and Samuel P. Huntington, "The Modest Meaning of Democracy," in *Democracy in the Americas*, ed. Pastor, pp. 11–16.
19. See Germaine A. Hoston, *Marxism and the Crisis of Development in Prewar Japan* (Princeton: Princeton University Press, 1986), chap. 1 passim; Kato Shuichi, "Taishō Democracy as the Pre-Stage for Japanese Militarism," in *Japan in Crisis: Essays on Taishō Democracy*, ed. Bernard S. Silberman and H.D. Harootunian (Princeton: Princeton University Press, 1974); and Germaine A. Hoston, "The State, Modernity, and the Fate of Liberalism in Prewar Japan," *Journal of Asian Studies*, forthcoming.

tional arrangements that were established in the Meiji era and provided for the "era of party rule"[20] in the 1910s, 1920s, and 1930s offered the basis for the military authoritarianism of the 1940s. Thus, while Japan is commonly described as having been "fascist" during the war, unlike the fascist regimes of Hitler's Germany and Mussolini's Italy, Japan's military authoritarianism thrived during the war without jettisoning the structures of parliamentary democracy.[21]

In the postwar period, Japan is now endowed with all the accoutrements associated with democracy, including popular, rather than imperial, sovereignty. Yet many, both within and outside Japan, question the extent to which this system functions in a truly democratic manner. Since 1955, Japan has been ruled by a single party, a Liberal Democratic Party that is neither liberal nor democratic nor, many would argue, even a party. The party does not even follow its own rules in selecting its president, who is invariably the country's Prime Minister.[22] The five major and other minor opposition parties have succeeded in gaining 49.5% of the vote in the recent past (1983), but single-party dominance is self-perpetuating, and not only because of the tremendous role that money plays in the process.[23] The

---

20. Peter Duus, "The Era of Party Rule: Japan, 1905–1932," in *Modern East Asia: Essays in Interpretation*, ed. James B. Crowley (New York: Harcourt, Brace & World, 1970).
21. Indeed, the persistence of the dominance of the bureaucracy and the centrality attributed to the Imperial Household—which were blamed by critics for the undemocratic aspects of the previous era—may be credited with having prevented the emergence of a single, dictatorial leader. Cf. Ben-Ami Shillony, *Politics and Culture in Wartime Japan* (Oxford: Oxford University Press, Clarendon Press, 1981), pp. 173ff.
22. Over the past 30 years, the presidential selection process has been dominated by irregularities that allow behind-the-scenes factional negotiations to determine the country's next prime minister. When an attempt was made in the mid-1970s to democratize the system by introducing a two-stage election system in which all party members would vote in a primary, and the two candidates receiving the most votes would compete in a run-off election in the party's convention, factional competition was simply intensified. As a result, in 1981, the party again changed its rules, now requiring that the first-stage primary election be suspended unless more than three candidates were nominated. At the same time, a measure was implemented to make it less likely that enough candidates would be nominated to require the open primary: candidates would have to be endorsed by 50 LDP Diet members to be nominated, instead of only 20, as formerly required.
23. Fukui and Fukai estimate that the LDP expends well over $1 billion in an election year, while in the 1983 British general election, the Liberal, Labor,

longer the dominance of the single party that controls the bureaucracy that in turn overshadows the Diet (parliament) continues, the more revolutionary and thus unlikely an alternative outcome becomes.[24] The result is that certain popular interests are systematically excluded from meaningful participation in the decision-making process. Almost one-third of those who sit in the House of Representatives are so-called *nisei* legislators—that is, their fathers, and in some cases, even grandfathers and great-grandfathers, were also legislators; and *nisei* legislators comprise 46% of the ruling LDP contingent. This is a product of what Haruhiro Fukui and Shigeko Fukai have characterized as "informal politics," politics not "subject to regulation by rules made and enforced by formal institutions of the state."[25] The way informal politics operate clearly is related to the customs and values that prevail in society in general.

These features of Japanese politics have drawn sharp criticism. T.J. Pempel and Keiichi Tsunekawa have characterized Japanese politics as "corporatism without labor,"[26] while Satō Seizaburō, Inoguchi Takashi, and Ellis Krauss and Muramatsu Michi have qualified the pluralism of Japanese democracy as "bureaucracy-cum-LDP-guided pluralism," "bureaucracy-led mass-inclusionary pluralism," and "patterned pluralism," respectively.[27] More importantly, within Japan, there has emerged a

and Conservative parties expended about $3 million, $9 million, and $15 million, respectively. Haruhiro Fukui and Shigeko N. Fukai, "Informal Politics and One-Party Dominance in Japan: A Case Study and a Rudimentary Theory" (Paper prepared for presentation at the 1990 Annual Meeting of the American Political Science Association, San Francisco, August 20-September 2, 1990), pp. 5, 8.

24. See the discussion in Germaine A. Hoston, "Between Theory and Practice: Marxist Thought and the Politics of the Japanese Socialist Party," *Studies in Comparative Communism* 20, no. 2 (Summer 1987), pp. 175–78, 206–7.

25. Ibid., p. 12 and passim.

26. T.J. Pempel and Keiichi Tsunekawa, "Corporatism Without Labor? The Japanese Anomaly," in *Trends Toward Corporatist Intermediation*, ed. Philippe Schmitter and Gerhard Lehmbruch (Beverly Hills: Sage, 1979), pp. 231–70.

27. Satō's expression is *jinmin-kanchō kongōtai ni hōkō-zukerareta tagen-shugi*, and Inoguchi's *kanryō shudō taishū-hōkatsu-kata tagen-shugi*. See Satō Seizaburō and Matsuzaki, "Jimintō chōchōki seiken no kaibō" (Autopsy on the super-long-term reign of the LDP), *Chūō kōron* (November 1984), pp. 66–100, especially pp. 70, 73–74; and Ellis Krauss and Michio Muramatsu, "The Conservative Policy Line and the Development of Patterned Pluralism," in *The Political Economy of Japan: The Domestic Transformation*, ed. K. Yamamura and Y. Yasuba (Stanford: Stanford University Press, 1987).

scholarly group called the civil society school (advocating a *shimin shakai-ron*, theory of civil society), which has recognized the centrality of the character of Japan's civil society to the debilities of its democracy. This group emerged in the late 1960s, just as accelerating economic growth was positioning Japan securely among the leading industrial nations of the world. Led by Uchida Yoshihiko and Hirata Kiyoaki, this school developed a critical perspective on Japanese politics and economics based on the concept of civil society. Although it is not always clear how the notion of civil society is to be distinguished from simply capitalist society,[28] civil society school theorists have returned to Marx, Weber, Gramsci, and even Hegel to conceive it as "a society in which [men and women have] freed[d] themselves of feudal or premodern communities in order to become independent individuals and enjoy liberty and equality legally and morally." This is a society in which "the identity between labor and property" prevails, i.e., "property based on each individual's [own] labor." Although the argument is made that this notion is to be taken not as a historical category, but rather as a "methodological concept," the West European experience is clearly the model for their construction of the concept.[29]

There is much that is suggestive in the theses of the civil society school about the prospects for democratization in Eastern and Central Europe. First, they support the notion that it is possible to have institutional arrangements within the realm of state power that accord with what is deemed necessary for democratic politics, but these may not in fact prove to be *sufficient* to realize political democracy. It is important to note, as

---

28. See, for example, the muddled discussion in Hirata Kiyoaki, *Shimin shakai to shakai-shugi* (Civil society and socialism) (Tokyo: Iwanami Shoten, 1969), pp. 51ff, where civil society is both identified with capitalist society and identified as that which made "a continuous turn into capitalist society."

29. Yamada Toshio, "Les tendances du marxisme japonais contemporain" (Trends in contemporary Japanese Marxism), in *Actuel Marx*, no. 2: *Le marxisme au Japon* (1987), p. 39. It is important to note that in the usage of these theorists—who are descendants of the prewar Marxist faction called the Kōza-ha—familial ties, which are identified with Confucian social relations viewed as "feudal" in character, are excluded from civil society, while in Hegel familial ties would have been included as part of the civil societal framework. These theoretical concerns are properly the subject of a separate study. It is sufficient to note here that even in Western parlance, there are at least two possible treatments of the family in the notion of civil society

Taylor does, that this is not a matter of a "chauvinistic idea that representative institutions cannot take root outside their home culture."[30] Rather, the critical point offered by the *shimin shakai-ron* self-critique of Japanese democracy is that Japan developed precisely such representative institutions at the same time as it modernized economically; indeed, it achieved "super-modernization," but its historical development omitted the creation of a true civil society.[31]

The burden of the civil society school's argument has to do with the remanence of "premodern" elements in Japanese society and culture, which ironically, in their view, accelerated Japan's extraordinarily rapid pace of industrial development after World War II.[32] This point is significant for what it asserts concerning the persistence of modes of behavior and thought— what might be called political culture—from previous social formations. Such remnants, especially as they are reflected in ethnic intolerance and antagonisms remaining from the pre-Stalinist era, constitute one of the greatest challenges for those who would build working democracies in Eastern and Central Europe. In Japan, the persistence of old "feudal" allegiances has meant that "all exigencies imposed by capital could easily be realized to the detriment of civil interests and without regard to human rights," including rights to decent living conditions, quality of the natural environment, and other considerations[33] that have not traditionally been embraced by Western liberal politics. In addition, Uchida has noted the supremacy of the state over civil society in Japan. Quoting the early Marxist Kawakami Hajime, Uchida contends, "In Europe, God endowed the rights of man, and then men gave rights to the state. In Japan, by contrast, with its state religion, one did not question the raison d'etre of the state: rather 'God created *Staatsrecht* first and then the state gave men rights.' "[34] Consequently, while capital and the state grew, civil society in Japan "remained powerless." The paradox here lies in the fact that while civil society is historically identified with the advent of capitalism,

---

30. Taylor, "Modes of Civil Society," p. 101.
31. See Uchida Yoshihiko, *Nihon shihon-shugi no shisō zō* (Images of the thought of Japanese capitalism) (Tokyo: Iwanami Shoten, 1967), pp. 242, 336.
32. Ibid., p. 334.
33. Yamada, "Les tendances du marxisme," p. 39.
34. Uchida, *Nihon shihon-shugi no shisō zō*, pp. 351–52.

whereby men and women in Europe made the transition "from relations of personalistic dependence to relations of material dependence,"[35] in Japan capitalism prospered precisely because of "the weakness of its civil society."[36]

What is important here is less the contrast between Japan and Europe than the significance attributed to the existence of an independent, autonomous civil society for the maturation of democratic politics. The point is not that Japanese, as non-Europeans, were somehow unable to evolve democratic institutions, for this they did. The problem was rather the persistence of pre-democratic modes of social interaction. In other words, what determines whether the outcome of the activity of democratic state institutions is in fact *democratic* lies not merely in the realm of the state and in the institutional arrangements made in its sphere, but in the realm of civil society. Thus, it may ultimately be less useful to focus on how activist the state is vis-à-vis civil society than to concentrate on the implications of *how* the state is activist—how the state's activities affect the maturation of a vital civil society. Thus, this chapter focuses on the role of the Japanese state in two realms that carry great significance for the democratization process—industrialization and education. After examining state activism in these realms in the Meiji (1868–1912) and postwar Occupation periods, observations relevant to the current challenges of democratization in Eastern and Central Europe will be offered.

■ A New Leadership in Pursuit of "Modernity" in Meiji Japan

The Meiji Restoration offers fertile ground for the exploration of the impact of specific state policies on the process of democratization. The Meiji leadership undertook two sets of measures that would have a profound impact on the development of Japanese civil society, and thus on democratization. At the outset, it is important to note that the Meiji oligarchs did not value political democracy per se, but rather introduced democratic institutions in order to convince the Western powers that Japan was a sufficiently "civilized" society, that Western unequal treaties should be renounced, and that Japan should be treated as an equal in the international system. To this end—

---

35. Ibid., p. 337.
36. Yamada, "Les tendances du marxisme," p. 40.

much as the desire to be accepted into the European Community motivated democratizing changes in Spain and Portugal a century later—the Meiji leadership deemed it necessary to demonstrate that Japan was worthy of such respect by adopting the representative constitutional system and institutions that were viewed as advanced in the West. It will be recalled that the legitimacy of the old Tokugawa shogunate had been founded on military supremacy. Impotent in the face of the superior Western technology with which it was confronted when Commodore Matthew Perry arrived on Japan's shores in 1854 demanding that Japan be opened to trade with the West, the shogunate quickly lost the support of the lower stratum of a warrior ruling class whose members were experiencing a decline in their economic circumstances.[37] During the Tokugawa period, there had already emerged a group of dissenters, scholars of Dutch learning who were convinced that Japan could not compete successfully in the Western international system without acquiring Western science and ethics. This view quickly prevailed over the xenophobic *sonnō jōi* ("revere the emperor and expel the barbarian") slogan that had propelled the overthrow of the Tokugawa shogun for its impotence in the face of Western encroachment. Within a few years after the beginning of the era of "enlightened rule" (*Meiji*), the new leadership had established a government with a tripartite separation of executive, legislative, and judicial powers; the Iwakura Mission was dispatched to ascertain what other elements of Western government might be suitable for adaptation to Japan, and to persuade the powers to modify the unequal treaties. Although the Meiji oligarchs did not succeed in the latter, they did return with insights on the institutional arrangements of modern Western-style representative government.[38]

Such initiatives by major political leaders, combined with independent efforts among intellectuals and grassroots activists to disseminate Western liberal political ideals, resulted in the promulgation of a constitution in 1889. Political associations

---

37. See the discussion of the factors contributing to the downfall of the Tokugawa and the rise of the new Meiji regime in Germaine A. Hoston, "Conceptualizing Bourgeois Revolution: The Prewar Japanese Left and the Meiji Restoration," *Comparative Studies in Society and History* 33, no. 3 (July 1991), pp. 539-581.
38. For details of these and other points in the succeeding pages, see W.G. Beasley, *The Meiji Restoration* (Stanford: Stanford University Press, 1972).

such as the Sanshisha (Society of Mihara District Teachers) and the Aishinsha (Society for Mutual Regard), inspired by Western natural rights theory, called for the establishment of a national representative assembly.[39] To promote the liberal ideals of Western thinkers from Montesquieu to Rousseau among Japanese youth, the Sanshisha founded an academy whose students were recruited to the Jiyūtō's (Liberal Party) rebellion against Meiji authoritarianism in the early 1880s.[40] Liberal Enlightenment scholars soon clashed with a state that imposed restrictions on the press when scholars boldly ventured in public discourse issues that approached the substance of politics.[41] Convinced that the Charter Oath with which the new regime had been founded in 1868 had provided for the establishment of popular assemblies, Fukuzawa Yukichi, Nishi Amane, and Ueki Emori pressured the regime for a fully representative constitutional order. Their efforts converged with those of the political party movement, in which the Constitutional Progressive Party (Rikken Kaishintō) advocated a parliamentary system on the English model, while the Liberal Party was drawn to more radical French revolutionary ideals.

The regime's response to these twin pressures was twofold. On the one hand, it resorted to repression, culminating in the implementation of the Peace Preservation Law of 1887, which permitted the removal of any person deemed a threat to public peace. At the same time, the leadership took positive measures to implement some form of constitutional government. The first step was to dispatch Itō Hirobumi to Europe, whence he brought German political theorists, the most important of whom was *Staatsrecht* theorist Hermann Roesler, to advise the Meiji leaders on the Japanese constitution.[42] By the time the constitution was

---

39. Shōji Kichinosuke, *Nihon seisha seitō hattatsu shi* (History of the development of political societies in Japan) (Tokyo: Ochanomizu Shobō, 1959), pp. 13–15.
40. Roger W. Bowen, *Rebellion and Democracy in Meiji Japan: A Study of Commoners in the Popular Rights Movement* (Berkeley and Los Angeles: University of California Press, 1980), pp. 216–28, 8–28.
41. For more detailed treatments of the popular rights movement in Meiji Japan, see Thomas R. H. Havens, "Scholars and Politics in Nineteenth-Century Japan: The Case of Nishi Amane," *Modern Asian Studies* 2, no. 4 (October 1968), pp. 315–24; and Shigeki Tōyama, "Reforms of the Meiji Restoration and the Birth of Modern Intellectuals," *Acta Asiatica*, no. 13 (1967), pp. 55–99.
42. On the details of the amalgamation of German state sovereignty theory with indigenous Japanese thought, see Joseph Pittau, *Political Thought in*

actually promulgated in 1889, the primary institutions of the new political order already existed and were in operation—except, significantly, the bicameral Diet. The resulting institutional structure provided the instruments for a potentially democratic representative government, along with a legitimizing myth based on premises that inhibited even the egalitarianism of Meiji liberals.[43]

Meanwhile, the Meiji leadership at once undertook revolutionary economic changes to bring Japan into the age of industrial modernity while implementing measures to ensure social and political stability in the face of these dramatic changes. The Western theorist Niccolò Macchiavelli once advised a prince to found a wholly new political order because the prince could convince his subjects that "nothing has changed."[44] The challenge for the Meiji regime was to defend the new order by persuading its people at once that everything had changed—the power to rule (tōchiken, or sovereignty) had been restored to the imperial authority from whom it had been usurped by the shogun—and yet that nothing had changed: This was the same imperial household that had always headed the Japanese body politic, at least in theory, in better, more halcyon days.[45] This the Meiji leadership accomplished, with the assistance of leading scholars of constitutional law, by propagating a new political myth, one that drew on both traditional Japanese beliefs about the social and political order and ideas about representative government imported from the West. Together with Meiji policies on industrialization, efforts to perpetuate this myth through universal education had significant effects on the articulation of a civil society in newly industrial capitalist Japan.

Early Meiji Japan, 1868–1889, Harvard East Asian Series, no. 24 (Cambridge: Harvard University Press, 1967); and Hori Makoto, "Meiji shoki no kokka ron" (The theory of the state in the early Meiji period), in Kokka gakkai gojū shūnen kinen—Kokkagaku ronshū (Commemoration of the fiftieth anniversary of the Kokka Gakkai: A collection of essays on state theory) (Tokyo: Yūhikaku, 1937), pp. 711–44.

43. On the nuances of Japanese liberals from Meiji (1868–1912) through Taishō (1912–1926), see Hoston, "The State, Modernity, and the Fate of Liberalism in Prewar Japan."

44. Niccolò Macchiavelli, The Discourses, ed. Bernard Crick (Harmondsworth: Penguin Books, Ltd., 1970), pp. 176–77.

45. In fact, of course, for most of Japan's long history, actual power had been separated from the imperial household, just as it was in the Tokugawa era, but the belief in imperial power was a matter of myth.

The Meiji State and the Rise of Industrial Capitalism

Under the slogan *fukoku kyōhei* ("wealth and power"), the Meiji leadership instituted measures that would support the transition to industrial capitalism in late 19th-century Japan. First, like 16th- through 19th-century European monarchs and parliamentary regimes, the Meiji leaders indirectly bolstered the rise of capitalism by providing the infrastructure to support an integrated national market.[46] These measures facilitated the consolidation of the sovereign's territory as a national state by centralizing governmental controls over subnational units and constructing effective systems of communications and transport. Then there were measures that—much more directly than those undertaken by the British Parliament, such as enclosure[47]—supported the emergence of indigenous industrial enterprises. Under the first set of measures, the Meiji leadership boldly engineered a transition from the already centralized feudalism of the Tokugawa shogunate to a still more centralized capitalist national state. The imperial capital, heretofore located in Kyoto, hundreds of miles from the shogun's headquarters in Edo (now Tokyo), was moved to Edo, and the shogun's castle became the imperial castle. The nearly 300 feudal *han* (domains) were abolished and replaced by a system of 75 prefectures (*ken*) in 1871, which was further centralized into a smaller number of prefectures in 1889. The now bankrupt *daimyo* (feudal lords) were not in a position to resist either this initiative or the establishment of a central imperial military force and the enactment of a Conscription Law in 1873 that eradicated the traditional status differentiation between warrior (samurai) and commoner. Samurai were no longer permitted to carry their traditional long and short swords, and they lost their legal

---

46. For accounts of these measures in the West, see the essays collected in Charles Tilly, ed., *The Formation of National States in Western Europe*, Studies in Political Development, no. 8 (Princeton: Princeton University Press, 1975); Otto Hintze, "Economics and Politics in the Age of Modern Capitalism," pp. 422–52, and Otto Hintze, "The State in Historical Perspective," pp. 154–169, both in *The Historical Essays of Otto Hintze*, ed. Felix Gilbert (New York: Oxford University Press, 1975).
47. For an insightful discussion of the impact of the enclosure movement in Britain in facilitating the country's transition from a rural agrarian to an urban industrial society, see Barrington Moore, *Social Origins of Dictatorship and Democracy: Lord and Peasant in the Making of the Modern World* (Boston: Beacon Press, 1966).

privileges. Moreover, ironically, although the Meiji leadership itself was comprised of samurai who had opposed the shogunate, the fate of the samurai as a social grouping was to fall still further. Samurai stipends were reduced and then finally commuted to bonds, and many samurai households fell into poverty. The 1873 expedition against Korea and the promise to establish local assemblies were but two measures taken to defuse the resulting samurai discontent. The measures were supplemented by actions taken to ensure that power in localities would lie in the hands of those sympathetic to the regime's goals. Since many such supporters were lower- and middle-rank samurai, a new emphasis on ability rather than inherited privileges in awarding political office served this purpose well and mollified those who advocated a more egalitarian society.[48]

Other policy initiatives more directly targeted the creation of a capitalist economy. The Meiji oligarchs eliminated the Tokugawa prohibition on the buying and selling of land, and, most importantly, implemented the land tax reforms that would provide the state with the capital it needed for industrialization. Driven by financial distress both within and outside the state—accentuated by peasant revolts, almost half of which were inspired by the new tax policy[49]—the new leaders implemented a reform that promised tax relief to peasants while ensuring the government a more reliable income. Under the old system, the land tax had been figured as a percentage of the yield of a holding, while the new system established the tax as a fixed monetary amount based on land value. This meant that the government's budget would not fluctuate wildly from year to year, so that effective planning for investment could occur.[50] Of course, the measure hurt the poorest among the peasantry. Tenancy rose sharply in the countryside, and rebellions reflected peasants' discontent with their worsened lot.[51] On the

---

48. See Beasley, *Meiji Restoration*, chap. 8, especially pp. 337ff.
49. Ibid., p. 391.
50. Ibid., pp. 390ff; and E.H. Norman, *Origins of the Modern Japanese State: Selected Writings of E.H. Norman*, ed. John W. Dower (New York: Pantheon, 1975), pp. 245ff.
51. Significantly, peasant revolts, which had begun before the Restoration, reached a peak in the year of the land tax reforms. See Tanaka Akira, "Meiji hansei kaikaku to ishin kanryō" (The Meiji reform of han rule and the Restoration bureaucracy), in *Meiji kokka keisei katei no kenkyū* (Studies on the process of the formation of the Meiji state), ed. Waseda Masatsugu (Tokyo: Ochanomizu Shobō, 1966), p. 114. The rate of land

other hand, its benefits to the regime were undeniable: the land tax provided over 90% of the government's tax revenues.[52]

This capital was of tremendous significance to the industrialization effort. The Meiji leaders already possessed some advantages in the legacy of the Tokugawa era. Under the shogunate, the Tokugawa and other *han* such as the Satsuma and Hizen had invested successfully in Western technologies such as iron smelting and shipbuilding. The Meiji government took over the two major shipyards at Yokosuka and Nagasaki and built another at Hyōgo (now Kobe). The state directly operated munitions factories and developed the communications (telegraph) and transportation networks (railways and steamer lines) essential to the functioning of a national capitalist economy. The government also began to operate coal, iron, and copper mines, although most investment in these areas remained private.[53]

At the same time, the state encouraged the growth of industry in Japanese textiles, an important potential export that could earn much-needed foreign currency. Japan's silk industry had flourished long before the Restoration, but the Meiji state had to encourage the very beginnings of the woolen and cotton textile industries.[54] Combined with its support of strategic industries, the role of the state in Japan's industrialization in these years was appreciable and effective. As economists Kazushi

tenancy was about 32% in 1873, increased to 37% in 1883, and was 39.99% in 1892. Note that the most significant increase occurred immediately after the land tax reforms. See Hirano Yoshitarō, *Nihon shihon-shugi shakai no kikō: shiteki katei yori no kyūmei* (The structure of Japanese capitalist society: An examination in terms of historical process) (Tokyo: Iwanami Shoten, 1934), p. 46–48; cf. Tsuchiya Takao and Okazaki Saburō, *Nihon shihon-shugi hattatsu shi gaisetsu* (Outline of the history of the development of Japanese capitalism), 2nd. ed. (Tokyo: Yūhikaku, 1937, 1948), pp. 220–22.

52. See William W. Lockwood, *The Economic Development of Japan: Growth and Structural Change, 1868–1938* (Princeton: Princeton University Press, 1964), p. 17. Cf. G.C. Allen, *A Short Economic History of Modern Japan, 1867–1960* (New York: Praeger, 1963), pp. 41–42.

53. Lockwood, *Economic Development of Japan*, pp. 14, 15; and Ōuchi Tsutomu, Kajinishi Mitsuhaya, Katō Toshihiko, and Ōshima Kiyoshi, *Nihon shihon-shugi no seiritsu* (The establishment of Japanese capitalism), vol. 2, *Shihon no genshi-teki chikuseki* (The primitive accumulation of capital), Nihon ni okeru shihon-shugi no hattatsu (The development of capitalism in Japan), 13 vols. (Tokyo: Tōkyō Daigaku Shuppan-kai, 1956), pp. 329–46.

54. See Hattori Shisō, "Ishin shi hōhō-jō no sho mondai" (Methodological problems in the history of the Restoration) (April-June 1933), in *Hattori Shisō chosaku shū* (Collected works of Hattori Shisō), 7 vols. (Tokyo: Riron-sha, 1955, 1960), vol. 1, p. 123.

Ohkawa and Henry Rosovsky have noted, "Government investments generally exceeded those of the private sector until World
War I: In 1884 they were 66 percent and in 1901 54 percent of the
total."[55] In part as a consequence of this activist role of the state,
Japan enjoyed spectacular growth from the 1880s until the end
of World War I without having to rely excessively on exports.[56]

This rapid growth did not occur without setbacks; yet the
Meiji state's initial involvement in heavy industry and the
manner in which it resolved its difficulties by retreating from
some of its direct involvement in the economy had a decisive
impact on the subsequent evolution of the relationship between
the state and private capital in the Taishō (1912–1926) and
Shōwa (1926–1989) eras. As a result of the 1876 decision to make
bond payments to samurai and *daimyo* and the 1877 Satsuma
samurai rebellion, the Meiji state experienced serious financial
difficulties, which were compounded by the costs associated
with the development of the northern island of Hokkaidō and
the expense of operating its own enterprises—many of which
were incurring heavy losses. In 1880, rampant inflation had set
in, and the value of the yen had declined by almost 50%. The
government immediately embarked on a policy of financial
retrenchment, and was forced to sell all its nonstrategic industrial enterprises at a substantial loss. Because so few private
capitalists could make such purchases, the enterprises were sold
to a small number of businessmen and officials, many of whom
were closely associated with the Meiji leaders. This, along with
the government's reliance on a few major companies in establishing its banking, minting, and industrial enterprises, helped to
accelerate the concentration of capital that would become much
more evident in the Taishō era. Indeed, by the mid-Meiji period,
the neologism *tokken-seisho* (politically privileged merchants)
had emerged to describe merchants who had been accorded

---

55. Kazushi Ohkawa and Henry Rosovsky, *Japanese Economic Growth: Trend
    Acceleration in the Twentieth Century*, Studies of Economic Growth in
    Industrialized Countries (Stanford: Stanford University Press, 1973), p.
    16.
56. Lockwood, *Economic Development of Japan*, p. 188. Significantly, the most
    rapid economic growth in pre–World War II Japan occurred during
    periods of war: the Sino-Japanese and Russo-Japanese Wars and World
    War I. Lockwood estimates that "total production and real income in
    Japan, allowing for the rise in prices, may have increased by 80 to 100
    percent in the quarter century ending in 1914" (p. 20; see also the table on
    p. 135).

privileges by the government or had accumulated wealth as purveyors for the government during the crucial early years of the Meiji's state-led industrialization.[57]

Let us look more closely at this phenomenon. Its roots actually lie in the Tokugawa era, when the Mitsui, for example, had been engaged in money-changing and tailoring "by appointment to the shogunate." When they saw the shogun would fall, they supported the Restoration movement in 1867. In exchange for helping to defeat the shogunate, in 1868 the Mitsui were charged with raising funds and issuing Cabinet notes for the encouragement of industry. Three years later, on their own initiative, they collected metals for currency and exchanged the old and new currencies, "thus performing the functions of an executive organ of the new government in the sphere of government finance." Accumulating capital through these activities, late in the 1870s, they founded the Mitsui Bank and Mitsui Bussan; in the former, 43% to 53% of deposits were government funds, while the latter profited from winning the sole right to sell coal from the government's Miike Coal Mine. Similarly, Mitsubishi profited from involvement in the government's early industrializing efforts. In 1874, the government asked Mitsubishi to run 13 steamships in its Taiwan expedition, and in 1875 to establish a steamer line to Shanghai. The company also received subsidies from the government to establish Japanese shipping routes, an enterprise that enabled the company to branch out into financing, insuring, and warehousing commodities for the small merchants who used the routes. In marine transport, Mitsubishi had only one major competitor, Kyōdō Transportation Co., with which it merged through government mediation in 1885. At this point, Mitsubishi owned "77 percent of the total registered gross tonnage in the country, 88,765 tons, comprising 228 vessels."[58]

---

57. In the 1880s selling-off of government enterprises (*kangyō haraisage*), the Mitsui and Mitsubishi companies, later Japan's two leading *zaibatsu*, "both obtained mining and other producing sector undertakings and caused the archetype of their diversified management to come into being." In addition, Shibagaki Kazuo notes that by 1884, 52.8% of the total deposits held by the Mitsui Bank (founded in 1876) were government deposits. Kazuo Shibagaki, "The Early History of the Zaibatsu," *The Developing Economies*, Special Issue: *The Modernization of Japan* 4, no. 4 (December 1966), pp. 538–40; Ōuchi et al., *Nihon shihon-shugi no seiritsu*, vol. 2, pp. 411–41; and Lockwood, *Economic Development of Japan*, p. 13.

58. Shibagaki, "Early History of the Zaibatsu," pp. 538–44. For a more detailed discussion of the growth of the *zaibatsu*, see Shibagaki Kazuo,

The history of close relations with the Meiji state set the stage for the expansion of these two companies into Japan's two largest *zaibatsu* (financial cliques) by the end of World War I. Along with the Japanese economy as a whole, both companies, like other large companies, profited disproportionately from economic booms during the war years, especially World War I, and the concentration of capital accelerated as they and other *zaibatsu* assumed the form of the "comprehensive *konzern.*"[59] While total manufacturing production rose dramatically by 78% from 1914 to 1919,[60] the value of commodities traded by Mitsui Bussan, for example, increased 279% from the 1911–1915 to the 1916–1920 periods; where Mitsui Bussan had handled 10% of the country's total imports and exports in the 1890s, it managed 20% thereof in 1920.[61] The Mitsui, Mitsubishi, Sumitomo, and Yasuda firms became large combines through financial investments directed from holding companies and through banks at their centers into the subsidiary companies that represented both vertical and horizontal industrial organization.[62] The growth of the concentration of capital was such that by 1944, Mitsubishi controlled 25% of Japan's shipping and shipbuilding industry and 21% to 35% of the country's electrical equipment.[63] The number of banks decreased during the 1920s by 50%, in part through state policies that encouraged the "rationalization" of

Nihon kin'yū shihon bunseki—zaibatsu no seiritsu to sono kōzō (Finance capital in Japan: a study of the process of the formation and the structure of the zaibatsu) (Tokyo: Tōkyō Daigaku Shuppan-kai, 1965).

59. Typically, the *konzern* "was topped by a holding company and . . . spread its wings in diversified management through share holdings over practically the whole field of undertakings in production, commodity circulation and finance." Shibagaki, "Early History of the Zaibatsu," p. 535. Cf. Lockwood, *Economic Development of Japan*, pp. 218–19.

60. Kato, "Taishō Democracy as the Pre-Stage for Japanese Militarism," p. 218.

61. Shibagaki, "Early History of the Zaibatsu," p. 557.

62. The Mitsui had as many as 300 to 350 subsidiary companies. By 1929 there were 12 industrial cartels involving the *zaibatsu*. See Hayashi Yū'ichi, "Dokusen shihon-shugi kakuritsu-ki: dai-ichiji taisen kara Shōwa kyōkō made" (The period of the establishment of monopoly capitalism: From World War I to the Shōwa panic), in *Nihon nōgyō shi: shihon-shugi no tenkai to nōgyō mondai* (History of Japanese agriculture: The development of capitalism and the agrarian problem), ed. Teruoka Shūzō (Tokyo: Yūhikaku, Yūhikaku Sensho, 1981), p. 118; and Shibagaki, "Early History of the Zaibatsu," p. 549.

63. Lockwood, *Economic Development of Japan*, p. 217.

the Japanese economy.[64] By 1929, the "five large banks" (Mitsui, Mitsubishi, Sumitomo, Dai'ichi, and Yasuda), four of which were at the core of leading *zaibatsu*, controlled over 34% of the nation's total bank capital.[65]

As for industrializing state policies, while these should not be exaggerated as a peculiar feature of Japanese capitalism, the government did continue to offer subsidies to support its development program by encouraging the expansion of transport and the oil, iron, automobile, and chemical industries. In addition, the state remained directly involved in industrial production. As of late 1928, "the capital of state enterprises in production areas ha[d] reached the huge figure of 4.28 billion yen" in mining, industry, and transportation. Since the private capital in these areas totalled 8.4 or 8.5 billion yen, "state capital comprise[d] 34 percent of all capital" in these spheres.[66] Indeed, state capital merged with private capital in the Southern Manchuria Railway, Sakhalin Mining, Japan Radio, and Japan Airlines, and state control expanded during this period at the expense of private monopoly capital. Finally, the state was involved with finance capital through semi-public banks it had founded to expand the nation's credit system. These included the Bank of Japan, the Bank of Taiwan, and the Industrial Bank of Japan, among others, which together held about 4 billion yen in currency.[67] The state-managed banks tended to operate in close cooperation with the Big Five banks, supplying the main source of capital for industry and serving the government's purposes in its imperialistic expansion abroad.[68] Moreover, the state also maintained a close, direct relationship with the large private banks associated with the *zaibatsu*: Of the 400 million yen in local bonds and 2.4 million yen in state bonds held by banks, 60%

---

64. Ibid., pp. 60, 507.
65. Takahashi Kamekichi, *Nihon shihon-shugi hattatsu shi* (History of the development of Japanese capitalism), rev. and enlgd. ed. (Tokyo: Nihon Hyōron-sha, 1929), p. 255.
66. Inomata Tsunao, *Kyoto-Tō ni okeru teikoku-shugi* (Imperialism in the Far East), Keizai-gaku zenshū (Complete economic works), no. 24 (Tokyo: Kaizō-sha, 1932), pp. 374–76; and idem, *Nihon no dokusen shihon-shugi— kin'yū shihon no kyōkō taisaku* (Japanese monopoly capitalism: The policy of finance capital in response to the panic) (Tokyo: Nanboku Shoin, 1932), pp. 110–11, 113.
67. Inomata, *Kyoku-Tō ni okeru teikoku-shugi*, pp. 376–79; and idem, *Nihon no dokusen shihon-shugi*, pp. 113–17, 122–25.
68. Lockwood, *Economic Development of Japan*, pp. 514–17.

were concentrated in the hands of 12 large banks, and 40% were held by the five largest banks.[69]

As the figures on the ratio of government investment cited above indicate, the state continued to play a major and direct role—albeit reduced in favor of the *zaibatsu*—in Japanese economic development throughout the prewar era. It is significant that the Meiji oligarchs were able to take major steps in launching their industrializing revolution from above with very little direct political input from societal forces. But what were the consequences of these efforts for the emergence of Japan's civil society? The concentration of capital in the prewar *zaibatsu* held ambiguous implications. On the one hand, although Mitsui and Mitsubishi secured their dominant positions in the Japanese economy in large part as a product of state initiative,[70] after the government divested itself of significant holdings in the late 1870s, the relationship between the government and large business was reversed, as the state became more dependent on these *zaibatsu* for crucial financial and heavy industrial resources. Thus, it could be argued that the state's early endeavors effectively strengthened a non-state set of institutions. At the very least, the 1920s and 1930s saw the expansion of the political role of Japan's new bourgeoisie, particularly with the liberalization of financial requirements for voting in 1919 and the passage of universal manhood suffrage in 1925. If the state had, as it began to do in the late 1870s, continued to withdraw from direct involvement in the economy and had not so aggressively promoted the interests of the combines, then the state's early activism might be viewed as a salutary force that promoted the transition from a feudal economic and political order to a capitalist and democratic one. On the other hand, the concentration of capital in the *zaibatsu* and the government's need to pursue policies that would not be disadvantageous to them, as the core of the Japanese economy, contributed to the perception that the *zaibatsu*, along with the bureaucracy and the military

---

69. Inomata, *Nihon no dokusen shihon-shugi*, pp. 119–21; idem, *Kyoku-Tō ni okeru teikoku-shugi*, pp. 381–82; and Inomata Tsunao, *Gendai Nihon kenkyū* (Studies on contemporary Japan) (Tokyo: Kaizō-sha, 1928, 1929, 1934), pp. 125–28.

70. Shibagaki notes, "Their sources of funds were above all government funds and also early monopoly profits" and that they prospered in large part through their positions as "merchants by appointment to the government." Shibagaki, "Early History of the Zaibatsu," pp. 544–45.

services, constituted an elite in Japanese politics that had interests that were opposed to the public interest and exercised an influence that prevailed over that of the common people.[71] It is important to note that this phenomenon, while particularly pronounced in Japan's case, was not unique to Japan. As indicated above, similar critiques have been made of advanced capitalist societies in general. Likewise, the interpenetration of the state and the private sector in Japan as described above resembled what Habermas would come to describe as a phenomenon common to industrial capitalist societies: the truncation of the range of the public sphere. To think of it another way, the concentration of so much economic power into so few hands meant that fewer were enfranchised politically and economically, and fewer underwent the psychic transformation and the development of a new private interiority, needed to nurture the development of an autonomous public.

Finally, the interpenetration of the state and the private spheres lessened the "space" available for the flourishing of civil society and discouraged those whose private economic interests might otherwise have inspired them to adopt a distanced and critical posture towards the state. Extreme examples of such truncation of the space available for an autonomous civil society may be found not only in Stalinist regimes, but also in Germany's experience in the Nazi period, when the state's "coordination" of all spheres of German life virtually obliterated the distinction between public and private and with it the space for an independent public.[72] The key point here, however, is that an economically activist state need not issue in such political repressiveness. The Japanese experience with the growth of democratizing forces before and after the militarist authoritarianism of the 1930s and 1940s is ratified in this respect by more recent experiences elsewhere, such as in Portugal, where state activism—even nationalization of industry—accompanied significant political liberalization. To the extent that the economic policies of the Meiji state encouraged the emergence of intermediate associations between the individual and his or her family and between the individual and the state, they laid the ground-

---

71. See Hoston, *Marxism and the Crisis of Development in Prewar Japan*, chaps. 1 and 7; and Shillony, *Politics and Culture in Wartime Japan*.
72. See the vivid description of this process in Germany in William Sheridan Allen, *The Nazi Seizure of Power: The Experience of a Single German Town, 1922–1945*, rev. ed. (New York: Franklin Watts, 1984).

work for a civil society that could have challenged the state. Yet in Japan, by 1940, the state itself absorbed civil society when all political and social associations were brought under the rubric of the Imperial Rule Assistance Association. The political parties that competed for leadership in the national Diet itself enthusiastically sacrificed their organizational autonomy by dissolving themselves so that their members might immerse themselves fully in the organic unity incarnate in the Imperial Household[73] (this led some to refer to Taishō as the "era of party rule"[74]). This outcome can be understood only with reference to other state activities in the realm of ideology and education.

Ideology and Education in Meiji Japan

The ability of the Meiji leadership to implement its revolutionary industrializing policies was enhanced by the institutional design of the central government and the elaboration of an effective political mythology in support of it. As noted, the 1889 Constitution reflected an admixture of the Western experience of constitutional government with indigenous Japanese elements, particularly concerning the pivotal position of the emperor. While the Meiji leaders drew heavily on the advice of the German *Staatsrecht* theorist Roesler, it was the special position of the Imperial Household and its advisors in the Meiji political system that provided an effective counterbalance to the civil societal forces set loose by the provision of local and national assemblies. The effectiveness of this mythology was then assured by educational provisions that at once guaranteed the formation of a highly educated public that might provide a broad popular basis for the sort of "rational-critical" discourse that Habermas has identified with the formation of a "public sphere of civil society" and disinclined that public to offer any effective contestation of the legitimacy of the Meiji state and its claim to imperial sovereignty.

The key to the invocation of the Meiji institutional configuration in support of authoritarian rule lay in article 1 of the Meiji Constitution. The Constitution materialized in response to public pressures as described above, and the institutions that it

---

73. See Shillony, *Politics and Culture in Wartime Japan*.
74. See Peter Duus, "The Era of Party Rule"; and idem, *Party Rivalry and Political Change in Taishō Japan* (Cambridge: Harvard University Press, 1968).

legitimated resembled a constitutional monarchy in which the Charter Oath's pledge that "'all matters of state shall be decided by public discussion' "[75] might be fulfilled. Yet the Constitution was said to have been "conferred" by the emperor rather than the product of popular initiative. The Constitution provided for a bicameral elected Diet: the upper chamber, the House of Peers, was to be comprised of higher-ranking nobility, delegates elected from among the lower nobility, and imperial appointees (such as celebrated scholars); the Lower House was to be elected by limited suffrage. (Adult males who paid at least a hefty 15 yen in taxes, only about 5% of the total adult male population at the time, could vote.) All permanent legislation and the budget required approval by both houses, but the actual power of the Diet was severely restricted by other arrangements concerning the role of the emperor. Article 1 specified that sovereignty or the "power to rule" (tōchiken) was invested in the emperor. The emperor could suspend the Diet, dissolve the Lower House and call new elections, and issue imperial proclamations in lieu of laws when the Diet was not in session. Furthermore, the Imperial Household had its own budget that was not subject to the control of the Diet; and the navy and army commands had the right to appeal directly to the emperor without consulting the cabinet or the Diet.[76] Although the emperor himself would not necessarily exercise these privileges in political practice, the stipulation of these imperial prerogatives enabled his formal and informal advisors in the government—in the Privy Council, originally created to approve the Constitution in the emperor's name, the Naidaijin (Lord Keeper of the Privy Seal or Inner Minister), the genrō (elder statesmen), and the Imperial Household Ministry, which was independent of the cabinet—to act in his name with considerable autonomy from the social forces represented in the Diet.[77] Finally, the cabinet, comprised of the Meiji leaders themselves as heads of various ministries, was established on the West European model; but the primacy of the emperor made them responsible directly only to him.

---

75. Beasley, *Meiji Restoration*, p. 323.
76. See Kato, "Taishō Democracy as the Pre-Stage for Japanese Militarism," p. 225.
77. See Miyazawa Toshiyoshi, *Nihon kensei shi no kenkyū* (Studies on Japanese constitutional history) (Tokyo: Iwanami Shoten, 1968), pt. 2; and David Anson Titus, *Palace and Politics in Prewar Japan*, Studies of the East Asian Institute, Columbia University (New York and London: Columbia University Press, 1974), chap. 3.

Although the Meiji emperor was as much a figurehead as the British monarch, what emerged out of this institutional design was not a parliamentary democratic system. Instead, what David Titus has called a "transcendental" imperial authority became an effective guarantor of state autonomy from civil society for the Meiji regime and its successors.

> If the imperial institution [as the "sacred and inviolable sovereign" of the state] was to be the eternal fount of political authority, ... measures had to be taken to ensure that political failures would not reach the emperor and that the emperor's human frailties wouldn't endanger the transcendental role of the throne in the Japanese polity.... The emperor was to ratify policies resolved upon by the officials who "advised and assisted" him. The emperor did not ratify policies as an individual monarch but as the representative of the Imperial Will—the bequeathed instructions of his ancestors "of a lineal succession unbroken for ages eternal." "Imperial Will" was thus to serve as a major political fiction for legitimizing decisions of the state while protecting the emperor from individual responsibility for the decisions he ratified.[78]

But what was to ensure the efficacy of this device? It is here that the Meiji regime's involvement in the realm of education becomes critical to an appreciation of the impact of state action on the creation of a civil society.

It was precisely to guarantee that the "political fiction" of the Imperial Will would work effectively that supporters of the Meiji leadership fashioned the political myth of the *kokutai* (body politic) family conception of the state and used the new educational system to propagate it in accordance with the 1890 Imperial Rescript on Education. The government's involvement in education proceeded through several stages. Initially, state initiative arose out of a Confucian emphasis on the importance of education in the cultivation of virtue and a utilitarian commitment to provide citizens with appropriate skills for an industrializing society. Continuity with the traditionally high valuation of education assured that Iwakura and other Meiji leaders viewed education as a legitimate function of the state. Under the Tokugawa, the upper strata of Japanese society had received a classical Chinese education, and in the late years of the period

---

78. Titus, *Palace and Politics in Prewar Japan*, p. 6.

new schools were established by several individual *daimyo* to teach Dutch learning.[79] What was new in the Meiji period was a much more utilitarian conception of the need for education, which flourished under the influence of "American ideas concerning democracy and utilitarianism in education."[80] After a false start in 1869, when an effort simply to continue the three Tokugawa schools of Western, Confucian, and medical studies collapsed in conflict over whether Chinese, Japanese, or Western learning should be provided,[81] a new Ministry of Education (Monbushō) was established in 1871. On the French model, the new ministry envisioned a new universal educational system, from primary schools (one for every 600 children) through higher technical schools in fields such as medicine. At the apex of the system would be Tokyo Imperial University (and subsequently other imperial universities) to provide a training ground for the civil service and take the lead in research.[82]

The new educational system bolstered the effort to eliminate feudal status differentials and privileges. The Education Law of 1872 asserted that in the past "people have made a mistake of thinking that learning is a matter for those above samurai rank." Now, however, "it is intended that henceforth universally (without any distinction of class or sex) in a village there shall be no house without learning and in a house no individual without learning."[83] Most of the burden for this was undertaken by the state, although there were also private institutions such as Keiō Gijuku Daigaku, founded by the Enlightenment thinker Fukuzawa. Even private education, however, was closely monitored by the Ministry of Education, which prescribed standards to be observed universally. The Meiji leaders made remarkable progress in creating an educated populace: by the turn of the century, almost all children were attending primary school,[84] and although higher education tended to be

---

79. Under the Tokugawa's policy of isolation, the Dutch were the only Westerners permitted to trade with Japanese, and their residence was limited to the island of Deshima. Not surprisingly, the domains in which Western scholarly influence was most pronounced were also those that played leading roles in the anti-shogun movement.
80. Lockwood, *Economic Development of Japan*, p. 510; cf. Chitoshi Yanaga, *Japan Since Perry* (New York, 1949), chap. 7.
81. Beasley, *Meiji Restoration*, p. 359.
82. Lockwood, *Economic Development of Japan*, p. 510.
83. Beasley, *Meiji Restoration*, p. 360.
84. Ibid., p. 361.

available in practice only to upper-stratum boys, students in colleges and universities numbered 15,000. (Lockwood notes in contrast that school attendance in England for children twelve and under became compulsory only in 1876, and general education became "generally available at public expense" only in 1890.) There were also 240 technical schools, in addition to technical colleges in the universities, and 1,000 "continuation" schools for part-time study in practical skills needed for economic activity in industry, agriculture, and commerce.[85]

By this time, however, some in the increasingly nationalistic Meiji leadership became alarmed at the utilitarian approach, and efforts were made to enhance the role of education in inculcating appropriate civic virtues. These certainly could have been democratic virtues, as they would become after the war, but those who were alarmed by the pressures levied by the civil rights and party movements thought it essential that the educational system be used rather to emphasize obedience and order. Thus the Imperial Rescript on Education advised the emperor's subjects to observe traditional Confucian values such as filial piety and social harmony rather than dissent, and to "'always respect the Constitution and observe the laws.' "[86] It came to be in the highest institutions of the nation's school system that the political myth celebrating these virtues was articulated, and through the universal educational system they were inculcated into several generations of children. At this point, the Meiji state's role in education came to exercise a detrimental impact on the emergence of a vigorous civil society in Japan.

Here the significance of the political mythology of the family conception of the state, of the *kokutai*, is not to be underestimated. By exploiting the traditional religious attachment of the Japanese people to the emperor and combining that with Confucian ethical principles on the natural harmony between ruler and ruled and German *Staatsrecht* thought, the Meiji devised the quintessential Socratic noble lie[87] and used it to establish and maintain the passive consent of the people.

---

85. Lockwood, *Economic Development of Japan*, p. 511; cf. David S. Landes, "Japan and Europe: Contrasts in Industrialization," in *The State and Economic Enterprise in Japan: Essays in the Political Economy of Growth*, ed. William W. Lockwood (Princeton: Princeton University Press, 1965), pp. 106–7.

86. Cited in Beasley, *Meiji Restoration*, p. 361.

87. " 'Could we,' I said, 'somehow contrive one of those lies that come into being in case of need, of which we were just now speaking, some one

In the *kokutai* myth we find two critical elements of the Socratic lie: first, there was an organic conception of the state, a notion that the political community had actually preceded the formation of the state. This contention conflicted with the conception of civil society as it evolved historically in Western Europe as a realm distinguishable and potentially autonomous from the state. In addition, the myth gave "divine sanction to the natural hierarchy of human talents and virtues" and provided "that unequal men receive unequal honors and unequal shares in ruling."[88] This contrasted with a conception of natural law that endowed human beings equally with rights as well as obligations. The family conception of the state, in which the emperor (*tennō* or *mikado*) played a pivotal role, provided both these elements in *kokutai* thought. In this view, the Japanese nation was a single extended family, of which the emperor himself, of divine origins, was head. The unity here between the realms of religious authority and political authority also contrasts with what Taylor has identified as an important precondition of the emergence of the modern West European conception of civil society: the separation between church and state, the "bi-focal" character that granted that there were two sources of authority, rather than a single unitary one.[89] This provided a basis for the contestation of the authority of the secular sovereign. In the notion of the *kokutai*, however, Confucian bonds of unquestioning loyalty and filial piety that existed within a properly Confucian family characterized the polity as well.[90] This element of myth is expressed forcefully in the words of a Ministry of Education textbook:

> Our country is a great family nation, and the Imperial Household is the head family of the subjects and the nucleus of national life. The subjects revere the Imperial Household, which is the head family, with the tender esteem [they have] for their ancestors; and the Emperor loves his subjects as his very own. [Author's note: Another word for "subjects,"

---

noble lie to persuade [of the legitimacy of the power of the rulers], in the best case, even the rulers, but if not them, the rest of the city?' " *The Republic of Plato*, trans. with an interpretive essay by Allan Bloom (New York and London: Basic Books, 1968), p. 93.

88. Bloom, "Interpretive Essay," in ibid., p. 366.
89. Taylor, "Modes of Civil Society," p. 102.
90. A definitive explication of the *kokutai* idea is offered in Ishida Takeshi, *Meiji seiji shisō shi kenkyū* (Studies on the history of Meiji political thought) (Tokyo: Mirai-sha, 1954), pp. 3–149.

sekishi, is here used, which carries with it an idea of endearment, frequently translated as "children."[91]

In this imagery, the concepts of nation and state were conjoined, and the emperor was at the apex of both, as the patriarchal head of the uniquely Japanese *kokutai*, incorporating race, ethnicity, and spirituality into a single concept, and as the political ruler of a constitutional monarchic form of state (*seitai*). Within the competitive international system to which the Meiji Restoration itself was a response, then, the emperor was at once "(1) a constitutional monarch, the monarch of an authoritarian state as established by the Meiji constitution granted by the emperor; (2) the generalissimo (*daigenshi*), the monarch as the summit of authority of the supreme command over the armed forces; and (3) a monarch of divine right, a monarch representing religious or spiritual authority in place of that of the West's Christianity."[92]

Indigenous perspectives on the emperor as a locus of moral and spiritual value had the effect of moderating the substantial influence of German constitutional scholars—Rudolf von Gneist, Lorenz von Stein, Albert Mosse, Karl Rudolf, Hermann Roesler, Georg Jellinek, and Johann Kaspar Bluntschli—on the making of the Meiji Constitution.[93] It was Bluntschli's *Allgemeines Staatsrecht*, translated into Japanese between 1871 and 1875, that exercised the most decisive German influence. Japanese enlightenment scholar Katō Hiroyuki discovered in Bluntschli an "organic theory of state sovereignty," which portrayed the state as a masculine body politic analogous to the feminine body of the Christian Church. The combination of a theory of state sover-

91. Japan, Department of Education, *Kokutai no Hongi: Cardinal Principles of the National Entity of Japan*, trans. John Owen Gauntlett, ed. with an introduction by Robert King Hall (Cambridge: Harvard University Press, 1949), pp. 89, 90 (insertions by Hall). This emphasis had become a prominent theme of educational texts by late Meiji (1910). See Harold Joseph Wray, "Changes and Continuity in Japanese Images of the *Kokutai* and Attitudes and Roles Toward the Outside World: A Content Analysis of Japanese Textbooks, 1903–1945" (Ph.D. diss., University of Hawaii, 1971), p. 103; and Ishida Takeshi, "Ideorogii to shite no tennō-sei" (The emperor system as ideology), *Shisō*, no. 336 (June 1952), p. 39.

92. Takeda Kiyoko, "Tennō-sei shisō no keisei" (The formation of the emperor system ideology), in *Iwanami kōza: Nihon rekishi* (Iwanami symposium: Japanese history), 21 vols., vol. 16: *Kindai* (Modern times), vol. 3 (Tokyo: Iwanami Shoten, 1962), p. 269.

93. Pittau, *Political Thought in Early Meiji Japan*, p. 132; and Takeda, "Tennō-sei shisō no keisei," pp. 273–74.

eignty with an organic theory permitted the Meiji oligarchs to reconcile a "modern" Western treatment of sovereignty with the traditional Japanese attachment to a divine emperor whom they viewed as the patriarch of the extended Japanese family-nation. The German formula was altered to attribute the "right to rule" to the emperor, who thereby held the right to promulgate a constitution. The font of power and legitimacy lay in the father-like emperor, believed to be divine, rather than in the much more dangerous popular will.[94] As German advisors Stein and Gneist recognized, this admixture implied strong imperial authority and a weak Diet and party system.[95] Roesler exercised the greatest influence in defining the role of the emperor as a suprapolitical actor who would transcend the privatistic infighting of party politics. Although he did not subscribe to the mythological content that in practice sustained the emperor in his transcendental role,[96] the constitutional arrangements Roesler helped to devise reinforced the *kokutai* myth. This mythology of the family state became so powerful that even civil rights activists no longer questioned the legitimacy of the emperor system. With the establishment of universal education, this conception was taught in the schools, and at the imperial universities founded to train future civil servants, it was systematized and propagated in the theory of imperial sovereignty, even absolutism, in the work of constitutional scholars such as Hozumi Yatsuka and Uesugi Shinkichi.[97]

---

94. S. An, "Meiji shoki ni okeru Doitsu kokka shisō no jūyō ni kansuru ichi kōsatsu: Burunchuri to Katō Hiroyuki o chūshin to shite" (The reception of J.C. [sic] Bluntschli's theory of the state by Hiroyuki Katō in early Meiji Japan), in *Nihon seiji gakkai nenpō, 1975: Nihon ni okeru Sei-Ou seiji shisō* (Western political thought in Japan) (Tokyo: Iwanami Shoten, 1976), pp. 121, 140–42.

95. Pittau, *Political Thought in Early Meiji Japan*, p. 145; Takeda, "Tennō-sei shisō no keisei," pp. 274–75; and Ishida Takeshi, "Kokka yūkitai setsu" (The organic theory of the state), in *Kōza: Nihon kindai hō hattatsu shi* (Symposium: The history of the development of modern Japanese law) (Tokyo: Keisō Shōbō, 1958), passim.

96. For a detailed discussion of the myth surrounding the emperor, see Robert Cornell Armstrong, *Light from the East: Studies in Japanese Confucianism* (Toronto: University of Toronto, 1914).

97. Interview with Ishida Takeshi, Tokyo, August 11, 1979. See especially Uesugi Shinkichi, *Kenpō jutsugi* (Explication of the constitution) (Tokyo: Yūhikaku, 1916), pt. 1; and Uesugi Shinkichi, "Kokutai ni kansuru isetsu" (Different views concerning the *kokutai*), in *Taishō shisō shū* (I) (Collection of Taishō thought, vol. 1), comp. Imai Sei'ichi, Kindai Nihon shisō taisei (Outline of modern Japanese thought), no. 33 (Tokyo: Chikuma Shobō,

Significant here is the fact that the Ministry of Education reserved the right to approve textbooks, and it did so in such a way that, in the first decades of the 20th century, school textbooks increasingly emphasized the nationalist and authoritarian implications of the family-state conception. Despite the advent and increasing popularity of Minobe Tatsukichi's challenge to the orthodox authoritarian interpretation of the Meiji Constitution[98]—an interpretation that would have enhanced the power of the Diet—in 1935 the Diet itself repudiated the emperor-organ theory and voted to censure Minobe and remove him from his post at Tokyo Imperial University.[99] Meanwhile, as early as 1910 school textbooks approved by the Monbushō clearly indicated a reaction against Western liberal legalistic conceptions of the nation-state. School textbooks of 1903 had stressed the theme of *chūkun-aikoku* (loyalty to the monarch and patriotism toward the state), and by 1910 this was replaced by a theme that accentuated still further the patriarchal authority vested in the emperor: the unity of filial piety with loyalty in Japanese sentiment toward the emperor.[100]

1979), pp. 3–13. Cf. Kakei Katsuhiko, *Dai Nihon teikoku kenpō no konpon gi* (The basic meaning of the Greater Japanese Imperial Constitution) (N.p., n.d.) for emperor-centered state theory following Hozumi and Uesugi. The Hozumi-Uesugi theory of imperial sovereignty was articulated in late Meiji and early Taishō.

98. The emperor-organ theory of Minobe Tatsukichi, a Tokyo Imperial University professor of constitutional law, maintained that Japan's emperor should be treated on the same basis as all national monarchs. The state was a sovereign organic body, and the emperor, as a legal but not divine person, was but the highest of its many organs, and the Diet thus shared the power to rule with the emperor. See Minobe Tatsukichi, "Kunshu no kokuhō-jō no chi'i" (The position of the monarch in state law), *Hōgaku shirin* 50 (November 15, 1903), pp. 1–6; and idem, *Kenpō satsuyō* (Outline of the constitution) (Tokyo: Yūhikaku, 1924). For an English-language treatment, see Frank O. Miller, *Minobe Tatsukichi: Interpreter of Constitutionalism in Japan* (Berkeley and Los Angeles: University of California Press, 1965), p. 65 and passim.

99. See the memoir of Minobe's son, late Governor of Tokyo Minobe Ryōki-chi, "Sore de mo tennō wa kikan de aru: Aru kenpō gakusha no shōgai" (Even so, the emperor is an organ: The life of a certain constitutional scholar), in *Kumon suru demokurashii* (Democracy in anguish) (Tokyo: Bungei Shunjū Shinsha, 1959), pp. 61–96; cf. Miyazawa Toshiyoshi, "Kikan setsu jiken to Minobe Tatsukichi sensei" (Professor Minobe Tatsukichi and the organ theory affair), *Hōritsu jihō* 20 (August 1948), pp. 42–44.

100. Wray, "Changes and Continuity in Japanese Images of the *Kokutai*," p. 103; Ishida, *Meiji seiji shisō shi kenkyū*, pp. 7–8; and idem, "Ideorogii to shite no tennō-sei," p. 39.

It is important to note two points of consequence for the emergence of a civil society and democratic politics in Japan. First, the family conception of the state obviated the sort of trifold distinction between family, civil society, and the state that was crucial to Hegel's conception of a civil society in terms of bodies interposed between the individual and the state. Indeed, it did not permit a clear delineation between state and nation or society and state. Rather, *kokutai* was clearly distinguished from *seitai* or form of state—the institutional configuration of the state— but in Japan the *kokutai* was the basis for the *seitai*, and the position of the emperor was unalterable. It was this position, of course, that was key to the absolutist interpretations of the Constitution offered by orthodox scholars Uesugi and Hozumi.[101] Second, as illustrated by the activities of the Aishinsha and the Sanshisha and the emergence of the political party movement in the 1870s and 1880s, there were signs of a nascent civil society in Meiji Japan that appeared along with the industrialization process. Essentially what the Meiji leadership sought to do by energetically propagating absolutist orthodoxy and its supporting mythology through the educational system was to close up the space available for the formation of a civil society, to discourage the formation of associations that would mediate the relationship of the individual to the state. The Peace Preservation Law of 1887 allowed the removal of any person deemed a threat to public peace, and the Peace Police Law of 1900 was promulgated in an effort to control the labor and agrarian movements that emerged after the Sino-Japanese War. This law further curtailed civil liberties by allowing police to disperse public gatherings, requiring groups to request permission from the police to meet publicly, restricting the formation of labor unions, and prohibiting strikes.[102] To be sure, these efforts were not successful during the late Meiji and Taishō eras, which saw the proliferation of illegal labor unions, tenants' unions in the countryside, a popular—and ultimately successful—movement

---

101. These appear in, for example, Uesugi, *Kenpō jutsugi*; Uesugi Shinkichi, *Kokutai kenpō oyobi kensei* (The kokutai constitution and constitutional government) (Tokyo: Yūhikaku, 1916), pt. 1; and Kakei, *Dai Nihon teikoku kenpō no konpon gi.*
102. *Nihon shi jiten* (Encyclopedia of Japanese history), rev. ed. (Tokyo: Ōbun-sha, 1978), s.v. "ch'ian keisatsu hō." See also Richard H. Mitchell, *Thought Control in Prewar Japan* (Ithaca: Cornell University Press, 1976), pp. 22–27.

for universal manhood suffrage, the formation of the Japanese Communist Party in 1922, and the flourishing of a vigorous independent press that published much that was politically critical. Nevertheless, the state's efforts in the field of education contributed to the authoritarian and militarist outcome of the 1930s. The enactment of universal manhood suffrage in 1925 was offset by the implementation of a new Peace Preservation Law that made it illegal to contemplate "altering the *kokutai*," and the repression of those with "dangerous ideas," primarily on the left, intensified.[103] Once Japanese army officers launched a full-scale invasion of China in the 1930s, the imperative to unify the country in support of the war effort intensified reactions against Western liberalism and its accoutrements. In accord with the mythology of a unified polity without meaningful divisions, when Prince Konoe Fumimaro offered his vision of a "New Order" in Japanese politics in mid-1940, the existing political parties promptly dissolved themselves, and their members united under the umbrella organization, the Imperial Rule Assistance Association. This development, considered alongside the 1935 censure of Minobe, testifies to the enduring power of a conception of the body politic that asserted unity between the emperor and his subjects and perceived intermediate bodies as threatening to that unity. In the postwar period, Occupation officials believed that the key to democratizing Japan lay in dismantling crucial components of that ideological structure and in reforming education to serve the needs of a democratizing society.

■ Economic Recovery, Occupation, and Democratization in Postwar Japan

The US Occupation of Japan after the war offered a new opportunity to achieve both economic growth and democratization at once. Interestingly, SCAP (Supreme Commander for the Allied Powers) authorities agreed with Japan's prewar left on the intimate linkage between politics and economics in their analysis of the ultimate causes of the war. Both groups held that the rise of authoritarianism and militarism was attributable to "the social and economic condition of

---

103. For a discussion of these developments, see Hoston, *Marxism and the Crisis of Development in Prewar Japan*, chap. 1.

the Japanese countryside,"[104] the concentration of economic power in the hands of the *zaibatsu*, and the power of the authoritarian state-centered ideology of the *kokutai*. SCAP's goal was initially to undertake reforms that would prevent the resurgence of such authoritarianism and militarism, and thus SCAP authorities sought to eliminate the economic and ideological forces that had led to the tragedy of the 1930s and 1940s.

What is important here is the extent to which SCAP authorities tried to realize these goals through economic and educational reforms. In their conceptualization and implementation, the reforms would profoundly affect the relationship between the state and the economy and the content of the state's role in education. Not all these reforms were fully realized, however. While in their initial intent, they were to weaken and even destroy Japan's military machine, many such reforms were abandoned abruptly with the shift of the Occupation to a "reverse course" in 1947. The sudden chill in US-Soviet relations, the deepening of the Cold War, dictated that Japan would no longer be treated as a vanquished enemy to be disarmed, but rather as the bastion of US support in the Cold War in the Pacific.[105]

At the outset, however, the point was "to democratize the country by encouraging a wider diffusion of wealth and political and economic power."[106] To this end SCAP undertook dramatic economic reforms in both city and countryside. Most significant of these were the agrarian land reform and the attack on the *zaibatsu*. As in the Portuguese decision in 1975 to expropriate latifundia in order to disperse land ownership into more hands,[107] the intent was to create a class of smallholding farmers who would hold a significant stake in a democratic polity. While specific provisions of the land reform varied by locality, generally lands owned by absentee landlords and in holdings greater

---

104. See R.P. Dore, *Land Reform in Japan* (London: Oxford University Press, 1959), p. 115.
105. Takafusa Nakamura, *The Postwar Japanese Economy: Its Development and Structure*, trans. Jacqueline Kaminski (Tokyo: University of Tokyo Press, 1981), pp. 23–25.
106. Allen, *Short Economic History of Modern Japan*, p. 172.
107. See Kenneth Maxwell, "Regime Overthrow and the Prospects for Democratic Transition in Portugal," in *Transitions from Authoritarian Rule*, ed. O'Donnell, Schmitter, and Whitehead, pp. 126–27; and John L. Hammond, *Building Popular Power: Workers' and Neighborhood Movements in the Portuguese Revolution* (New York: Monthly Review, 1988), pp. 178ff.

than ten acres per household were bought by the government and resold to former tenants who could secure loans at low interest rates. By 1950, land tenancy had declined from a rate of nearly 50% to only 10%, and rent controls had reduced the onus of high rents on agrarian households.[108]

More significant for the issue of state activity was the effort to dissolve the *zaibatsu*. In the view of SCAP authorities, the powerful financial cliques had been used "as a tool of war" and had inhibited the growth of smaller-scale capitalism and democracy:

> The responsibility of zaibatsu for Japan's aggression overseas was not personal but mainly institutional, in that individual zaibatsu organizations were turned into convenient tools of military aggression. Japanese industry was under the control of a small number of large zaibatsu, which were supported and strengthened by the Japanese government. Concentration of control over industry encouraged the continued existence of quasi-feudal relations between labor and capital, lowered wages and prevented the development of labor unions. It also prevented independent entrepreneurs from starting new business and hindered the rise of a middle class in Japan. Because such a middle class was absent, Japan until today lacked the economic basis for individual independence; therefore, forces to counter the military clique did not develop nor for that matter was there any development of democratic, humanistic national sentiment that might serve as a counterforce against military designs.[109]

In an initial round of reforms, 83 *zaibatsu* holding companies were dissolved, "*zaibatsu* leaders including members of the founding families were purged and were prohibited from further activity in the financial world," *zaibatsu* shareholdings were redistributed, and antimonopoly laws were passed.[110] Business leaders who had helped to administer the war economy, for example, by heading the "control associations" (*tōseikai*) the wartime government established to coordinate economic planning and production, were purged from their positions. These moves were to be followed by a second wave of dissolutions

---

108. Dore, *Land Reform in Japan*, chaps. 6–8, especially p. 175, table 8.
109. These are the words (retranslated from Japanese) of Corwin D. Edwards, head of the State-War Mission on Japanese Combines, quoted by Kazuo Shibagaki, "Dissolution of Zaibatsu and Deconcentration of Economic Power," *Annals of the Institute of Social Science*, no. 20 (1979), pp. 11–12.
110. Shibagaki, "Dissolution of Zaibatsu," pp. 24ff.

affecting over 1,000 additional companies in February 1948. This plan was abandoned, however, with the shift to a reverse course. SCAP authorities were beginning to notice that these and other democratizing reforms were interfering with Japan's economic recovery and thus were at cross-purposes with the aims of the reverse course.[111]

Interestingly, Shibagaki notes that "banking institutions were left completely untouched" by the reforms that dissolved the two largest trading companies in Japan, the Mitsui Trading Company and the Mitsubishi Trading Company. The omission of the financial institutions, which SCAP perceived as separate from industry and commerce,[112] came to be critical to the reintegration of the business networks (keiretsu) that have gained increasing attention as a major source of friction in the problematic US-Japan trade relationship. In addition, the abandonment of the effort to deconcentrate capital in other companies left Japan's basic industrial structure intact, although the body charged with carrying out this mission, the Deconcentration Review Board, claimed on its own dissolution in 1949 that "excessive concentration of economic power in Japan was completely broken and a condition of free competition in all fields had been created."[113]

This reverse course in industry was matched in the sphere of labor relations. The early Occupation authorities promoted progressive labor legislation, and the proportion of workers unionized soared from zero to almost 60% between 1945 and 1949. SCAP authorities were also tolerant of the former Communists who had been released from prison, and of the fact that the unions quickly fell under the influence of the reconstituted Japanese Communist Party and the new Japanese Socialist Party. Under the reverse course, however, SCAP suppressed a general strike that the left-wing union Sangyōbetsu Rōdō Kumiai Kaigi, or Sanbetsu, had planned for February 1, 1947. In 1948, SCAP issued political order no. 201, making it illegal for government employees to strike, and the following year, early liberal labor laws were revised in a restrictive direction. These efforts culmi-

111. Nakamura, *Postwar Japanese Economy*, pp. 23–25; Allen, *Short Economic History of Modern Japan*, p. 172; and Shibagaki, "Dissolution of Zaibatsu," p. 14.
112. E.M. Hadley, *Antitrust in Japan* (Princeton: Princeton University Press, 1970), p. 33.
113 Ibid., p. 180, cited by Shibagaki, "Dissolution of Zaibatsu," p. 36.

nated in 1950 in a "red purge," in which Communist leaders were removed from labor unions.[114] Clearly these measures inhibited developments that SCAP leaders had earlier believed to have been essential for the development of a vital civil society and a democratic Japan. As we will see in the sphere of education as well, these regressions picked up momentum once the Occupation was over and Japanese leaders, many depurged in the reverse course, were in control of their own political circumstances. The police that had been decentralized were recentralized in 1954, and police powers were enhanced in the late 1950s to respond to riots and other perceived threats to internal security. Similarly, local administration was recentralized, recalling the power of the Home Ministry that had been abolished in 1947,[115] as was educational policy.

Educational policies in occupied Japan reflected an appreciation of the role of education in political socialization. The government would continue to have a role, but that role—and the content of its influence on the system—would be different, under the intentions of Occupation policy, from what it had been in the prewar era. Indeed, the Constitution did no more than stipulate that Japanese people had a right to education, and by making no further provision joined the Fundamental Law of Education in attempting "to formally guarantee the independence of education from state control." The Diet passed legislation that prevented the state from adopting any particular political doctrines to be reflected in the educational system.[116] But the specific purpose of the educational system was articulated clearly in the Fundamental Law: to create autonomous individuals through the full development of the personality, young men and women who would participate actively in the democratic process.[117] This involved above all a change in the content of education; for example, freedom of thought and belief as in tolerance towards religion would be taught in the

---

114. Nakamura, *Postwar Japanese Economy*, pp. 28–29; and Robert A. Scalapino, *The Japanese Communist Movement, 1920–1966* (Berkeley: University of California Press, 1967), p. 68.
115. Kurt Steiner, *Local Government in Japan* (Stanford: Stanford University Press, 1965), pp. 92–93, 107.
116. Teruhisa Horio, *Educational Thought and Ideology in Modern Japan: State Authority and Intellectual Freedom*, ed. and trans. Steven Platzner (Tokyo: University of Tokyo Press, 1988), pp. 128, 149.
117. Ibid., pp. 108, 114.

schools.[118] Just as significantly, much about the way schools operated would itself also be changed. Control of the schools would devolve from the central government to the localities, with publicly elected local school boards bearing the major responsibility for educational policy.[119] In addition, the publication of textbooks by private bodies, rather than the Ministry of Education (Monbushō), was authorized, and local administrators were empowered to consult with teachers in selecting the texts.[120] Teachers were provided with broad outlines according to which to choose teaching strategies, but these left them fair latitude in pursuing their vocation.[121] Finally, efforts were made to create a more egalitarian system of higher education with standards relaxed for private universities, with a view towards enabling them to compete more successfully with the prestigious state universities.[122]

Not surprisingly, these changes were also reversed dramatically with the shift in the overall objectives of the Occupation. As the Cold War intensified, in 1953, US leaders conferred with Japanese leaders to launch a campaign against the "excesses of democracy." Suddenly it was deemed important to use the educational system to instill nationalism so that Japanese would support the country's position in US strategy in the Pacific. More importantly, critic Teruhisa Horio argues, the system could not encourage democracy in practice because it was the state, rather than the people, that pursued education. The reversal of direction in education policy was facilitated by the fact that, despite the creation of a League of Political Education for Democracy in August 1947, the Occupation authorities had not significantly purged the Ministry of Education along with other government bureaus more directly associated with wartime mobilization.[123]

---

118. Ibid., p. 119.
119. Ibid., p. 150; Steiner, *Local Government*, p. 421; and Lawrence H. Redford, *The Occupation of Japan: Economic Policy and Reform: The Proceedings of a Symposium by the MacArthur Memorial* (Norfolk, VA: The MacArthur Memorial, 1980), p. 27.
120. Yamazumi Masami, "Textbook Revision: The Swing to the Right," *Japan Quarterly* 28, no. 4 (October-December 1981), p. 475.
121. Horio, *Educational Thought and Ideology*, p. 172.
122. See William K. Cummings, Iko Amano, and Kazuyuki Kitamura, eds., *Changes in the Japanese University: A Comparative Perspective* (New York: Praeger, 1979), pp. 33–35, 143.
123. See Appendices A and B in *Political Reorganization of Japan, September 1945 to September 1948*, Report of the Government Section, Supreme Commander for the Allied Powers, vol. 2.

The retrenchment of democratic efforts in the realm of education was reinforced under direct Japanese rule when the 1955 Law on Local Administration replaced the publicly elected school boards with appointed ones, opening the way for school boards to be subordinated to the central bureaucracy.[124] Teachers increasingly came into conflict with the state, as the Ministry of Education sought to crush the Teachers' Union by requiring principals to rate teachers on their "efficiency" every year.[125] New, strict guidelines were established on textbook inspection. Previously, textbooks could be screened only if they violated the Fundamental Law of Education, but the law itself was changed in 1958 to delete the phrases "the spirit of peace" and "respect for truth and justice." The impact of this apparently minor change was to make it easier for the Monbushō to increase the screening of textbooks. The same year, the ministry legalized a single course of study, mandating that teachers in all schools follow it. Finally, in 1963, the government passed the Law Concerning the Free Provision of Textbooks in Compulsory Education. This law increased centralization by according authority to municipal governments—which are not completely autonomous of central government authority[126]—to select texts, and assigning their publication to a limited number of companies deemed to have a high enough concentration of capital to achieve sufficient economies of scale for the state to provide the textbooks gratis.[127] In recent years, education has been targeted from both the left and the right for reform. On the right, Prime Minister Tanaka Kakuei moved in 1974 to reinstate the Imperial Rescript on Education of 1890, arguing that it promoted universal moral values that were being neglected by the excessive emphasis on intellectual development.[128] These trends reached a zenith in the early 1980s with the outcry generated by the

---

124. Horio, *Educational Thought and Ideology*, pp. 121, 142–50.
125. Masami, "Textbook Revision," pp. 476–77.
126. See Akira Amakawa, "The Making of the Postwar Local Government System," in *Democratizing Japan: The Allied Occupation*, ed. Robert E. Ward and Sakamoto Yoshikazu (Honolulu: University of Hawaii Press, 1987), pp. 276ff.
127. Horio, *Educational Thought and Ideology*, pp. 151, 165–73; Masami, "Textbook Revision," pp. 477–78. The 1958 Course of Study reintroduced the *"Kimi ga yo"* as a required song for schools. The song was reintroduced as the national anthem in 1978.
128. Masami, "Textbook Revision," p. 478.

Monbushō's revision of textbooks to omit critical references to Japan's role in World War II.

Thus, the postwar era has seen the sphere of education as a vehicle for state activism; first, in the initial years of the Occupation for the promotion of democratization, but later, in the late Occupation and post-Occupation eras for molding citizens to state ends. The point was not whether or not the state should be used, but how it was used. Moreover, a critical question was whether it was the central government itself or official bodies at the local level with significant autonomy from the center that were making decisions about curriculum and teaching methods. At the level of local parent-teachers' associations and school boards, parents and teachers can feel that they exercise a democratic control over matters in their own communities. At this level, the state is the state "writ small rather than large," at least as it is perceived by the actors involved. Individuals are encouraged to participate, because it is clear that if they do not mobilize themselves to act in their own best interests, no one else—except perhaps those with agendas that might be in conflict with those interests—will do so.

■ Conclusions: Japan and the Challenges of Democratization in the "East" of Europe

What do these two historical experiments in democratizing Japan have to offer to our appreciation of the opportunities and obstacles for democratic change in Eastern and Central Europe? The Japanese case can be highly instructive, because despite the conspicuous cultural and other contextual differences, Japan shared with Eastern and Central Europe certain key circumstances. Like the societies where the revolutions of 1989 occurred, Japan was a late industrializer relative to Western Europe, and like Poland, the Czech and Slovak Federal Republic, and Hungary, its leaders looked westward for models of the desirable polity. As in Eastern and Central Europe today, Japan's modernizers recognized that a constitutional system endowed with institutions of representative government was essential to the country's acceptance in the Western-dominated international order. Thus, while Poland, Hungary, and the CSFR may lay claim to indigenous roots of democratic values, such claims may not suffice to defuse nativist and nationalist counter-claims in the face of external pressure.[129] Nor is this the only sense in which nationalism has proven to be as problematic for aspirants to democracy in Eastern and Central Europe as it was in prewar Japan. Much more burdensome has been the link between the quest for nationhood and the nature of state power as state building is pursued along with democratization. To be sure, while the immediate objective of the new leaderships has been to dismantle much of the repressive apparatus of the totalistic Stalinist *anciens régimes,* the dual task of state building and democratization, historically associated with the rise of the bourgeoisie in Western Europe, has not been left behind in these societies. There is an important sense in which these peoples are, like the Meiji oligarchs, engaged in a process of building the nation-state as they seek to replace quasi-colonial outposts of the Soviet empire with self-assertive national units (a project that requires that they tackle unresolved ethnic tensions to define anew the nation).

This coupling of the tasks of achieving significant economic development with democratization produces a shared context that is fraught with tensions concerning the state-society relationship. How does one balance the need for state initiative in achieving large-scale economic growth with the importance of societal initiative in achieving working democratic politics? What can the state do to promote democratization when it is the primary agency available with the resources to promote developments within society that are essential to the realization of democratic politics? These questions require that one move beyond the simple antagonistic state-society dichotomy and rethink critically what elements in the domains of both state and society are required to realize democratic politics.

The Japanese case is useful precisely because of the contentiousness of the issue of the extent to which democracy prevails there. Because of the historic leadership that the Meiji state assumed in engineering Japan's industrial development, this question is intimately bound up with the assessment of the nature of the role the state plays in economic life, in "civil society" narrowly construed. On this point, there is considerable disagreement among Western scholars. Some have portrayed

---

129. See the more extended discussion of this problem in Germaine A. Hoston, *The State, Identity and the National Question* (Princeton: Princeton University Press, forthcoming), chap. 10.

the Japanese state as a fairly autonomous force that is extremely effective in guiding Japan's industrial development,[130] while others insist that it is the private sector that manipulates the policy-making process for its own ends, so that it is virtually fortuitous if state objectives are met.[131] More importantly, there is a strong sense among many Japanese that the close relationship between business and political elites that has persisted since the prewar period has been detrimental to Japanese democracy. Much as Habermas deplores the diminution of the public realm by the forces of domination, Hirata Kiyoaki has pointed to the role of "patronal associations, linked to bureaucracies, beginning with MITI," the enterprise-based (rather than occupation-based) union, and the "invention of diverse forms of participation" (*ringi* for middle managers and "quality circles" for workers)—all these, in his view, perpetuate the impact of Japan's statist ideology on Japan's weak civil society. The problem is not simply the state's support of industrial development, but rather the interpenetration of the public and private spheres. The close linkages between the conservative LDP in power with industrial associations that negotiate with labor every year through the coordinated *Shuntō* (spring battle), and the proliferation of *shingikai* (deliberative councils) to resolve conflicts before they manifest themselves in the parliamentary process—these to Hirata signify "parliamentary democracy linked to political corporatism." They reflect an economy that he characterizes as "cooperative capitalism," in large part because of the leading role of the industrial *keiretsu* (loose industrial groups descended from the prewar *zaibatsu*)[132] with their high levels of intra-*keiretsu* shareholding.

There are really two problems here that are of significance for the transitions under way in Eastern and Central Europe. The first, for Japan's civil society school theorists, lies in the persistence of ties considered to be premodern. The second, related point is that it is not enough to have the institutional

---

130. See Chalmers Johnson, *MITI and the Japanese Miracle* (Stanford: Stanford University Press, 1982); and Daniel I. Okimoto, *Between MITI and the Market: Japanese Industrial Policy for High Technology* (Stanford: Stanford University Press, 1989).

131. See Richard J. Samuels, *The Business of the Japanese State: Energy Markets in Comparative and Historical Perspective* (Ithaca, NY: Cornell University Press, 1987).

132. See Hirata Kiyoaki, "La société civile japonaise contemporaine," in *Actuel Marx*, no. 2: *Le marxisme au Japon* (1987), pp. 67–69.

structures of democratic politics. What matters is how the institutions work in practice. Here the obstacles and opportunities for the fruition of true democracy lie not only in the state but in the realm of informal, societal relations. To be sure, in the Meiji era, alongside the bicameral parliament and embedded in the constitutional structure were formal arrangements that proved to be detrimental to democracy. The transcendent monarch, the special privileges of the military high command, and the Privy Council helped to promote the curious combination of rigid hierarchy with leadership that lacks a responsible center that Karel van Wolferen has identified. That he can claim that this problem persists to the present despite the elimination of these special institutional arrangements signals the tremendous significance of informal social relations in Japanese politics.[133] Such informal patriarchal and hierarchical relations hamper the full flowering of democracy in Japan, diminishing the competitiveness of the political system, inhibiting the free and open exchange of views that defines the "public sphere," obstructing "the recognition of the principle of the legitimacy of opposition and dissent,"[134] and vesting the bureaucratic apparatus of the state with an authority with which the representative structures of the Diet (and its opposition parties) can ill compete.[135] These relations are evidenced in voting behavior heavily conditioned by personal ties, "organizations and social networks"[136] in an electoral pattern that privileges the sons and other relatives of those who are already in power. *Nisei* (second-generation) candidates comprised 40% of all LDP candidates in the 1983 general elections, and 43% in the 1986 general election and "roughly the same proportions of the LDP winners in both cases."[137] This

---

133. See Karel van Wolferen, *The Enigma of Japanese Power* (New York: Knopf, 1989); and idem, "The Japan Problem," *Foreign Affairs* (Winter 1986/1987).

134. Bradley M. Richardson and Scott C. Flanagan, *Politics in Japan* (Boston and Toronto: Little, Brown and Company, 1984), p. 73.

135. In Japan, approximately 60% to 70% of all bills introduced into the Diet are sponsored by the ministerial bureaucracy, and a much higher proportion of cabinet-initiated bills (89.2%) than Diet member-sponsored bills (26.6%) are passed. See ibid., p. 347; and Nobuo Tomita, Akira Nakamura, and Ronald J. Hrebenar, "The Liberal Democratic Party: The Ruling Party of Japan," in *The Japanese Party System: From One-Party Rule to Coalition Government*, ed. Ronald J. Hrebenar (Boulder: Westview, 1986), p. 272.

136. Scott C. Flanagan, "Electoral Change in Japan: A Study of Secular Realignment," in *Electoral Change in Advanced Industrial Democracies: Realignment or Dealignment?* (Princeton: Princeton University Press), p. 186.

137. Ibid., p. 9; Curtis, *Japanese Way of Politics*, p. 95.

trend was reinforced in the 1989 upper house elections. The lack of any alternation of the party in power for 35 years is consistent with this pattern.

These observations return us to the importance of the cultivation of a strong and vibrant civil society in promoting democratization. Where totalistic regimes existed in Eastern and Central Europe, there is an even more urgent need than in Japan to create and nurture civil societies where only nascent ones exist. The achievement of modernization in economic and democratic terms will require the eradication of old as well as new traditions. The resurgence of longstanding ethnic antagonisms that have torn asunder the CSFR and Yugoslavia reveal the remanence of strong traditions—some of them dating to periods as recent as the 1920s and 1930s—beneath the suppression imposed by the Soviet-supported communist states. The impact of old regimes in destroying the traditional bases of civil societies in the articulation of conflicting class or occupational interests has enhanced the significance of such ethnic or personalistic ties viewed by many as premodern. As in Japan, the challenge of superseding such premodern ties is intensified by the fact that, unlike the process in Spain, for example, democratization is being pursued simultaneously with economic development.

The pressures of resolving dire economic difficulties render the task of democratization that much more onerous. The latter comes into conflict with the urgent economic need to rely on the expertise of old elites. This difficulty is amply illustrated in the incompleteness of the postwar purge and SCAP's anxious de-purging of Japan's prewar elites. Personnel changes at the top of the bureaucracy must be accompanied by changes in personnel at lower levels, where democratizing policies in such vital areas as education are implemented. Moreover, the expertise supplied by administrative top-down initiatives must be tempered by the encouragement of popular participation as an educational process in itself. As the Japanese case reveals, a universal educational system without a specifically authoritarian political agenda can create an educated populace with the basic skills to enable it to participate in governing itself. Enhanced with an agenda to promote civil liberties, and operating under methods that encourage the active democratic participation of citizens themselves in the education of their children, a state-sponsored educational process can further magnify the benefits to democratization of a universal education system.

The Japanese experience also highlights the dual problem of bureaucracy and accountability. It is not sufficient for bureaucratic power to be "rationalized," as in the Weberian paradigm. To guard against the potential *anti*-democratic influence of remanent elites of the old regimes, bureaucratic power must be held accountable. Here the role of political parties that articulate competing societal interests is crucial. This has been achieved only partially in both Meiji and postwar Japan. Likewise, in East Central Europe, where nascent parties are even less organically linked to articulate constituencies, we have yet to see the emergence of viable political parties that articulate competing interests and preferences of individuals rather than nostalgic yearnings for premodern, precommunist, predominantly ethnicity-based communities.

At the same time, it is precisely because of the appeal that nationalism has demonstrated anew in Eastern and Central Europe that one must call into question the Japanese civil society theorists' assumption of that which comprises the desideratum of civil society. How satisfying can relationships of "material dependency" be as an objective of social life? Is there not a danger of the reproduction of an anomic society, the sort of atomization—in a changed form, to be sure—that characterized the old totalism? The strength of the nationalist impulse suggests precisely such a fear. It thus compels us to consider how the comfort of community, of intersubjectivity, might be restored and strengthened, even as old, patriarchal, hierarchical relations are replaced by new democratic norms.

Finally, the commitment to industrialization and democratization in Central and Eastern Europe will entail a coming to terms with elements of the past and indeed with national identity itself. Japan's experience would appear to be irrelevant in this respect, given its excessively vaunted myth of ethnic homogeneity. Yet, as both prewar Marxist controversies on the left and the Shōwa Restorationist movements on the right of the 1920s and 1930s demonstrate, Japanese have had to confront fundamental issues concerning the implications of the pursuit of modernization for Japanese national identity. The endurance of the issue through the postwar era—as represented in the phenomenon of *Nihonjin ron*[138]—underscores its significance, de-

---

138. *Nihonjin ron* is a genre of literature that emerged in the 1960s examining what was unique about Japanese.

spite Japan's strong national tradition of syncretism. Unlike Japanese, Hungarians or Poles will not be laboring under the sense that the modernity they are seeking is alien. Yet the possibility Taylor suggests, that the emergence of the public sphere coincided historically in the West with the assertion of a "sense of the nation,"[139] underscores an important urgency stressed in other chapters in this volume: the need to bridge the gap between the intellectual elites who spearheaded the revolutions of 1989 and those non-elites who comprised what in the French Revolution was—when the nation (*la patrie*) came to conjoined with the notion of the popular masses—*le peuple*. Together, they must adopt political democracy as a goal that is consistent with their own indigenous traditions. Together, they must build a civil society, a new public sphere, and achieve mutual trust if true democratization is to be achieved.

---

139. Taylor, "Modes of Civil Society," p. 108.

PART II

CENTRAL EUROPEAN CASE STUDIES

4

Regime Transformation and the Mid-Level Bureaucratic Forces in Hungary

TAMAS L. FELLEGI

■ *Introduction*

This chapter concerns the role of mid-level bureaucratic forces in the transition process from communist post-totalitarianism[1] to democracy in Hungary. Unlike during previous regime changes in modern Hungary,[2] state bureaucracies and their personnel remained in place during the agony and the transformation of the communist regime in 1988–1990.[3]

I would like to thank Rudolf L. Tőkés, Henry Krisch, and Matthew D. Lyon (all of the University of Connecticut) for their suggestions and advice in writing this chapter. I am also indebted to Philippe C. Schmitter (Stanford University), Germaine A. Hoston (University of California, San Diego), and Henryk Szlajfer (Polish Institute of International Affairs) for their comments on the draft version of this paper.

1. It is beyond the scope of this chapter to engage in a discussion about the utility and possible definitions of concepts like post-totalitarian or communist authoritarian. To avoid any confusion, I will use these terms interchangeably, based on the definition of post-totalitarian regimes provided by Juan J. Linz, "Totalitarian and Authoritarian Regimes," in *Handbook of Political Science*, vol. 3, *Macropolitical Theory*, ed. Nelson Polsby and Fred Greenstein (Reading, MA: Addison-Wesley, 1975), pp. 175–354. The "postcommunist" adjective is getting more fashionable both in the scholarly literature and in journalism. To the best of my knowledge, the term was originated by Zbigniew Brzezinski, *The Grand Failure: The Birth and Death of Communism in the Twentieth Century* (New York: Scribner, 1989).
2. By previous regime changes I mean the 1918 collapse of the Austro-Hungarian Empire, the 1919 collapse of the first democratic republic, the 1919 defeat of the short-lived communist regime, the 1944–1945 collapse of the rightwing conservative regime of Admiral Horthy, and the communist takeover in 1945-1949.
3. There are different options for setting the time frame of transition: 1968, 1978, 1981, 1988. Most observers designate the Communist Party's national conference in May 1988, which removed the Kádárist Old Guard from office, as the immediate start of the transition.

The transition took place rapidly but gradually, through constitutional and legal reforms underlining the role of, and the need for, a functioning and disciplined state bureaucracy. Not only did this process avert any form of revolutionary mobilization or radical rupture, but it permitted the nomenklatura to "transform" itself into "converted democrats," small entrepreneurs, or even capitalists. The incomplete transition process itself permitted strongholds of the top governmental and regime elites and the mid-level state bureaucratic forces to remain in place within the public administration, the police and the military, the judiciary, and the economy.

Continuity prevented overt power struggles between the new regime and the administrative elites (bureaucrats) inherited from the old regime. Domestic and international circumstances have made any attempt by domestic or international forces to restore the communist regime extremely unlikely, if not impossible. The state bureaucracy today serves the new regime as readily as it once served its communist masters. Consequently, the main analytical issue here is the impact of the state, including its bureaucracies, on the process of transition, and not the specific personnel changes in these bureaucracies.

This chapter will focus on the changing role and position of the mid-level bureaucratic forces in the dynamic processes of regime transformation in Hungary. The main purposes are (1) to illuminate those critical junctures at which state bureaucracies have played a decisive role; (2) to shed light on theoretical problems pertaining to the concepts of regime and state in transitional postcommunist politics; and (3) to assess the future relationship of the inherited bureaucratic forces and the new regime.

It is a major thesis of this chapter that, contrary to general expectations generated during the transition from authoritarian rule to democracy in Hungary, there has been an ongoing effort by the new government to reestablish the wide scope of bureaucratic control over society that had been there for the preceding decades of communist and noncommunist, but nondemocratic, rule.

I assume that the increase in bureaucratic governmental control can be attributed to the ruling center-right coalition's[4]

---

4. There are six parties in the Hungarian Parliament. The Hungarian Democratic Forum, the Independent Smallholders' Party, and the Christian

political effort to handle political and economic conflicts by taking advantage of the inherited institutional control mechanisms of resource allocation and public ownership of land, productive facilities, and other economic resources. Since it took power in the summer of 1990, the ruling coalition has— deliberately or instinctively—relied on the bureaucratic power of the state and tried to recentralize governmental control, thus weakening the effect of market changes introduced in 1988– 1990.

In what follows, I discuss basic terms that relate to the topic, namely, *bureaucracy*, *regime transformation*, and *regime* and *state*. Then I analyze the process of regime change with regard to the bureaucracies, and finally assess the survival strategies available to the bureaucrats in the new regime.

■ *The Bureaucracy*

I do not intend to provide a sociological analysis of the bureaucratic personnel, nor am I able to offer detailed statistics on the topic. There are two main reasons for these limitations. First, as of yet, there has been no significant research conducted on the role of the mid-level bureaucratic forces in the context of transformation. Inquiries have focused mainly on the elites, the political parties, and the first multiparty elections, and have tended to overlook the role of the state and its bureaucratic forces. In addition, Hungarian studies of elites are inclined to ignore the difference between government elites and mid-level bureaucratic forces.[5] Due to these constraints, any investigation at this stage is rather speculative in nature and has to follow the logic of deductive analysis.

Second, I do not believe that either the development or the collapse of communism can be adequately and meaningfully

---

Democratic People's Party have forged a center-right, national-conservative coalition with about 58% parliamentary support. Two liberal democratic parties, the Alliance of Free Democrats and the Federation of Young Democrats, and the Hungarian Socialist Party (the reformist wing of the former Communist Party) have been in opposition.

5. György Szoboszlai, "Elections and political system change in Hungary," in *Demokratikus átmenetek* (Democratic transitions), ed. György Szoboszlai (Budapest: Hungarian Political Science Association, 1991); Rudolf L. Tőkés, "Hungary's New Political Elites: Adaptation and Change, 1989–1990," *Problems of Communism* (November-December 1990); Ákos Róna-Tas, "The Selected and The Elected: The Making of the New Parliamentary Elite in Hungary," *East European Politics and Societies* 5, no. 3 (Fall 1991), pp. 357–93.

described by the analysis of bureaucracy. Although bureaucracy and bureaucratization are inseparable from both the idea and praxis of state socialism, as Kaminski reminds us, "to portray the system as a bureaucracy that displays patterns of behavior similar to those of any large organization does not offer any insights about its evolution."[6] After the early period of revolutionary mobilization, communist development displayed the characteristics of a system employing routinized procedures, large organizations, and a pattern of division of labor in which specified individuals dealt with specific issues, using specific methods and resources on a professional basis. Nevertheless, the existence of administration, bureaucrats, and routinized procedures does not necessarily fit the Weberian definition of bureaucracy. State socialism is a system of bureaucratic domination; to paraphrase Lincoln, a government of the bureaucrats, for the bureaucrats, by the bureaucrats.

Empirically, decision-making power rested with the bureaucrats of the political and economic apparatus in the state and the Communist Party.[7] The vast majority of society's resources were at the disposal of these bureaucracies. Two functions of critical importance grew from the predominant role of the bureaucracies: the command of the economy (fiscal power and property-management rights) and the power of appointment (nomenklatura) specifically in the hands of the party apparatus. Under state socialism, there did not develop a Weberian professional bureaucracy,

> a system of administration carried out on a continuous basis by trained professionals according to prescribed rules. . . . which professional administration embodies a double contrast: first, between administration and policy making, which is the responsibility of the association that employs the bureaucracy, and to which it is legally subordinate; second, between modern and traditional methods of administration, which are arranged on non-professionalized lines.[8]

6. Bartlomiej Kaminski, *The Collapse of State Socialism: The Case of Poland* (Princeton: Princeton University Press, 1991), p. 6.
7. Maria Hirszowicz, *Coercion and Control in Communist Society: The Visible Hand in a Command Economy* (New York: St. Martin's, 1986), pp. 4–11; Erzsébet Szalai, "The metamorphosis of power?" *Valóság*, 1991, no. 6, pp. 3–6.
8. David Beetham, *Bureaucracy* (Minneapolis: University of Minnesota Press, 1987), pp. 3–4.

Nevertheless, over time there developed a system of management and regulations that generated bureaucratic routines, techniques, methods, and even a limited scope of meritocracy within professional or semi-professional organizations.

The state and party bureaucracies had various hierarchical levels. Each level was set apart from the lower and upper levels by its role in the division of labor and by its own administrative duties. Decision-making power was delegated from the upper level, ultimately away from the national party-state leadership, but the rules of the game were not formally defined. The upper echelon, nonetheless, retained the authority to recentralize decision-making authority at any time. Bureaucratic competency and authority flowed from the political hierarchy, not from the internal rules of a professionally bureaucratic system. Because the institutionalization of political procedures and decision-making powers was incomplete, whenever a discrepancy arose between formal bureaucratic requirements and political demands, the latter prevailed. This was one of the reasons that reforms aiming at decentralizing the communist system failed. During the policy of decentralization, formal decision-making powers and obligations were delegated to different levels in the bureaucratic hierarchies, while the real decision-making authority, especially the disposition over economic resources, remained in the political hierarchy.

The bureaucracies and bureaucrats were divided along various political, economic, and social lines demarking conflicting sectoral interests. Such cleavages might have caused the misperception of a pluralistic power structure evolving under communism.[9] However, social forces had no better and freer access to political-economic power outside the bureaucratic framework of the party and the state. The regime prevented any groupings in society, let alone autonomous organizations, from emerging as political forces. Socioeconomic conflicts and cleavages did not take political forms, but remained within the closed circles of a fragmented bureaucratic system. Even if these divisions often represented real social conflicts, bureaucrats ap-

---

9. In the late 1960s there emerged a whole body of literature mistakenly describing the post-Stalinist regime as moving toward a pluralistic power system. See H. Gordon Skilling and Franklyn Griffiths, eds., *Interest Groups in Soviet Politics* (Princeton: Princeton University Press, 1971); Jerry Hough and Merle Fainsod, *How the Soviet Union is Governed* (Cambridge, MA: Harvard University Press, 1979).

peared as "political forces" only vis-à-vis the other segments of the same bureaucratic system. Because the term "political force" had, at best, limited meaning in state socialism (where the economy was overpoliticized and the polity was depoliticized),[10] "pluralism" does not seem to be the proper term to characterize the politics of fragmented bureaucracies.

With this in mind, one can speak about mid-level bureaucratic "forces." Bureaucrats and bureaucracies themselves were the party-state system. Political and sociological analyses suggest that the mid-level bureaucracies right beneath the top party and state leaders were the critical agents of commanding the economy and administering society.[11]

In my definition, mid-level bureaucrats are those individuals whose paid job is to occupy:

- the cabinet-level leading administrative and decision-making positions in the government ministries and in the prime minister's staff under the position of secretaries of state;

- the leading administrative and decision-making positions in the nonministerial but cabinet-level state agencies (*országos hatáskörü szervek*) with institutional channels to the cabinet or to the prime minister's staff;

- the leading administrative and decision-making positions in the nonministerial or subcabinet-level state agencies with institutional channels to the cabinet or to the prime minister's staff;

- the leading administrative and decision-making positions in the county- and city-level administration (self-government) in actual charge of administering the given political-geographic unit;

- the permanent envoys of the prime minister or the cabinet representing the central government at the county or municipal level.

A 1988 estimate put the number of nationally or locally decisive leaders in the range of 25,000.[12] Included in this group were the apparatchiks of the party bureaucracy (5,000–8,000), the Communist Youth League (2,000–3,000), and the trade unions (from the high hundreds to the low thousands). In the new

---

10. Kaminski, *Collapse of State Socialism*, pp. 3–4.
11. Ibid., pp. 135–94; Hirszowicz, *Coercion and Control in Communist Society*, pp. 1–23, 127–47; and Szalai, "Metamorphosis of power."
12. Mihály Bihari, "Changes and unchanges," in Sándor Kurtán, Péter Sándor, and László Vass, eds., *Magyarország politikai évkönyve 1988* (Political yearbook of Hungary, 1988) (Budapest: Okonomia Alapitvány-Economix Rt., 1988), p. 56.

noncommunist regime, the bureaucracies and the bureaucrats of the Communist Party and its auxiliary ("transmission-belt") organizations have disappeared. The widely shared estimate is that approximately 10,000 to 12,000 individuals have been elected or appointed to leading positions of national importance since the transfer of power in 1990.[13] The number of the top political elite, meaning the members of Parliament (386), high government officials (150), and the leadership of the major parties and political organizations (300–500), total approximately 1,200. Thus, according to my arbitrary and conservative estimate, the number of mid-level bureaucrats might be in the range of 8,000 to 10,000.

■ Transition and Regime Transformation

To analyze the role that different political forces perform in the process of regime change, the concepts of transition and regime transformation have to be defined. *Transition* is a multidimensional and open-ended process that refers to "the interval between one political regime and another."[14] It is a sequence of related yet autonomous processes, moving from the disintegration of the *ancien régime*, through the emergence and gradual implementation of new forms, and finally to the consolidation of the new regime. Each stage has its own unique political configuration, dominant institutional and individual actors, major socioeconomic and political objectives, and domestic and international challenges and conflicts. By setting the pace and direction of political and socioeconomic changes, the interplay of these factors determines the different modes of regime transformation.[15]

---

13. Mihály Bihari, "Regime and power change in Hungary," in Sándor Kurtán, Péter Sándor, and László Vass, eds., *Magyarország politikai évkönyve 1991* (Political yearbook of Hungary, 1991) (Budapest: Ökonomia Alapitvány-Economix Rt., 1991), p. 35.
14. Guillermo O'Donnell and Philippe C. Schmitter, *Transitions from Authoritarian Rule: Tentative Conclusions About Uncertain Democracies* (Baltimore: Johns Hopkins University Press, 1986), pp. 6–7.
15. In the transition literature there are several categories to describe the different modes of transition. The most frequently cited are those of Mainwaring and Share, Huntington, and Linz. Donald Share and Scott Mainwaring, "Transitions Through Transactions: Democratization in Brazil and Spain," in *Political Liberalization in Brazil: Dynamics, Dilemmas, and Future Prospects*, ed. Wayne A. Selcher (Boulder: Westview, 1986); Samuel P. Huntington, *The Third Wave: Democratization in the Late Twentieth Century*

At the core of the concept of transition is the notion of *regime transformation*, which refers to the political process in which a characteristically new political and social regime emerges and consolidates itself. In this sense, transition is the broader and more technical term that concerns the fact of change, whereas transformation is the "substance" of regime change. Transformation implies active participants, i.e., transformers, with the intention of changing the system, strategies, resources, resource mobilization, and individual or collective strategic decisions.[16]

Regime transformation directly addresses the Lasswellian question of "who gets what, when, and how?" Indeed, regime transformation has, by its nature, three dimensions that one can distinguish for analytical purposes: (1) the redistribution of political power within the changing composition of elites; (2) constituency building (partisanship and realignment); and (3) the redefinition of property rights and the allocation of public assets (including privatization). The role of political forces ought to be examined in the context of these three dimensions.

The position and role of the mid-level bureaucratic forces in the first phase of the transition process in Hungary are determined by two separate tendencies: one is the effort by the new government to "bring the state back in,"[17] and the other is the movement by the top bureaucrats toward the private sector either as entrepreneurs or managers. The former relates to the new governing coalition's efforts to centralize political decisions in the hands of government bureaucracies and make use of the bureaucratic forces in pursuing its political agenda in regime transformation. The latter tendency pertains to a particular individualistic adaptation strategy by the members of the mid-level bureaucracies.

As for the first political tendency, one can observe an increase in the scope of bureaucratic state intervention vis-à-vis

---

(Norman, OK: University of Oklahoma Press, 1991); Juan J. Linz, *Crisis, Breakdown and Reequilibration* (Baltimore: Johns Hopkins University Press, 1978).

16. This is one possible way to differentiate between reformers, whose main purpose is to make the existing regime more viable without changing its underlying premises, and transformers, who want to replace the existing regime with a new one.

17. This is, of course, the title of Peter B. Evans, Dietrich Rueschemeyer, and Theda Skocpol, eds., *Bringing the State Back In* (Cambridge: Cambridge University Press, 1985).

Parliament and civil society, compared to the earlier stages of transition.[18] This is especially striking considering that two major objectives of regime transformation were to reduce the strong interventionist state, and to prevent any one political party from taking hegemonic control of the state and the new regime.

■ The Mode of Regime Transformation in Hungary

Communist regimes disintegrated from within and eventually ceased to exist under international conditions conducive to regime change.[19] In Hungary, communism did not collapse under unbearable external and internal pressures. It was gradually rejected by society and abandoned by a large segment of the political and economic nomenklatura elite that had occupied critical positions over a long period of time in the economy, the legal system, and public administration. Transition was precipitated by two decades of liberalization under the control of a regime or party-state elite that became increasingly fragmented and incapable of performing essential tasks of management and system maintenance.

Ultimately, after years of political upheaval within the party, within the leadership, and within society, the regime elite, offering little or no resistance, surrendered its political power through negotiations to a selective group of nine opposition organizations (parties and proto-parties). In this sense, the transfer of political power took the form of transformation through transactions.[20] The speed and direction of political events were subject to political pacts negotiated between the reformist segments of the regime elite and the emerging opposition elites without significant mass participation.[21]

---

18. László Kéri, *Összeomlás után* (After the collapse) (Budapest: Kossuth, 1991).
19. By favorable conditions I mean three factors: the impact of Gorbachev's perestroika and new foreign policy; the economic and political pressures exerted by the West, including the IMF and private banks, on these countries to further liberalize their polities and economies; and the demonstration effect of the simultaneous changes occurring in the neighboring communist countries (ripple effect).
20. This phrase was originated by Share and Mainwaring, "Transitions Through Transactions."
21. There have been different opinions as to whether the Hungarian transition was mainly an elite transaction. Some argue that it was: see Tőkés, "Hungary's New Political Elites"; László Bruszt, "1989: Hungary's negoti-

It is, however, of critical importance to note that throughout the periods of liberalization and transition there were no master plans, ready-made blueprints, or strategies pursued by the regime elite.[22] As Hungarian political scientists have pointed out, the Hungarian communist regime was best described as a web of personal and bureaucratic loyalties, a complex fabric of intra-leadership and clientelistic relations.[23] The Hungarian period of economic liberalization (1968–1989) was marked by policy zigzags and elite infighting. To a significant extent, decisions and contingency choices were the outcomes of interpersonal bargaining processes that in turn were heavily influenced by leadership ambitions.[24] This latter feature became especially evident during the period of 1988–1989, when the ruling Communist Party fell victim to paralyzing internal power struggles in which the different factions closed ranks behind leading personalities.[25]

Nevertheless, by the late 1980s, as the social bases of the regime evaporated or turned rebellious,[26] the reformist segments of the elites came to recognize that the regime, including the Communist Party, was obsolete in its then current form because of its inability to solve the protracted economic and

---

ated revolution," in Sándor Kurtán, Péter Sándor, and László Vass, eds., *Magyarország politikai évkönyve 1990* (Political yearbook of Hungary, 1990) (Budapest: Okonomia Alapitvány-Economix Rt., 1990). Other observers put more emphasis on the social and economic changes precipitating and accompanying the changes: Kéri, *Összeomlás után.*

22. It is beyond the scope of this chapter to discuss this important point in detail. I would like to suggest that although blueprints were missing, political and socioeconomic expectations rose in society and within the elites concerning the directions and pace of reforms and liberalization of the regime.

23. See, e.g., Elemer Hankiss, *East European Alternatives* (Oxford: Clarendon Press, 1990); László Kéri, "A Kádár-korszak fölbomlása (The disintegration of the Kádár regime) (Manuscript, Budapest, 1991), p. 16; and Mária Csanádi, "Structure, Cohesion and Disintegration of the Hungarian Party-State System," in *Democracy and Political Transformation*, ed. György Szoboszlai (Budapest: Hungarian Political Science Association, 1991).

24. László Lengyel, "1990," in Kurtán et al., *Magyarország politikai évkönyve 1990*; Bihari, "Regime and power change in Hungary"; Kéri, *Összeomlás után*; and idem, "A Kádár-korszak fölbomlása."

25. From early 1988 on, five potential contenders emerged as short-term or prospective successors to János Kádár: Károly Grósz, János Berecz, Imre Pozsgay, Rezsö Nyers, and Miklós Németh.

26. From the second half of 1988 the country experienced unprecedented strikes across the nation, and in 1989 the reform circles within the Communist Party gave rise to the political alternative that paved the way to the dissolution of the ruling Communist Party and the formation of the Socialist Party.

political crisis. In 1989, a reformist leadership emerged, taking positions in the government and state bureaucracies[27] and ready to act upon this realization. As an Italian observer rightly noted, compared to the rest of Eastern Europe, "the Hungarian leadership was better disposed towards reform, until ultimately it [the rest] became set on it."[28]

■ Regime, State, and Government

There are several reasons for placing the policy analysis of the mid-level bureaucratic forces in the context of state-regime relations. First of all, both tendencies that I have listed as conditioning the current position and role of the mid-level bureaucratic forces are central to the state-regime relations. The government bureaucracies that exercise the monopoly of the state's coercive and executive powers are the central components of all bureaucratic forces. Reallocation of power and property in postcommunist Hungary is inseparable from the state and its bureaucracies.

Second, the state and its bureaucracies operate in a deeply embedded etatist historical-cultural mold in Hungary.[29] In a deeply paternalistic political culture, the state has been looked upon as the provider of welfare and livelihood and as the protector of society.[30] State bureaucracies have penetrated society and especially the economy; therefore, the agenda of a yet-to-be-implemented democratic reallocation of power and property in postcommunist Hungary is as much a part of the problem as of the solution.

27. Prime Minister Miklós Németh, Ministers of State Imre Pozsgay and Rezsö Nyers (all in the four-member presidency of the Communist Party), and Foreign Minister Gyula Horn, presently the Chair of the Socialist (former Communist) Party.
28. Pietro Grilli di Cortona, "From Communism to Democracy: Rethinking Regime Change in Hungary and Czechoslovakia," *International Social Science Journal*, 1991, no. 128, p. 318.
29. Andrew C. Janos, "The One-Party State and Social Mobilization," in *Authoritarian Politics in Modern Society*, ed. Samuel Huntington and Clement Moore (New York: Basic Books, 1970); and idem, "The Politics of Backwardness in Continental Europe, 1780–1945," *World Politics* 41, no. 3 (April 1989), pp. 325–58.
30. For the relationship between paternalism and infantilistic political attitudes, most importantly dependency on the state, see Elemer Hankiss, "Reforms and the Conversion of Power," in *Upheaval Against the Plan*, ed. Peter Weilemann, Georg Brunner, and Rudolf L. Tőkés (Oxford/New York: Berg, 1990), pp. 55–59.

Third, in the midst of volatile political and social conditions of regime transformation, state bureaucracies represent stability and continuity, and thus offer themselves to the governing coalition as a predictable and loyal, though not necessarily enthusiastic, political constituency.

Conceptual clarity concerning regime, state, and government is of critical importance in studying the impact of state bureaucracy on the transition process. The term "regime" here is understood as a way of organizing political power,[31] a particular way of establishing and regulating relations between the state, the government, and civil society. It is defined as

1. a known and practiced set of patterns that determines the forms and ways of elite recruitment and access to governmental and other principal decision-making positions in and out of the state;
2. the actors and their attributes (such as social status), whether or not they are admitted to or excluded from this access;
3. the available resources to gain or maintain such access.[32]

By contrast, the "state" is a more permanent structure of domination and coordination that includes the coercive apparatus and means for governing society.[33] The state is not merely a battleground where different interests and political forces fight one another.[34] Nor is it a fortress that can be seized and monopolized by a political force from without; contrary to Marxism-Leninism, the state is not a mere coercive arm of a ruling class.[35] It is rather an autonomous entity in constant interaction with society at large and with the dominant political forces therein. As an autonomous entity, the state has its own organizations,

---

31. Jeane Kirkpatrick, *Dictatorships and Double Standards* (New York: American Enterprise Institute and Simon and Schuster, 1982), p. 96.
32. See Guillermo O'Donnell, *Bureaucratic Authoritarianism: Argentina 1966–1973—In Comparative Perspective* (Berkeley: University of California Press, 1988), p. 6; and Guillermo O'Donnell and Philippe C. Schmitter, *Transitions from Authoritarian Rule: Tentative Conclusions* (Baltimore: Johns Hopkins University Press, 1986), p. 73.
33. Robert M. Fishman, "Rethinking State and Regime," *World Politics* 42, no. 3 (April 1990), pp. 434–43.
34. Theda Skocpol, "Bringing the State Back In: Strategies of Analysis in Current Research," in Evans, Rueschemeyer, and Skocpol, *Bringing the State Back In*, p. 4.
35. Alfred Stepan, *The State and Society* (Princeton: Princeton University Press, 1978), pp. 20–22; Ralph Miliband, *The State in Capitalist Society* (New York: Basic Books, 1969), p. 6.

personnel, resources, and interests that can diverge from or converge with the interests of other social-political forces.[36]

With all this in mind, the state is conceived of as a complex set of institutional arrangements and organizations (administrative, policing, and military) directed by an executive authority. The state, operating through continuous and regulated activities of individuals acting as occupants of offices (bureaucracy), is designed to rule and govern. Through its bureaucracies, the state extracts resources from society and redistributes them by utilizing state power that flows from the administrative and coercive organizations.[37]

"Government" is the most specific of the three concepts, referring to the personnel in charge of the executive and legislative branches of the state. The two most prominent institutions are the cabinet, the focus of the executive branch, and the Parliament, the supreme legislative body and the institutional embodiment of popular sovereignty. The Parliament, as the political battlefield of all parties elected by the public and the source of the cabinet's authority, is a regime-like institution, in that it embodies a broader concept of representation and interest aggregation than the executive. The Parliament is the core institution for controlling and overseeing the ruling parties' activities in the government. Moreover, it is the sole *constitutional* vehicle available for the opposition and the public to promote changes in the policies and personnel of the executive.

In the Hungarian context, this conceptual differentiation is of essential importance. Under state socialism, the lines between state and regime were blurred; the government was little more than the executive arm of the regime. State and regime were intertwined, and the state's primary task was to provide the communist regime and its basic institutions with a protective umbrella against external and internal shocks.[38] Moreover, regime and state were interwoven to the extent that regime

---

36. For analyses see Eric A. Nordlinger, *On the Autonomy of the Democratic State* (Cambridge: Harvard University Press, 1981); Skocpol, "Bringing the State Back In."

37. Theda Skocpol, *States and Social Revolutions: A Comparative Analysis of France, Russia, and China* (Cambridge: Cambridge University Press, 1979), p. 29; Gianfranco Poggi, *The Development of the Modern State: A Sociological Introduction* (Stanford: Stanford University Press, 1978).

38. Philippe C. Schmitter, "Liberation by Golpe: Retrospective Thoughts on the Demise of Authoritarian Rule in Portugal," *Armed Forces and Society* 2 (November 1975), p. 10.

institutions, most importantly the Communist Party and the official trade unions, assumed functions and powers normally reserved for the government, thus sharing the monopoly of coercive force with the state.[39] Prime examples were the Communist Party's powers to directly govern the military, the secret police, and foreign affairs, or the trade unions' decision-making powers in managing the state's social security and pension funds.

At the center of the party-state system, the single ruling party operated with politically and constitutionally unrestricted power to penetrate both the state and society. The autonomy of social, professional, political, and even state organizations was defined with reference to the party. Between state and party a symbiotic relationship developed; state and party hierarchies in state socialist systems are organically linked.[40] The party in particular assumed the powers to do the following:[41]

1. set the political, and frequently the professional, agenda for any party and non-party state organizations, including government agencies;
2. appoint and nominate to leadership positions in non-party and state organizations, including government agencies;
3. maintain and operate primary party groups within non-party and state organizations, including government agencies;
4. demand party discipline over any forms of professional, organizational, membership, or bureaucratic loyalty.

As a legacy of the party-state system and the communist economic structure, the state involves large public assets, including property and management rights. Due to this nature of the postcommunist state, political and bureaucratic forces that take charge of the government might take full control of the nation's assets and make use of them for their own political and economic purposes. To avoid the resurrection of the party-state under a different political label in the process of democratization, all political groups ought to be prevented from taking hegemonic control of the government. Toward this end, a democratic, multiparty parliamentary supervision of governmental management of public assets and proprietary rights ought to

---

39. Kaminski, in *The Collapse of State Socialism* (pp. 7–8), calls the symbiosis of state, regime, and society the fusion principle.
40. Ibid.; see also Csanádi, "Structure, Cohesion and Disintegration," pp. 327–28; and Hirszowicz, *Coercion and Control in Communist Society*.
41. Csanádi, "Structure, Cohesion and Disintegration," pp. 328-30.

be implemented. As we will see later, this is why the separation of the state and the government is a major political issue between the governing coalition and the opposition.

■ *The Private Sector Alternative*

The private sector as an alternative realm of full-time professional or business careers started to evolve in 1986-1987.[42] Its emergence gained momentum in 1988 when the regime approved the first large-scale transactions turning state property into privately owned or managed assets.[43] By 1989, the evolving private sector, based on the transfer of state and party properties, grew large enough to provide the nomenklatura elite with a secure and desirable strategy of adaptation. Party assets were converted into private businesses under the ownership or management of party leaders and bureaucrats.[44] State enterprises were turned into joint stock companies, converting nomenklatura managers into CEOs, shareholders, and board members under the process of "spontaneous privatization."[45] Government experts and mid-level bureaucrats established consulting, accounting, and privatizing firms to both lay down the infrastructure of capitalism and assure their future economic power in postcommunist Hungary.

Compared to any other East European country, Hungary during the 1980s went furthest in reducing central planning, implementing individual material incentives, and extending the scope of private ownership in the economy. The newly born private sector transformed party and state bureaucrats into a new managerial-entrepreneurial class. Uniquely in Hungary, the privatization of state properties and party assets not only offered the economic and political nomenklatura an alternative strategy of adaptation to the changes, but to a certain extent it made transformation economically desirable for them. This way

---

42. The growth of the private sector gained momentum by the legal recognition of private enterprises in 1982.
43. István Csillag, "Magyarország" (Hungary), in *Privatizáció Kelet-Európában* (Privatization in Eastern Europe), ed. Ervin Apáthy et al. (Budapest: Atlantisz/Medvetánc, 1991), pp. 105–7.
44. It was as late as July 1989 when the still communist majority Parliament reluctantly put a legal ban on selling out the party's huge real estate properties.
45. Csillag, "Magyarország"; Zita Mária Petschnig et al., *Reports from the Tunnel: On the State of the Hungarian Economy, 1989* (Budapest: Financial Research Ltd., 1990).

it served as a safety valve that vastly contributed to the peaceful and resistance-free transfer of political power.

"In contrast to Czechoslovakia and Poland, Hungarian opposition was reinforced by reformist drive from above, initiated by pragmatic segments of the ruling elite."[46] Unlike the ruling elites elsewhere in the region, the Hungarian nomenklatura became politically and economically interested in initiating and directing the transition process. Consequently, regime transformation has to a large extent been the transfer of political power to the opposition and the transfer of economic and business power to the nomenklatura and the all-powerful industrial-managerial lobbies.

Economic transformation is at the heart of regime transformation. The consolidation of democracy hinges on the success of structural economic reforms. The economy is where the new regime faces the most severe challenges: the twin burdens of the inherited economic crisis[47] and bureaucratic state control of the economy. There is a widespread consensus that a major restructuring of the redistributive governmental system and the privatization of the state economy need to be the central components of any economic transformation. For decades, it was the state administration, primarily the mid-level bureaucratic forces in the government organizations, that was in control of both steering resource allocation and administering state property and management rights. Therefore any change in these fields necessarily modifies the position and role of the mid-level bureaucratic forces in the new regime.

■ State and Government: The Instruments of Transition

Between 1987 and 1989, two fundamental processes laid the foundations of the remarkable changes of 1990: state-regime relations underwent radical changes, and the political and economic nomenklatura started to reorient itself toward the evolving private sector.

---

46. Grzegorz Ekiert, "Democratization Process in East Central Europe: A Theoretical Reconsideration," *British Journal of Political Science* 21, pp. 285–313, here p. 307.

47. The inventory of adverse economic conditions is impressive: inflation, unemployment, fiscal crisis, foreign indebtedness, and the collapse of traditional (former communist) foreign markets.

By the second half of 1989, the government became so separate and independent from the Communist Party's control that it turned out to be the critical instrument of transforming the communist regime. During that year, the evolving opposition became organized[48] and, in a series of roundtable talks with the beleaguered and retreating party-state leadership, forced the Communist Party to open the legal-constitutional way for regime transformation. Further, after two years of power struggles at the top, and rank-and-file revolts at the bottom, the Hungarian Socialist Workers' Party collapsed in October 1989 and gave way to the Hungarian Socialist Party, a self-proclaimed reform communist/social-democratic party. During the period up to the March-April 1990 free elections, the last Communist-Socialist government of Miklós Németh acted on its own, without any real party or parliamentary support.

Paradoxically, however, both the strength and the weakness of the Németh government stemmed from the same fact: it was a transitional government. It did not have solid backing in the last Communist-dominated Parliament, nor did it gain legitimacy from the nation through democratic means.[49] Its strength and freedom of action derived from the fact that it remained the only functioning governing institution in the country in the wake of the collapse of the Communist Party. Moreover, as a cabinet of experts, the Németh government, under the pressure of the IMF and the World Bank, put into effect several unpopular and politically suicidal economic decisions, thereby saving the opposition from the need to implement them later on.[50] This way, in late 1989 all political forces, opposition and regime alike, had a strong interest in the survival of the Németh government until the free elections, which were scheduled for March 1990.

To its credit, the Németh cabinet went beyond its own political and ideological limitations and pushed through the last

---

48. In April 1989, nine leading opposition organizations established the Opposition Round Table, an umbrella organization designed to facilitate opposition cooperation and unity vis-à-vis the Communist Party. In the summer of 1989, opposition candidates handed down humiliating defeats to Communist Party candidates in a series of by-elections.
49. Zita Mária Petschnig et al., *Reports from the Tunnel: A Summary of the First Year of the Antall Government* (Budapest: Financial Research Ltd., 1991), pp. 7–9.
50. Zita Mária Petschnig, "Gazdasági átalakulás—Gazdasági rendszerváltás magyarországon" (Economic transformation—economic regime change in Hungary) (manuscript, Budapest, 1991), pp. 8–11.

communist Parliament the "essential acts" of regime transformation that had been negotiated during the national roundtable talks between the nine leading opposition organizations and the regime in the summer of 1989.

The full explanation of the Communist Party's self-destruction in 1988–1990 is too complex to present here. But I will elaborate on one powerful reason that combines the survival instincts of the nomenklatura and the mid-level bureaucratic forces with the gradual separation of state and regime.

Due to 20 years of liberalization and an increasingly professional state bureaucracy,[51] by the mid-1980s the party leadership, however reluctantly, relinquished its governing power to the party bureaucracy and to the mid-level state bureaucracies. This was especially true in the field of economic management, where "hands-on" bureaucratic control prevailed from the early 1980s on. Information gathering and dissemination became monopolized by the state mid-level bureaucratic forces. The party leadership was increasingly at the mercy of state bureaucracies for daily information about the economy. Decisions were made in a web of bargaining processes involving party and state bureaucratic forces representing conflicting bureaucratic and sectoral interests as well as the managerial oligarchies. A Hungarian economist called this system a "party-state interlocking directorate."[52] In this web of bureaucratic and sectoral interests, neither decision-making powers nor responsibilities were clearly defined.[53]

By the late 1980s, the party sank deeper and deeper into crisis, and most of the power and resources to govern the country were transferred to the government and its bureaucracies. The mid-level bureaucracies and the consultative and advi-

---

51. For this see Ferenc Gazsó, "A Káderbürokrácia néhány szociológiai jellemzöje" (Certain sociological characteristics of the cadre bureaucracy) (manuscript, 1990); István Harcsa et al., *Vezetök a nyolcvanas években* (Leaders in the 1980s) (Budapest: KSH, 1991).
52. Mária Csanádi, "Party-State Interlocking Directorate: Economic and Political Decision Making in Hungary" (manuscript, 1989).
53. Valerie Bunce's description of state socialism as a system of uncertain and invisible procedures but certain outcomes might be an interesting framework of analysis. See Valerie Bunce, "The Struggle for Liberal Democracy in Eastern Europe," *World Policy Journal* 7, no. 3 (Summer 1990), pp. 395–430. It is also a major theme of democratic reforms in Adam Przeworski, *Democracy and the Market: Political and Economic Reforms in Eastern Europe and Latin America* (Cambridge: Cambridge University Press, 1991).

sory bodies of several government agencies, such as the Ministry of Finance or the banking sphere, became the headquarters of the anti-regime (not anti-communist) reformist internal opposition, or to use Juan Linz's category, semiopposition.[54] Nevertheless, the Communist Party and the regime elite retained their hold on the strategic decisions, including the power of appointment (nomenklatura), generating a war of attrition between state experts and party officials, economic interests and bureaucratic interests.[55]

The "scores of semi-autonomous, or autonomous 'policy relevant' [circles] in and out of the official party and government power structure"[56] flooded Hungary with their reform proposals.[57] Research institutes, university faculties, the Hungarian Academy of Sciences, and professional associations of lawyers and businesses bombarded the party, the government, and the public with policy papers and analyses proposing or demanding reforms. A substantial body of these reform blueprints aimed at "upgrading" the state-party (regime) relations that would have

---

54. Semiopposition encompasses those social-political groups that have some "share in the government or in the political power structure but oppose some aspects of it, advocating certain policies . . . or some long range objectives. . . . Being partly 'out' and partly 'in' power, or even in the government, makes it difficult for the semiopposition to serve as a political alternative and to be perceived as such. Often the semiopposition is more a pseudo-opposition. The regime tends to function like a permanent coalition with shifting balances of power." Juan J. Linz, "Opposition in and Under an Authoritarian Regime: The Case of Spain," in *Regimes and Oppositions*, ed. Robert Dahl (New Haven: Yale University Press, 1973), p. 192. The semiopposition is strictly related to the regime and its power structures. In the absence of institutionalized pluralism, its social bases exist within the regime's institutions, namely the Communist Party and its auxiliary organizations. Semiopposition groups can be found in the realms of regime bureaucracies (such as trade unions), education and professional organizations, and business associations. However, "the most effective arrangement [for the semiopposition] is the growth of factionalism around particular bureaucracies closely linked with particular interests and the 'colonization' of ministries and agencies by persons with similar political outlooks" (p. 199).
55. This was the latest and last manifestation of the conflict between ideologues and technocrats so characteristic of the communist regime. In the literature it is referred to as the Reds versus the Experts.
56. Rudolf L. Tőkés, "A Második átmenet politikája magyarországon: Az elit kilátásai és küzdőterei" (The politics of second transition in Hungary: Elite perspectives and policy arenas), in Kurtán et al., *Magyarország Politikai Évkönyve 1991*.
57. Kéri, *Összeomlás után*; and Lengyel, "1990."

corresponded to the state's new power position.[58] While the opposition focused on environmental issues, human rights, and civil society activities, the internal dissent hoped to reform the regime by pushing the Communist Party to gradually relinquish its remaining operative powers to the state, and by gradually emancipating the state and elevating it to a new power position vis-à-vis the Communist Party. Most of the reformist groups took either South Korea or Franco's Spain as a model for a regime in which decision-making power would rest on the state and its bureaucracies under the oversight of the political power center, i.e., the party reigns but does not rule. Proposals written by state experts particularly favored some rather neo-corporatist and state capitalist solutions.[59] Moreover, by the mid-1980s, the idea of the restoration of a genuine multiparty system cautiously but overtly circulated in political and academic circles.

The separation of powers between state and party corresponded to a widening gap between the state and the regime segments of the nomenklatura. Hungarian sociologist Ferenc Gazsó concluded that in 1989, the critical year of the transition, 71.4% of the state bureaucrats had "convertible skills,"[60] compared with only 28.5% of the party bureaucrats.[61] In other words, whereas more than two-thirds of the high- and mid-level bureaucratic forces in the state apparatus had alternative career paths to survive, more than two-thirds of the bureaucrats and political cadres belonging to the regime's institutions, most importantly to the party, had no alternative but the regime itself.

A double movement was observable in the wake of the inertia of the regime leadership, generated by the deepening succession and economic crises. First, the reform communist political leaders flocked into the state leadership as the signs of the evident collapse of the regime became numerous.[62] State power was perceived as more valuable than the regime's institutions. Second, the disillusioned and exhausted political and social groups that had supported the liberalized communist

---

58. Hankiss, *East European Alternatives*.
59. Ibid.
60. By "convertible skills" one understands a degree in law or economics, proficiency in at least one major Western language, Western economic, political, or professional connections, long bureaucratic experience, and good personal connections to the economic and political elites, communications and computer skills.
61. Gazsó, "A káderbürokrácia," pp. 20–22.
62. See note 27.

regime started to desert both the regime and the state. The all-powerful industrial and agricultural managerial oligarchies, the state experts, the middle class, and the intelligentsia with more than one source of income all turned their back on both the communist state and the communist regime.[63] Using Albert Hirschman's categories, one may suggest that the reformist political elite chose the voice, the rest of the power bases of the regime opted for the exit option.[64] The regime virtually decomposed and the political system became an empty shell of institutions and organizations.

The period between 1987 and 1990 gave rise to the "parachutist phenomenon."[65] The term refers to those political appointees of the communist nomenklatura who, making use of their privileged positions in the party and state bureaucracies, "ejected" themselves from the "cockpit" of the power structure and landed somewhere in the (nonpolitical) public sector or the economic-managerial sector. In 1988 and 1989, amid growing political, economic, and social uncertainty, numerous apparatchiks of the party or its transmission belts were relocated as school principals, factory directors, and local "nobilities." During this period, a relatively large number of strikes took place across the nation, from schools to printing shops, to protest the unwanted appointment of former mid-level party bureaucrats and to protect the positions of the individuals who were to be replaced.

This operation accompanied both the self-transformation of top political appointees and leading bureaucrats into private entrepreneurs and the massive privatization of the Communist Party's assets.[66] The three simultaneous processes added up to a strategy of saving the economic foundations of the nomenklatura's power. In this way, not only did the nomenklatura find the individual strategy of survival, but it might lay down the foundations of its future economic, and therefore political, power.

---

63. Lengyel, "1990."
64. Albert Hirschman, *Exit, Voice, Loyalty* (Cambridge: Harvard University Press, 1970).
65. To the best of my knowledge, it is not known who invented this term. Nevertheless, it has become a familiar political slang expression in Hungary.
66. For an excellent summary of the privatization of party assets, see Endre Babus, "A hatalmi-politikai infrastruktura és rendszerváltás" (The infrastructure of political power and the regime change), in Kurtán et al., *Magyarország politikai évkönyve 1991*, pp. 156–86.

■ The Goals and Needs of the New Government

The coalition parties and the new government that came into office after the democratic elections in March-April 1990 faced two related tasks: (1) to finish the political transformation and establish itself; and (2) to proceed with the economic transformation at a pace and sequence acceptable to society and opposition alike.[67] At this stage, the position of the mid-level bureaucratic forces was basically determined by the needs and goals of the new government and the adaptation strategies available.

The new regime and the first democratic government inherited both the bureaucratic forces of the communist nomenklatura and the special interests of the former "party-state interlocking directorate." The inherited state was interventionist in nature, but politically weak. It had been and remained hostage to conflicting bureaucratic-sectoral interests and managerial oligarchies.[68]

In addition, the new government assumed power under adverse economic conditions and amidst growing social, economic, and political uncertainties that generated high expectations and anxiety in the public. As Tőkés has noted, the new regime and the new government had come into existence under systemic and situational constraints. By systemic constraints he understood the structural flaws inherited from the Kádár era; situational constraints involve the immediate socioeconomic and political conditions that inhibit the new regime's and government's freedom of action.[69]

A systemic constraint pertains to an inherent conflict of democratic transitions: "to bring about democracy, anti-authori-

---

67. Although several political forces favored a quick return to a market economy, no one really advocated the Polish "shock therapy" for Hungary.
68. This built-in conflict has been one of the main reasons for the government's inability to come forward with a consistent economic reform package. The first Minister of Finance, Ferenc Rabár, resigned only after six months in office. Soon the prime minister's chief economic adviser, György Matolcsy, left the cabinet. Today, the Ministry of Finance, headed by Mihály Kupa, and the Ministry of International Economic Cooperation, led by Béla Kádár (no relation to the communist leader János Kádár), represent two conflicting alternatives as to how to proceed with the implementation of a full market economy. Kádár's ministry is said to be the headquarters for the former CMEA lobbies.
69. Tőkés, "Hungary's New Political Elites," pp. 259–60.

tarian forces must unite against authoritarianism, but to be victorious under democracy, they must compete with each other."[70] Whereas to replace the authoritarian regime requires a framework of democratic institutions and procedures, to embark on a policy of economic and political transformation demands consensus on the core ideas of the substance of democratization. Discussing the substance versus procedure conflict in democratic transformations, Przeworski concluded that

> If the choice of institutions were just a matter of efficiency, it would evoke no controversy; no one would have reason to fear a system that makes someone better off at no cost to anyone else. But given the distribution of economic, political and ideological resources, institutions do affect the degree and manner in which particular interests and values can be advanced. Hence, preferences concerning institutions differ.[71]

During the 1989 national roundtable talks, the opposition favored the concepts of a powerful Parliament, a weak cabinet, and a weaker president. The negotiated political system was meant to enhance the positions of the opposition vis-à-vis the Communist Party, even a reformed one. Whereas the opposition had just started to build its political infrastructure and power base from nothing, the Communist Party had for more than 40 years been in total control of the state, its bureaucracy, and assets—virtually the whole economy. Under these circumstances, it was entirely unclear who would be in charge of the government after the free elections, despite the likelihood of a strong opposition showing in the future postcommunist Parliament.[72] For this reason, during the negotiations the opposition sought to weaken the government and to expand the powers of the Parliament. In addition, according to the polls, it seemed highly realistic at the time that Imre Pozsgay, the leading reform communist, would take control of the newly established presidency.

The reform communists suffered a crushing electoral defeat, and the three conservative Christian parties secured a

---

70. Przeworski, *Democracy and the Market*, p. 67.
71. Ibid., pp. 80–81.
72. The results of the summer 1989 by-elections, the November 1989 referendum on the party's assets and on the presidential elections, as well as public opinion polls indicated that the opposition might have the overall majority in Parliament.

stable majority in the Parliament. The incoming coalition's preference, then, shifted toward the concept of a weak Parliament and a powerful prime minister. The political philosophy and the personality of Prime Minister József Antall, as well as the high concentration of his personal power within the coalition, favored a highly centralized governmental structure around an all-powerful prime minister. Accordingly, in the evolving power structure, the Parliament and the president would have secondary functions vis-à-vis the cabinet.

All this led to a significant increase in agencies and bureaucrats directly or indirectly attached to the cabinet or to the prime minister's office. According to an estimate, the increase almost doubled the number of bureaucrats around the cabinet and prime minister, compared with the 400–500 under the Németh government.[73] "The standing committees of the government, the various agencies of the cabinet and the prime minister's office almost doubled the network of ministries, thus giving rise to a duplicated system of decision-making."[74] This structure, to a certain extent, reproduced the pathologies of the previous regime: decisions were being made at higher levels than necessary, the importance of personal relations and informal bargaining increased, and political and personal loyalty to the prime minister occasionally overshadowed professionalism.

In practical political terms, the more power the government (cabinet) has to determine the "substance" of regime transformation, and the less power the Parliament has to influence the pace and direction of changes, the less competitive the emerging democratic system is. Choice and competition appeared to be the main principles on which the institutional and procedural framework of democratic political transformation was meant to be built. The coalition's political will to neutralize the opposition and the bureaucrats of the former regime paved the way for governmental centralization. This process resulted in a decrease in the decision-making competency and effectiveness of the Parliament. The reduced parliamentary competence, in turn, decreased the political efficiency and efficacy of the postcommunist, liberal democratic and socialist, opposition.

Right from the outset, there was an obvious disagreement between the three coalition parties and the opposition as to how

---

73. Petschnig, "Gazdasági átalakulás," p. 6.
74. Bihari, "Regime and power change," p. 37.

to interpret the results of the first democratic elections. As far as the opposition was concerned, the elections authorized the coalition to govern the country for four years as representatives of one segment of the electorate. In this interpretation, the mandate required the government to continue the policy of negotiations and consensus seeking to build a new Hungary acceptable to all. In the winners' explanation, however, the elections rewarded them with a historic mandate to promote their own political and ideological agenda as if they had been elected by the whole nation and not for only four years.

Another aspect of this "mandatism" is what Przeworski calls "an impetus to pursue political unanimity."[75] As the conflict among the anti-authoritarian political forces over the substance of democracy becomes bitter and more passionate, the various political forces may claim the monopoly of representing *the* national interest. "Political forces do not see themselves as parties representing particular interests and particular views against representatives of other interests and projects. Since the nation is one body with one will, each of the political forces aspires to become the one and only representative of the nation, to cloak itself in the mantle of *el movimiento nacional*."[76]

Indeed, on numerous occasions, the prominent leaders of the governing coalition expressed the idea that belonging to their parties and supporting their government constitute one's genuine commitment to the nation, its traditions and values, and, of course, a better future. On one occasion in September 1990, Foreign Minister Géza Jeszenszky, addressing the Parliament, declared dissent in general, but social democracy and liberal politics in particular, un-Hungarian, and defined the notion of "Hungarian" in only Christian terms; the opposition walked out of the Assembly Hall in protest.

The ruling parties took control of the government without their own bureaucratic experts. Bureaucratic expertise became a precious commodity that was at the disposal of the former communist nomenklatura. The bargaining position of the holdover high-level and mid-level bureaucratic forces was enhanced by the urgent need to face the overwhelming challenges of regime transformation and the economic, social, and moral crisis of the nation. The government came under heavy pressure to

---

75. Przeworski, *Democracy and the Market*, p. 92.
76. Ibid., pp. 92–93.

deliver on its campaign promises and accomplish the transition rapidly and stabilize the country. These political and economic pressures on the new government helped the position of the mid-level bureaucracies become even stronger.

A leader of the smallest coalition party, the Christian Democrats, expressed the dilemma of experts this way:

> During regime change it is natural that the new leadership brings in its own personnel who have specific skills. However, these newcomers have been educated under the former regime; the overthrown regime's ideas reverberate in their expertise and philosophical outlook. Moreover, the "old" experts remained in place in the mid-level bureaucracies. Can this change, then, be described as regime change? Those, who from university chairs and leading research positions advocated the social and economic superiority of socialism are the real experts of nothing other than their own survival and career. Upon whom should we rely, then? Upon those who were pushed to the fringes [of professional life]. Every profession has its own martyrs, those who did not join the apogees [of socialism]. These were pushed to the periphery and were sentenced to silence. They are the honest and genuine supporters of regime change. We have to build on them, even if they have less public and informal connections due to their peripheral positions. In addition, there are people not indoctrinated [by socialism] living in the West, who can be considered experts. It is a false assumption that a new government with new experts who lack adequate skills and expertise cannot be productive. The inertia, chaos, deliberate misinformation and delay, intentionally misguided decisions, and the deliberate mishandling of expertise—all induced by the old experts—lead to real and much greater inefficiency and counter productivity.[77]

There were several factors that contributed to the government's effort in its formative months during the summer of 1990 to replace the lower- and mid-level decision makers of the old regime. Every incoming government has the legitimate right to practice political patronage. However, in transitional systems, where the institutionalization of politics is low and the rules of the game are fluid and vigorously contested, the line between legitimate political patronage and political clientelism is often

---

77. Miklós Hasznos, "Hit, remény és bizalom" (Faith, hope, and trust), *Pesti Hírlap*, March 9, 1991. Cf. Kéri, *Összeomlás után*, pp. 49–50.

fuzzy. The fact that at the highest level of the government many appointees had family connections or long-term friendships with Prime Minister Antall spawned the general perception that (1) promotion was based on personal connections rather than meritocracy; (2) regime change in fact was rather elite change; and (3) promotions were meant to strengthen Antall's position.[78] The campaign promise of "spring house cleaning," the perceived threat of the parachutists, and the desire to accomplish a rapid regime change also motivated the government's anti-mid-level leadership campaign of June-August 1990. The hastily launched and inconsistent campaign aimed to replace enterprise managers and company councils only elected in June 1990,[79] school principals and hospital directors, university chairs, and managers in the media. The Hungarian political scientist Mihály Bihari observed that "between spring 1989 and fall 1990, 80%-90% of the Hungarian political elite were replaced. The changes involved at least 10,000 persons, i.e., around 10,000 new individual actors got into the Hungarian political leadership in the first half of 1990."[80]

The interplay of governmental philosophies, political demands, economic needs, and social realities led to a paradox: although state penetration of society has been declining, bureaucratic governmental control has been on the rise. In the previous regime, the main conflict lay between state and society, that is, state control and social autonomy. In the transitional regime, these conflict lines can be found between political forces competing for the constitutional control of the government. "In this regime," argues Péter Szalay, "the struggle between the Parliament and the cabinet [government] is clearly the decisive factor."[81] The state is supposed to be independent and neutral, and no party may take it as its own political estate. The current government and the ruling coalition have overextended themselves in order to centralize decision-making powers on the direction and pace of socioeconomic transformation. This in

---

78. For this, see Attila Ágh, "A felemás fordulat éve" (The year of incomplete changes), in Kurtán et al., *Magyarország politikai évkönyve 1991*, pp. 16–19.
79. The enterprise or company council was a special form of employee participation in workplace management.
80. Bihari, "Regime and power change," p. 37.
81. Péter Szalay, "Rendszerváltozás és alkotmánymódositás—1990" (Regime change and amending the constitution: 1990) in Kurtán et al., *Magyarország politikai évkönyve 1991*.

turn has reestablished the central role of the mid-level bureaucratic forces. This contradiction has developed to its full capacity regarding the media and the privatization of state assets.

The media was one of the first realms where the communist nomenklatura converted party and state assets into private enterprises. Along with Maxwell, Murdoch, Bertelsman, and Axel Springer, the most powerful media czars are former communist and state leaders.[82] For a good many political, ideological, and economic reasons, the governing coalition perceived the privatization of the media as an attempt to create an antigovernment media. Instead, they offered to divide up the media into party spheres of influence, including the national television and radio. The conflicting interpretations of privatization, public service, political neutrality, freedom of the press, and public financing led to a war of attrition between the government and the media. In this conflict, the opposition straightforwardly supported the press. The government's response was to introduce strict bureaucratic control over the financing and printing of the nonprivatized press. In the latest round in October 1991, the Constitutional Court grappled with the question of whether the figurehead president has the constitutional authority to block cabinet appointees from accepting appointments in the single national TV and radio, financed through the state budget approved by the Parliament, even if their appointment is obviously politically motivated.

The negative impact of the inherited bureaucratic control and powerful interest groups (managerial oligarchies) is most strongly manifested in the economy. The government is torn apart by the same old bureaucratic and sectoral interests represented by the same old mid-level bureaucratic forces that undermined the communist state's capacity to handle the economy.[83] The Soviet Union has collapsed, and the Council for Mutual Economic Assistance is out of business, but the former CMEA lobby continues to pursue its own special interests to keep its inefficient factories afloat.[84]

---

82. Imre Nagy, the last First Secretary of the Communist Youth League, has become a media mogul and sits on the board of about three dozen companies. (No relation to the executed martyr prime minister of the 1956 revolution.)

83. See note 68.

84. Crane, "Institutional Legacies," p. 318.

Privatization was meant to free the economy from the dominance of political rationale, party considerations, and bureaucratic control. Originally, the management of state properties and the privatization of state assets were considered two different tasks, with two different government agencies under parliamentary control. Corresponding to the main objectives of regime transformation in Hungary, this system was designed to prevent any one political combination from monopolizing strategic decisions on economic management and privatization.

It was clear even before the transition process accelerated in 1989 that the privatization of state assets would be one of the keys to the success of regime transformation. Opposition and government alike realized that their political future would hinge on the success of economic restructuring, because this would be the critical factor in constituency building at the social as well as the political level.

The new political forces had to build their following and infrastructure from nothing. The pact-based and elite-controlled transfer of political power in 1989–1990 might have averted revolutionary mobilization and protracted transitional crisis; by the same token, however, the process left the participating elites and their political parties without well-defined and predictable popular support. With the probable exceptions of the rural-oriented Smallholders' Party and the Federation of Young Democrats, which owes its origin to an independent youth movement, other parties are amorphous entities displaying no clear class, age, gender, or residency (urban-rural) cleavages.

The redistribution of economic and financial resources and the privatization of the state-run economy offer the single most important means to (1) create a new class of owners; (2) promote certain social groups over others; (3) reward or punish political and ideological allegiance; and (4) build long-term political loyalty. The living legacy of an interventionist state, bureaucratic control over resources, and the inherited bureaucracies gave the new governing parties the edge. Not only were the mid-level bureaucratic forces the primary instruments of constituency building, but they also offered themselves as natural targets of constituency building.

Both the governing coalition and the opposition immediately recognized the enormous advantage of combining the political power of the Parliament (through a comfortable majority), the bureaucratic power of the government (through its expanded powers), and the management and property rights of the state (through the recentralization of resource allocation and privatization). The bitter, and at times abrasive, conflicts between the two sides reflect the opposition's desperate attempts to keep the Parliament in charge of the state institutions and assets, on the one hand, and the government's effort, on the other, to centralize all these resources.

The State Property Agency (SPA), initiated under Németh, was meant to be the chief state agency in charge of the privatization process under Parliament's supervision. The Antall cabinet gradually expanded the SPA's powers to not only control the buyouts of state assets but also to exert some managerial rights concerning all capital movements. Then it pushed the Parliament to pass legislation that put the SPA under direct government (that is, cabinet) control. Contrary to the original intent to keep it under Parliament's supervision, the SPA exercises bureaucratic control and management in the state economy: the SPA itself has become a mid-level bureaucracy.[85]

■ *Available Options*

During the first phase of the transition process and throughout the campaign for the first parliamentary elections, the Communist Party and the bureaucrats appeared to be the common enemies for the opposition to run against. Every party promised a virtually full replacement of the old administrative elites. Given the campaign rhetoric of the coalition parties, and indeed all noncommunist parties, it seemed that the mid-level bureaucratic forces would have to take all the blame for the previous forty-plus years. Bureaucracy became a curse, equivalent to corruption, unearned privileges, and waste. It embodied all the indecencies and humiliations that the regime or its agents had inflicted on their subjects.

Under the conditions of the new regime, the mid-level bureaucratic forces had two strategy options to adapt to the new realities: either to turn into a politically neutral civil service and loyally serve the political master, or to quit public service in order to pursue careers in the private sector. As I have already noted, a large portion of the top bureaucrats had skills and bureaucratic expertise marketable in the private sector. They left

---

85. Szalai, "Metamorphosis of power," p. 61.

the civil service, by and large en masse. For lack of political and career alternatives, the vast majority of lower-level state bureaucrats had no choice but to serve and hope for a better future.

In addition, wages and salaries have grown significantly higher in the private sector than in the public administration. With the same qualifications, the top mid-level bureaucrat may earn three to seven times more in the private sector than in civil service. Consequently, a bureaucratic career was devalued economically and socially, while selling one's bureaucratic skills became a desired career objective. The new banks, joint ventures, foreign companies, and law and accounting firms put great value on past position, political and bureaucratic connections, information, and expertise. In the first several months of the new government, state experts with convertible skills flocked into the private sector.[86]

■ *Conclusion*

The mid-level bureaucracies are in a peculiar situation in the context of regime transformation in Hungary. Politically, they are caught in a cross fire between the government and its opposition. No party, in or out of the government, trusts them, nor can these bureaucracies perceive their survival (career positions) as secure. Institutionally they are indispensable, but because of their political weakness they cannot take advantage of this fact. All centralization attempts in the government help enhance their institutional position. By carrying out their professional duties they lend their support, often involuntary, to the governing coalition. For a good many reasons, in part to compensate for this but also to keep open more avenues of future employment, many of the mid-level bureaucrats also work for the opposition, from leaking information to advising them.

The governing coalition has clearly demonstrated its ambivalence toward the "holdover" bureaucrats.[87] Early in its formative months, the government tried to purge the mid-level bureau-

---

86. According to unconfirmed information, of about 800 employees, 600 have left the Ministry of Finance. Interestingly, though not surprisingly, the changes were the lowest in the military, the police, and, up to the second half of 1991, in foreign affairs.

87. Describing the composition of the elite in Hungary, Tőkés, in "A második átmenet politikája magyarországon," coined the terms "old," "holdover," and "new" elites.

cracies under pressure to deliver on their campaign promises and to accomplish the political phase of regime change. It was, in part, an ideological campaign to restore justice and morality, to undo the damages done by the bureaucratic dictatorship of 1948–1989.[88] By the same token, the coalition's political campaign to reelect the workers' and managerial councils of companies, factories, and offices aimed at reallocating the critical mid-level decision-making positions—on a party loyalty basis.

The attempt failed because of two major reasons. First, the governing coalition did not calculate on the nature of regime-society relations in the last decade of communist rule in Hungary. The communist regime and society had developed a symbiotic relationship. The division between the regime and civil society was blurred, but at least by far not as sharp as the vehemently anti-communist electoral campaign might have suggested. Unlike in Poland, in Hungary up to mid-1989 there was no nationwide and organized political opposition with massive popular support. The resurrection of civil society in the 1980s was based on economic, cultural, and professional autonomies, not on alternative political bases. Consequently, the communist regime's historical obsolescence and performance failure did not necessarily have a devastating impact on the mid- and lower-level officeholders and employees. As a result, contrary to the coalition's expectations, the large majority of council members and other elected officeholders were reelected in the workplaces.

Second, the political and economic conflicts in and around the government and the pressing needs to stabilize the coalition's newly gained political power required a stable mid-level bureaucracy. Furthermore, the governing coalition did not have enough politically loyal bureaucratic experts to replace the "holdover" bureaucracy. The relationship between the new government and the mostly inherited mid-level bureaucratic forces is not an alliance. Rather, it is an uneasy coexistence or probably a marriage of convenience. Neither side is happy, but each needs the other to survive.

---

88. The Hungarian Democratic Forum put forward a highly controversial proposal, the "Justitia Plan," to list and compensate for the legal and moral damages inflicted on society by the communist regime.

5

Democracy in Hungary: The First Hundred Days and a Mid-Term Assessment

RUDOLF L. TŐKÉS

■ *Introduction*

In his May 1990 inaugural speech, Prime Minister József Antall asked the Hungarian people for patience so that the government might have a fair start with the task of transforming the country from a post-totalitarian to a liberal democratic state.[1] The Parliament modified the constitution and enacted several laws; the government abolished and created new ministries.

But as early as August 1990—the end of the "first hundred days"—even a national referendum could be held and largely ignored by the voters. The country's "transition to democracy" was on track, yet the public's mood was one of skepticism, or worse.[2] The Parliament was in disarray, and the opposition parties were already demanding the resignation of cabinet members and issuing scathing reports on the government's alleged mismanagement of the country's affairs. Drastic changes, especially the "spring housecleaning" of the old elites from their positions that the parties of the government coalition had promised, had not materialized. The frustrated electorate remained unconvinced that what had transpired in Hungary was a change

---

The conclusion of this chapter was written in January 1992; the earlier parts had originally been prepared for a conference on "Overcoming Obstacles to Democratization and Institution Building in Europe," sponsored by the Institute for East-West Security Studies and the Netherlands Institute of International Relations, The Hague, November 9–11, 1990.

1. Hungarian Parliament, Proceedings, Stenographic Minutes, 1st sess., May 22, 1990, cols. 190–214.
2. On this, see findings of national polls in *Világ*, July 12, 1990, pp. 22–23; *Figyelő*, Aug. 9, 1990, pp. 1, 5; and *Magyar Hirlap*, Aug. 17, 1990.

of the political system rather than a mere shuffle of the ruling elites.[3]

Assessing the political situation in Hungary in 1992, no less than in 1990, one must call attention to the burdens of the past that the leadership must overcome in order to build democracy. When reflecting on the Antall government's policy dilemmas, although the circumstances are quite different, one is reminded of the celebrated exchange between the Menshevik Julius Martov and the Bolshevik Lenin on the prospects of the Russian revolution. Martov was deeply pessimistic and cited Friedrich Engels' classic caveat in *The Peasant War in Germany*. As Engels saw it,

> The worst thing that can befall a leader of an extreme party is to be compelled to take over the government in an epoch when the movement is not yet ripe for the domination of the class which he represents, and for the realization of the measures which that domination implies. What he can do depends not upon his will but upon the degree of contradiction between the various classes, and upon the level of development of the material means of existence, of the conditions of production and commerce upon which class contradictions always repose. . . . What he can do contradicts all his previous actions, principles, and the immediate interests of his party, and what he ought to do cannot be done. In a word, he is compelled to represent not his party or his class, but the class for whose domination the movement is then ripe. In the interests of the movement he is compelled to advance the interests of an alien class, and to feed his own class with phrases and promises and with the asseveration that the interests of that alien class are its own interests. Whoever is put in this awkward position is irrevocably lost.[4]

The Hungarian Democratic Forum (HDF) is not an extreme party, and József Antall and his coalition government colleagues in the Smallholders' Party (SM) and Christian Democratic People's Party (CDPP) are not revolutionaries; nor is it suggested that Hungary's new leaders are "irrevocably lost." In fact, as will be shown below, they have a range of policy options available to

---

3. See László Kéri, "A magyar politikai élet szerkezete és mozgása a rendszerváltás után" (Hungarian politics: Its structure and dynamics since the change of the political system) (Unpublished, August 1990), p. 140. See also Béla Kurcz, "Jótündér" (Fairy godmother), *Magyar Nemzet*, Aug. 21, 1990.
4. Lewis S. Feuer, ed., *Marx and Engels: Basic Writings on Politics and Philosophy* (New York: Doubleday, 1959), p. 435.

overcome many of the obstacles that face the regime. The main point is that unlike Iliescu in Romania and the leadership of the pre-unification GDR, Antall and his colleagues are not presiding over the still-smoldering ruins of the old regime. They are beneficiaries of the yearlong process of nonviolent political transition that culminated in free elections in March-April 1990, bringing the HDF-SM-CDPP coalition to power.[5]

Hungary's negotiated revolution was peaceful. In fact, so peaceful that, as Antall put it, "not even a slap was heard."[6] Let us reflect on this statement. The stormy rebirth of democracy elsewhere in Eastern Europe may have had a desirable cleansing effect and served as a needed caesura between the old and the new. There were no cleansing political storms in Hungary.

Therefore, one might ask whether it was a good thing that the old regime failed to put up any resistance and almost gladly handed over the reins of the country to a freely elected government. And what about those who ran and woefully mismanaged the country in the preceding 42 years? Should they not be held accountable for their crimes against the people? Are they owed gratitude and forgiveness for not acting like Ceauşescu? And what should their place be in a new Hungary? Questions of this kind on the Hungarian transition agenda are symptomatic of the second thoughts that inevitably follow the overthrow, however peaceful, of a political dictatorship.

The flip side of the question is whether the country is politically mature enough to accept and support the policies of its freely elected legislature and government. Moreover, are not the social and economic circumstances that shape the political consciousness of the people and the elites still virtually the same as they were in the late Kádár years? Are the people not still captives to the thinking and values of the country's 42-year legacy of "existing socialism"? Therefore, are the interests that the new regime is expected to accommodate not the same as those of their discredited predecessors? Lenin and Stalin over-

5. See Rudolf L. Tőkés, *From Post-Communism to Democracy: Politics and Free Elections in Hungary, 1989–1990* (Bonn: Konrad Adenauer Stiftung-Forschungsinstitut, 1990). See also György Szoboszlai, ed., *Parlamenti választások 1990* (Parliamentary elections, 1990) (Budapest: Social Science Institute, Hungarian Academy of Sciences, 1990).
6. "Antall, Ministers Interviewed on 'Next 110 Days,' " Foreign Broadcast Information Service, *Daily Report—Eastern Europe* (FBIS-EEU-90-175, Sept. 10, 1990), p. 35.

came "Münzer's dilemmas" (whether to adapt to or forcibly overcome backwardness and societal resistance to change) in Russia, but their methods gave birth to the monster totalitarian state. Terror and dictatorship are neither available nor acceptable methods of building a liberal democracy in Hungary.

The thesis of this chapter is that the new leaders of Hungary must and will find a way to overcome the past, and, moreover, that the solution to this historic challenge will emerge from the interaction of the country's "old," "holdover," and "new" political elites and the Hungarian people. In what follows, I will concentrate mainly on the elite actors of Hungarian politics and identify the individual components of the three clusters of elites that are salient for the determination of political outcomes in the continuing transition period in Hungary.[7] Each of these elites should be seen as loosely connected clusters of several organized and unorganized interest groups, policy lobbies, and amorphous social entities, active and seeking to promote their interests in one or more of the eight "policy arenas" of postcommunist Hungary.[8]

Interest advocacy may take the form of cooperation, adaptation, or confrontation, or a mixture of the three, with the political incumbents. Though the "people" as such—either as concerned onlookers, or as the prize of inter-elite contestation—are always present, their wishes are barely discernible; reliable survey data on the public's beliefs and policy preferences in Hungary today are relatively sparse.[9]

■ Hungarian Elites in Transition: Preliminary Observations

Who are the elites in Hungary today? In a general sense, by "elites" I am inclined to follow Suzanne Keller's classification, and thus by this term understand both the

7. On the social origins of Hungary's new political elites, see Rudolf L. Tőkés, "Hungary's New Political Elites: Adaptation and Change, 1989–1990," *Problems of Communism* (November-December 1990), pp. 44–65.
8. The term "policy arena" and related conceptualizations have been adopted from Michel Oksenberg, "The Chinese Policy Process and the Public Health Issue: An Arena Approach," *Studies in Comparative Communism* 7, no. 4 (Winter 1974), pp. 375–408.
9. This is also true for the rest of Eastern Europe as well. See Timothy Garton Ash, "Eastern Europe: Après Le Déluge, Nous," *New York Review of Books*, Aug. 16, 1990, pp. 51–57.

"strategic" and "segmental" elites, as well as their division into (a) the current political elite; (b) the economic, military, and scientific elites; (c) elites exercising moral authority, such as clergy, philosophers, and educators; and (d) elites that "keep society knit together," such as leading cultural personalities.[10] All four types of elites are present in Hungary. They possess specific skills and resources that may be converted into influence over public opinion, hence into power with respect to capability to affect choices and outcomes in the realm of public policy.

It is axiomatic that elites seek to defend and promote their interests by way of constantly redefining, to their advantage, the terms of interaction with competitors in the pursuit of resources and public support. Though the process can be extremely complex, under "steady state" conditions of political stability, it is open to scrutiny by students of elite politics. This is particularly true for liberal democracies where the free press and the traditional rules of the political game help create a relatively open environment in which the participants of elite politics tend to comport themselves with due regard to accepted standards of civility and fair play.

The elite politics of political transitions, especially the type that involve changes of "revolutionary" magnitude (such as a 180-degree change of political direction from state socialism to liberal democracy), is extremely difficult to penetrate. As Guillermo O'Donnell and Philippe Schmitter put it,

> During these transitions, in many cases and around many themes, it is almost impossible to specify ex ante which classes, sectors, institutions, and other groups will take what role, opt for which issues, or support what alternative. Indeed, it may be that almost all one can say is that, during crucial moments and choices of the transition, most—if not all—of those "standard" actors are likely to be divided and hesitant about their interests and ideals and, hence, incapable of coherent collective action. Moreover, these actors are likely to undergo significant changes as they try to respond to the changing contexts presented them by liberalization and democratization.[11]

---

10. Suzanne Keller, "Elites," *International Encyclopedia of the Social Sciences*, vol. 5 (New York: Macmillan and the Free Press, 1968), pp. 26–28.
11. Guillermo O'Donnell and Philippe C. Schmitter, *Transitions from Authoritarian Rule: Tentative Conclusions about Uncertain Democracies* (Baltimore: Johns Hopkins University Press, 1986), p. 4.

Though the Hungarian transition has left a wide enough paper trail of published evidence, we know very little about the internal workings of the many scores of elite and sub-elite groups and organizations that played a role in the process. We know even less about the specifics of interpersonal relations, informal understandings, and confidential agreements among the old elite and between the old and new elites for future power sharing and redistribution of privileges.[12] However, what we do know is sufficient for the formulation of several general propositions about the elites' role in Hungary's political transformation, to wit:

- Until May 1988, all strategic decisions had been made by small elite groups in the Hungarian Socialist Workers' Party (HSWP).

- Well before the fall of János Kádár in 1988, there had been scores of semiautonomous or autonomous "policy-relevant" elites active in and out of the official party and government power structure.

- The number of elite groups involved in political decision making, either in a direct participatory or a consultative capacity, increased dramatically between June 1988 and the exit of Miklós Németh's government in May 1990.

- With the revival in the winter of 1988–1989 of many scores of "civil society"-type groups, clubs, and associations, and several political parties, the boundaries of elite politics expanded into the hitherto regime-controlled realm of mass politics.

- With the collapse of the HSWP's political authority and its surrender of the regime's nomenklatura privileges in the summer of 1989, a process of elite realignment began in anticipation of a transition toward a pluralistic postcommunist political system in Hungary.

- For different reasons, old and new Hungarian elite strategies of adaptation to a new political environment relied heavily on negotiations and other nonviolent means of conflict avoidance as instruments of choice for the objectives of salvaging the old nomenklatura elites' power, property, position, and related perquisites for the postcommunist era, and creating a political

---

12. A year after the signing of the national roundtable agreements on September 18, 1989, there were still all kinds of unanswered questions as to who said (or promised) what and to whom. On this, see Károly Vigh, "Asztalbontás után" (After the roundtable), *Magyar Nemzet*, Sept. 18, 1990; and "A Pozsgay-Orbán vita" (The Pozsgay-Orbán debate), *Magyar Hirlap*, Oct. 1, 1990.

environment conducive to peaceful transition to free elections and a multiparty democracy.

- To control for the vagaries of unpredictable electoral outcomes, several more or less well-financed elite groups chose to field candidates for the parliamentary elections of March-April 1990. Though neither the old elites' "Trojan horse" type of electoral alliances nor their individual candidates (save a few running as independents) gained parliamentary representation, most of them survived the transition to democracy with their organization, resources, and, more to the point, ambivalence or outright hostility toward popular sovereignty (i.e., the rule of non-elites) essentially intact.

In sum, Hungary is a small country where most players of elite politics have been recruited from the intelligentsia. In an East European, and certainly in a Hungarian, context the term "intelligentsia" connotes not a narrow circle of literati, or those exercising "moral authority," but educated people (most often university graduates) with a self-appointed responsibility for the nation's destiny.[13] The upper stratum of the Hungarian intelligentsia is made up of overlapping circles of articulate, clannish, and highly competitive groups positioned along a hierarchical continuum of power, status, and achievement. The Hungarian elites are not "friends of the people" in the Russian Narodnik sense; rather, they perceive themselves as guardians with a historic mission to protect the people from the powers that be. Not surprisingly, the "people's interests" invariably seem to coincide with those of the elites, and the postcommunist politics of Hungary is no exception.

■ Three Elites: Parallel or Convergent Paths?

There are three kinds of elites—"old," "holdover," and "new"—that are active, or at least present, in Hungarian politics today.[14]

By old elites, I understand (a) the extra-parliamentary political parties and electoral alliances under the leadership of still

---

13. The best overview of contemporary intelligentsia politics in Eastern Europe is by Timothy Garton Ash, *The Uses of Adversity: Essays on the Fate of Central Europe* (New York: Random House, 1990).
14. The taxonomy is mine, and the term "holdover elites" seeks to denote members of the functionally indispensable mid-level "meritocracy" of the old regime who continue to serve under the new one.

active political and social notables of the old regime; (b) corporatist interest groups such as the old/new Trade Union Federation (TUF) and the successor organizations to the Young Communist League; (c) the formal and informal political action committees of the old agricultural and heavy industry policy lobbies; (d) amorphous clusters of third-echelon elites formerly associated with the police, army, and the Workers' Guards; (e) scattered fundamentalist Marxist-Leninist intelligentsia groups; and, somewhat incongruously, (f) leaders of major religious denominations that had gotten along (some say only too well) with the old regime.

By holdover elites, I understand (a) the reappointed subcabinet- and ministerial-level executives; (b) appointed top civil servants in local and regional governments; (c) leaders and top members of corporatist entities such as the Academy of Sciences, the universities, and associations of creative intellectuals and technocrats; (d) executives, program managers, and senior editors in the print and audio-visual media; (e) military officers (field grade and above), the judiciary, and professional chambers of law, medicine, and engineering; (f) still serving appointed, or dubiously "elected," managers of industrial enterprises, state farms, and agricultural cooperatives; and (g) local, ostensibly nonpolitical, notables.

By new elites, I understand (a) the new government, the political appointees in the executive branch, and the newly elected Constitutional Court; (b) members of the Parliament; (c) newly elected mayors and top municipal councilors; (d) leaders of new lobbies, such as the independent unions, environmental groups, etc.; (e) civil society-type groups, clubs, and associations (17,000 of which were registered between 1988 and 1992); and (f) new business elites in the manufacturing, trade, and service industries, and executives of charter member firms (mainly banks) of the Budapest Stock Exchange.

What distinguishes the new elites from the other two is their active involvement, since the fall of 1988, in party politics and public affairs. Some of the new elites, especially the leaders of the "historic" SM, CDPP, and Social Democratic parties, and the HDF and the Alliance of Free Democrats (AFD) veterans of the 1956 revolution, are middle-aged or older people. On the whole, however, the average age of 45.8 years of the new members of Parliament in 1990 is a reasonably accurate indicator of the new elites' essentially "postrevolutionary" generational identity. In terms of past political record, many of them suffered persecution, ranging from prison terms to job discrimination and unemployment, under the Kádár regime. Still, no more than one-third of the parliamentary deputies had been active political dissidents prior to 1988. Moreover, since the trial and acquittal of Miklós Haraszti (an MP and a member of the AFD executive) in 1972, none of them had been imprisoned for their political beliefs or actions.

Thus, what legitimates the new elites' claim to power are the risks they took when they entered the political arena (there were no guarantees in 1988 and early 1989 against the return of a martial law-type regime), the political mandate bestowed on them by the people at free elections, and the moral, political, and economic support by Western liberal democracies that is unavailable to the old elites.[15] In any case, in addition to their electoral mandate, the new elites derive political support from the six parliamentary parties' approximately 250,000 dues-paying members. By contrast, it is well worth keeping in mind that the old elite-controlled and still unreformed Trade Union Federation has over 3.5 million members, who until recently supported the TUF through payroll-deducted union dues. (Since then, thanks to AFD-sponsored remedial legislation, Hungarian workers are free to choose whether or not to pay union dues.)

As a direct consequence of the change of the political system, the old elites are barred from any direct exercise of political power. Their constituencies are drawn from among the political and economic losers of Hungary's institutional transformation and economic restructuring from a centrally planned to a market economy. Chances are that a significant portion of the nonvoting public (about 35% of the eligible voters) and those 777,777 voters who cast their ballots at the March-April 1990 free elections for the old regime's successor parties and electoral coalitions are the old elites' potential supporters. On the other hand, an equally compelling case can be made for saying that after several years of political turmoil, political nonparticipation is a sign of exhaustion rather than opposition to the new regime.

Although they probably see themselves as suffering subjects rather than the beneficiaries of Hungary's political transformation, the holdover elites are the real winners of this process. All that is expected of them is to carry on with their work.

---

15. See Tőkés, "Hungary's New Political Elites."

Moreover, they are free to get on with their lives without any official expectation to become involved in politics. To the extent they articulate their current policy preferences, they speak for the passive and by-and-large silent majority of the Hungarian people. The holdover elites continue to serve the new regime, but not because they are democrats or are supportive of the values of the government or the opposition. Rather, they serve because they see no alternatives to the new status quo. They are the "missing middle" in Hungarian politics. Indeed, in many ways, it is the holdover elites' "negative consensus" that keeps the present, precariously balanced political system afloat and permits the new elites and the relatively few people they can mobilize to fight out their differences in Parliament, in the media, and at political rallies of the party faithful.

In sum, the three types of Hungarian elites may be likened to actors in a classical Greek morality play. The old, holdover, and some of the new elites' ideological preferences, habits of thinking, and ambivalence toward and fear of the uncertainties of liberal democracy (and of the sovereignty it confers on non-elites) are rooted in Eastern Europe's traditional political culture, as well as in the elites' shared experiences in the preceding 42 years of communist rule. Although the opportunities for their collective emancipation from the burdens of the past through the country's democratic transformation are there, the elite "actors," just as their Greek role models, seem unable to shed the divinely preordained fate that compels them to march inexorably toward their destiny. The outcome, however, need not be "tragedy." As the following discussion on the politics of the first 100 days of the Antall government and its opposition will indicate, superhuman efforts made by all concerned to "fool the gods" by staying the course, regardless of the obstacles to the building of democracy in Hungary, may have proved successful.

■ Elites: Policy Arenas and Issues

With the old regime gone since May 1990, Hungary has been in the process of "another transition" toward democracy.[16] However, democracy, as Adam Przeworski ex-

---

16. O'Donnell and Schmitter, *Transitions From Authoritarian Rule*, p. 12.

plains in his seminal essay, "institutionalizes uncertainty."[17] Therefore, from the new leadership's viewpoint, the outcome may be called the "captain's dilemma." While the destination is known, the waters are uncharted, the crew is inexperienced, and the "vessel" of the country's political institutions is overdue for refit. Still, ready or not, "navigate he must," for the passengers are restless and mutineers lurk among the crew.

The leading issues of the current transition period seem to fall within eight policy arenas. Each of these involves the active participation of two, or all three, of Hungary's political elites. The policy arenas may be labeled as follows: (a) institutional transformation, (b) the "missing left," (c) economic restructuring, (d) "moral regeneration," (e) political justice, (f) social justice, (g) self-government, and (h) "Hungary's place in the world."

Institutional Transformation

The new regime inherited a heavy backlog of unresolved issues. Prominent among these were the new constitution, the government's accountability to the Parliament, procedures for the election of the president of the republic and the powers of that office, and the scope of legislative issues that required a qualified, two-thirds majority of the Parliament for enactment into law.

Had the resolution of these matters been left to the new Parliament, legislative paralysis, political stalemate, and anarchy would have been the result. Instead, the five-part compromise package secretly negotiated by the HDF and the principal opposition AFD in late April 1990 was a bold but politically risky solution for both parties.[18] Preempting the freely elected Parliament's rule-making privileges by a political fait accompli left both sides vulnerable to charges of betrayal by their respective coalition partners and political allies. The "pact," as the agreement was dubbed by its many critics, also raised some troubling

---

17. Adam Przeworski, "Problems in the Study of Transition to Democracy," in *Transitions from Authoritarian Rule*, vol. 3, *Comparative Perspectives*, ed. Guillermo O'Donnell, Philippe C. Schmitter, and Laurence Whitehead (Baltimore: Johns Hopkins University Press, 1986), p. 58.
18. "Megállapodás" (Agreement), *Magyar Hirlap*, May 3, 1990. For an assessment of elite commentary on the "pact," see Kéri, "Hungarian politics," pp. 94–103.

questions about the nature of the party system in postcommunist Hungary.

Once the second-round (April 8, 1990) results of the parliamentary elections were at hand, many people, particularly the old and holdover elites, clamored for a "grand coalition" to guarantee stability. One suspects that what these elites had in mind was "continuity" in the sense of watering down both parties' electoral platforms and thwarting the Smallholders' radical land reprivatization scheme and the League of Young Democrats' (LYD) call for "new politics" in Hungary. Fears of divisive partisan battles between the government and a vigorous opposition were also shared by most Hungarians, long accustomed to a strong government and an occasionally noisy, but basically soporific, legislature.

By courageously opting for the "certainty of uncertainty" of a liberal democratic and de facto two-party system, the HDF and the AFD opened the Pandora's box of partisan politics in Hungary.[19] However, in doing so, they may have fatally undermined their credibility in the eyes of their respective partners on either side of the aisle in the "Esteemed House" of Parliament. While the HDF, as the senior partner in the government, had a tough but manageable problem of keeping the rambunctious Smallholders in line, the Alliance of Free Democrats lost, probably irrevocably, the trust of the small but dynamic LYD in their commitment to previously shared ideological goals.[20]

The new government has found itself in an adversarial relationship with the parliamentary opposition parties and other elites that had been stripped of political power. At issue here is the actual and perceived balance of power between the new political incumbents in possession of all the executive branch's power resources and their parliamentary and extraparliamentary critics. The matter revolves around each side's understanding of the outcome of the March-April 1990 elections. On the one hand, the government coalition, though controlling 59% of the

19. Beyond the usual parliamentary wrangling between the government and the opposition, the overheated atmosphere of partisanship also produced a dozen of what László Kéri calls "firecrackers," or "scandals of the week" over matters both trivial and profound. Kéri, "Hungarian politics," pp. 108–12.

20. Viktor Orbán, "A paktum" (The pact), *Magyar Narancs*, May 17, 1990; and József Szajer, "Térdig a paktumban" (On the pact), *Népszabadság*, July 19, 1990. Unlike the LYD leaders, 64% of the public did approve of the "pact." *Magyar Hirlap*, July 13, 1990.

seats in the legislature, derives its mandate from the affirmative votes of less than one-third of the eligible voters of Hungary; the opposition parties' electoral support is even more slender. On the other hand, the exclusion from power of six electoral finalist parties, as well as of the 30-odd additional parties that had fallen by the wayside at an earlier stage of the electoral campaign, tends to impose unspecified broad expectations on a government that claims to speak for the interests of the whole nation.[21]

In a different sense, the opposition is also a victim of electoral arithmetic. The ideological distance of the AFD and the LYD from the old elites is much greater than that which separates the parties of the government coalition from the old elites. Because the opposition also claims to speak for the nation, the result is massive disorientation concerning the interpretation and legislative implementation of the government's and opposition's respective electoral mandate. Moreover, the lack of overt resistance by the old regime and its elite allies to Hungary's political transformation has deprived the new elites of political justification for moving as fast and as far as they could have otherwise.

The new elites' cautious stance on many matters encouraged the hitherto silent old and holdover elites to question and criticize the government's right to implement its "secret pact" and dismiss the concerns of its "democratic" extraparliamentary critics.[22] Moreover, because the Alliance of Free Democrats was honor-bound to live up to the terms of the HDF-AFD agreement, the party was put in the untenable position of having to defend the government from these extramural critics, yet trying to remain the politically untainted leader of the government's "constructive opposition." (The AFD chairman, philosopher János Kis, must have found it ironic to have to grapple with his party's share of "Münzer's dilemma."[23])

---

21. On the then-new government's dilemmas, see the interview with József Antall in *Magyar Nemzet*, June 6, 1990.
22. See Károly Alexa, "Az MDF és a hatalom" (The HDF and political power), *Népszabadság*, June 18, 1990; Tamás Fricz, "Demokrácia—demokraták nélkül" (Democracy without democrats), *Figyelő*, June 21, 1990; and Attila Ágh, "Az MDF könnyű álmot ígér" (The HDF promises pleasant dreams), *Magyar Nemzet*, Aug. 18, 1990.
23. János Kis, "Majdnem száz nap után" (Almost one hundred days later), *Beszélő*, Aug. 11, 1990, pp. 4–6; and István Eörsi, "A pártfétis szívóssága" (The persistence of party fetishes), *Népszabadság*, June 15, 1990.

The arduous task of enacting into law even a small portion of the Hungarian government's legislative agenda would have taxed the energy and talents of seasoned lawmakers of a mature and well-established liberal democracy. The members of the Bundestag, the House of Commons, and the US Congress benefit from expert staff assistance, well-oiled public relations, routinized interaction with policy lobbies and interest groups, and reliable links with their parties and constituencies. None of this has been available to the 386 members of the Hungarian Parliament thus far. In view of these constraints, it is a wonder how much this group of enthusiastic political novices has accomplished at all.[24]

Still, Parliament's admirable achievements have incurred serious political costs to the incumbents. The most important of these is the growing distance between the six parties' parliamentary caucuses and the political movements whence they came.[25] Preoccupation with legislative and governing responsibilities left the field of interpreting and evaluating the new elites' record open to critics in the media and to word-of-mouth slander of their diehard enemies at the extreme left and right of the political spectrum.[26] Because of this, public support of the parliamentary parties (except the League of Young Democrats) declined and, as will be shown below, the nonparty "independents'" stock rose, as it did at the September-October 1990 municipal elections. The reincarnation over time of the old elites as "independents" is a trend well worth watching, as it may augur the partial dissolution and restructuring of the present Hungarian party system and, as a sort of Gresham's Law of postcommunist politics, its replacement by a reborn coalition of the old and holdover elites.

---

24. For two contrasting evaluations of the results of the first 100 days, see the Prime Minister's Office, "Az első száz nap" (The first hundred days), *Magyar Hirlap*, Sept. 1, 1990; and Fidesz (League of Young Democrats), *Az első száz nap* (The first hundred days), September 1990.
25. Mihály Bihari, "A pártosodás és az oligarchia vastörvénye" (Partification and the iron law of oligarchy), *Világ*, June 28, 1990. However, given the choice between the old and the new Parliament, two-thirds of the respondents preferred the latter. *Magyar Hirlap*, Aug. 3, 1990.
26. Views of this kind received extensive airing in *Szabadság*, the weekly of the Workers' Party (HSWP), and in *Szent Korona*, the weekly of the Christian National Union. See also the paid political advertisement by the HSWP in *Vasárnapi Hirek*, July 29, 1990.

The "Missing Left"

In 1989–1990, 45 political parties and groups received financial support for electoral campaign expenses from the Hungarian government.[27] Of these, six parties and seven independent or semi-independent MPs won seats in the Parliament. The remaining parties and groups may be divided into "left," "right," and single-issue clusters. Unlike the last two, which may not last once their one-time subsidies run out, the left, or actually its absence from the legislature, represents a political dilemma of considerable magnitude.

By parties and groups of the left, I mean largely six parties and electoral coalitions—the Hungarian Socialist Workers' Party (now renamed the Workers' Party [HSWP]), the Hungarian Social Democratic Party, the Agrarian Alliance (actually, the AA has one parliamentary MP), the Entrepreneurs' Party, the Patriotic Electoral Coalition, and the Hungarian People's Party, each of which failed to receive 4% of votes cast for the party ballot, yet together they received a total of 777,777 votes in the first round of balloting. Additionally, there are other "also-ran" parties, such as the Independent Social Democratic Party and the Hungarian Gypsies' Social Democratic Party, and groups such as the orthodox communist Ferenc Münnich Society.[28]

The parties of the "missing left" claim to represent the interests of "working peasants, industrial workers and those living on fixed incomes"—or about two-thirds of the Hungarian electorate. However, even if one were to accept this claim to apply only to those at the bottom of the social hierarchy, such as the hereditary poor, unskilled workers, pensioners, and Hungary's 500,000 Gypsies, we are still left with a formidable potential political constituency bereft of direct representation in the Parliament.

Of the parties of the left, it is the absence of social democrats that is the most keenly felt in Hungary's political life. Unlike the

---

27. *Figyelő*, May 31, 1990; and "Fantompártok, fantompénzek" (Phantom parties, phantom monies), *Világ*, July 26, 1990.
28. Ervin Csizmadia, "Pártok—parlamenten kivül" (Parties outside the Parliament), *Magyar Hirlap*, June 22, 1990; Rita Csik, "A párt elhagyta elnökét" (The party abandoned its chairperson), *Világ*, May 24, 1990; "TESZ lett a HNF-ből" (From the Patriotic People's Front to the League of Social Associations), *Magyar Nemzet*, June 25, 1990; Tamás Fricz, "És mi van a parlamenten kivül?" (And what is there outside the Parliament?), *Figyelő*, July 26, 1990, p. 5.

parliamentary Hungarian Socialist Party, which is the party of the holdover elites and of the socialist "middle class," the interests of organized labor, particularly those of the blue-collar unions, are still articulated by the leftover Stalinist apparatchiks of the old/new Trade Union Federation.[29] The "workers," both as a symbolic political entity and as voters to be wooed, have become objects of HDF-AFD parliamentary power plays and of government manipulation for strike prevention and political profit.

Given Hungary's occupational stratification and the public's extreme sensitivity to the loss of jobs by hundreds of thousands of semiskilled and unskilled workers, the present, at best indirect, representation of the interests of these normally politically passive segments of society carries with it the danger of drastic action by these designated victims of privatization and drastic economic reforms.[30] The available administrative firefighting devices, such as ad hoc "interest reconciliation" boards and one-on-one negotiations between the affected ministries and strike-bound mines, enterprises, and public utilities, only help to institutionalize anarchy.[31] Chronic labor strife is the last thing that the insecure new political elites can afford during Hungary's transition to democracy. The "missing left" is also a challenge to the parliamentary parties that are seeking to expand their constituencies among the have-nots and the politically inactive segments of the electorate. Whether the present Hungarian party structure is elastic enough to accommodate such potential protest voters, or a third social democratic political cluster will emerge to fill the void between the Christian national and the radical liberal ideological-political poles, is too early to tell. In the meantime, the field is wide open to the old and holdover elites for mischief and quick political profit.

---

29. To prevent this, the HSP proposes to speak for these constituencies in the Parliament. See "A parlamentben az egész baloldalt kell képviselnünk" (In the Parliament we must represent the entire left), *Uj Forum*, May 18, 1990. See also Zoltán Bárány, "The Fate of the Left," *RFE/RL Report on Eastern Europe*, Sept. 7, 1990, pp. 15–18.
30. See Attila Ágh, "A demokratura helyzete" (Democracy today), *Esti Hirlap*, Aug. 18, 1990; and László Thoma, "Prognózis az őszi robbanásra" (Forecast for fall explosions), *Népszabadság*, Aug. 11, 1990.
31. "Az Érdekegyeztető Tanács második ülése" (The second session of the Council for Interest Reconciliation), *Beszélő*, Sept. 8, 1990, pp. 17–18.

Economic Transformation

In one way or another, the budgetary process, taxation, and the privatization of the land and of other resources of the national economy affect citizens and elites alike.[32] The political essence of the matter is that neither the government nor the opposition (except the Smallholders with their land privatization platform) has a specific enough economic reform program for which it could be held accountable by the electorate. Brave but ambiguous statements such as "after an (unspecified) period of painful adjustments all will be well" have served as a political placebo to quiet demands for higher wages, lower inflation, and little or no unemployment.[33]

Of the wide range of issues in the economic policy arena, let us consider three representative items: the privatization of industrial enterprises, the privatization of the print media, and the prospects for small business people in Hungary today.

The politics of industrial privatization involves all three elites. The government wants to shed loss-making or marginally profitable enterprises by selling them to the presumably more efficient private sector. The term "presumably" is used not to question the inherent superiority of private enterprise over state management, but rather to suggest that upon the transfer of an enterprise to private hands, efficiencies are realized initially by the cutting of overhead, i.e., by firing much of the labor force. In any case, the passing of political responsibility for the much-needed trimming of the labor force to the private sector is a major motive behind such policies.[34]

The government has a political stake in the identity of the buyer of a presently state-owned enterprise. Although "leveraged buyouts" and the "fire sale"-type giveaways of assets by

---

32. For an overview of Hungary's economic dilemmas, see János Kornai, "Socialist Transformation and Privatization: Shifting from the Socialist System," *East European Politics and Societies* 4, no. 2 (Spring 1990), pp. 255–304. For the official position, see Mátyás Matolcsy, "Az uj gazdaságpolitika karaktere" (The characteristics of the new economic policies), *Magyar Nemzet*, Aug. 25, 1990.

33. "SZDSZ and Fidesz vélemény" (AFD and LYD views on the government's economic program), *Figyelő*, May 31, 1990, p. 5. For a nonpartisan view, see "Mit tegyen és mit ne tegyen a kormány? A Hid csoport ajánlatai" (What the government should and should not do: Recommendations of the Hid group), *Figyelő*, May 17, 1990, p. 9.

34. Katalin Botos, the State Secretary, Ministry of Finance, denies this in *Figyelő*, June 7, 1990.

the incumbent (holdover elite) managers are discouraged, joint ventures with Western investors are welcomed. That foreign investors tend to retain the current management is axiomatic, and so is the grassroots resentment of this process.[35] Since there are few foreign buyers for Hungary's rust-belt enterprises, the state is often stuck with them; yet, to salvage what it can, the government insists on holding new elections for top managers. The country's industries were estimated in 1990 as worth $32 billion, and thus the stakes in the future management of Hungarian enterprises are very high.[36]

Because the workers are fearful of drastic managerial changes, they often reelect the incumbent management in hopes that the state will sooner or later bail out the ailing enterprise.[37] The privatization process involves (in addition to the government) the old or "renewed" trade unions, local governments, the region's parliamentary MP, the scandal-hungry media, and local civic groups. The new elites' holdover proxies from the ministries, the banks, and the state's Agency for State Assets, and Western management consultants (including, more than likely, the home governments and local embassies of the latter) are also parts of the process. In sum, the atmosphere surrounding the process of industrial privatization resembles a three-ring circus.

The privatization of the print media has been the most publicized and politically volatile economic policy issue of Hungarian elite politics. The matter is complex, as it involves the disposition and editorial control of the top five national daily

---

35. Tamás Benedek, "Kit veszélyeztetnek a vegyes vállalatok?" (Who are threatened by the joint venture enterprises?), *Figyelő*, June 14, 1990, p. 9; and János Budai, "Rendszerváltás vagy elitváltás?" (Change of the system, or only of the elites?"), *Magyar Nemzet*, July 30, 1990; and János Budai, "Mi az uj elit érdeke?" (What are the new elite's interests?), *Magyar Nemzet*, Aug. 18, 1990.
36. "Borsodi Mozaik" (The Borsod mosaic), *Figyelő*, June 21, 1990 (the title refers to a conference on enterprise options). See also *The New York Times*, May 22, 1990.
37. Of the 86 state farms under enterprise council management, 61 voted to reappoint the incumbent general managers. *Heti Világgazdaság*, Sept. 29, 1990, p. 9. The results of elections at the 31 enterprises (of the top 100) under enterprise management proved that the highly qualified incumbent managers stood the best chance of reelection. For background information, see "A-listázás" (On job retentions), *Heti Világgazdaság*, Aug. 18, 1990; and Attila Hámos, "Őszi nagytakaritás?" (Fall house cleaning?), *Heti Világgazdaság*, Sept. 15, 1990, pp. 4–5.

newspapers, 20 regional ones, and several weeklies. Each of these publications has the capacity to shape public opinion for or against the new regime and its policies. Most of them had been owned or controlled by the HSWP or one of its front organizations. In the feeding frenzy for bargain-priced media assets between the fall of 1989 and the summer of 1990, several Western media conglomerates (e.g., Bertelsman, Maxwell, Murdoch, and the like) descended on Hungary and bought either controlling or substantial minority interest in all but one national and several regional newspapers.

In some instances, the change of ownership enriched the old Communist Party's "legal successor," the HSP, and, more importantly, left the incumbent editorial staff in place. Thus, quite unwittingly, media privatization with the participation of Western capital helped reinforce the position of hundreds of "holdover" journalists at newspapers controlling about 75% of the market. By contrast, it is worth noting that the combined circulation of the weekly journals sponsored by the HDF, AFD, SM, and LYD is less than one-third that of the now independent socialist *Népszabadság*—the successor of the old HSWP's daily by the same name.[38] The new elites' tenuous toehold in the print media is further attenuated by the unremitting hostility (or at best skepticism) of many key newspaper columnists toward the new regime, its inexperienced legislators, and their contradictory policies.[39]

The Antall government is no fonder of the critical media than are its Western, or indeed Russian, counterparts. In any case, "media battles" took up a disproportionate amount of time and public attention during the 100 days (and after).[40] The stakes remain high, for neither the parliamentary opposition, particularly the Alliance of Free Democrats, nor the old elites have reconciled themselves to the Christian national parties' electoral victory. Well into 1991, they were still in the "campaign mode" of seeking to discredit and, if possible, cause the downfall of the government. Opposition elites still see the media more

38. "Pártlapok—csak belső használatra" (Party press—for internal circulation only), *Világ*, July 12, 1990, p. 28.
39. Zoltán Farkas, "Hadijelentés. Harcok a sajtó körül—adatok egy vitához" (Report from the front lines: Press wars—background to a dispute), *Mozgó Világ* (July 1990), pp. 12–31.
40. Ervin Csizmadia, "A koalíció és a sajtó" (The coalition parties and the press), *Magyar Hírlap*, Oct. 1, 1990.

as a political weapon to undo the results of the last elections than as a vehicle to promote reasonable discourse among the people, the elites, and the regime.[41]

Unlike the seemingly intractable issues of industrial and media privatization and the ambiguous role played by the old and holdover elites in this process, Hungary's small business elites have no political competitors. Indeed, potentially there is a perfect political fit between the market-oriented government and the new entrepreneurial elites. To be sure, Hungary's 125,000 small business people and the growing number of newly prosperous professional people have yet to make an impact on national politics.[42] But the exponential growth of financial resources controlled by the new rich clearly destines the business community for a politically influential role in the 1990s.

A handful of wealthy private entrepreneurs who were said to have contributed significant sums of money to the AFD's campaign chest may be the harbingers of a new trend in Hungarian politics. In 1989, the number of taxpayers with a gross income of Ft 500,000 ($8,000) or more increased fourfold from the previous year, and the annual income of the top 10,000 taxpayers grew from Ft 800,000 to Ft 1.5 million in the same period.[43] It is more than likely that the top taxpayers included many former Communist Party apparatchiks, high ministry officials, leading enterprise managers (the "red barons"), and their rural brethren (the "green barons").[44] Their future political loyalties are likely to go to the highest bidder—almost certainly in the monetary rather than ideological sense.

The least visible yet most powerful of Hungary's political kingmakers are the senior executives of the top dozen commercial banks. Benefiting from an annual profit margin of 40% and more, these financial institutions dispose of significant discretion-

---

41. Gáspár Miklós Tamás, "Demokratikus illemszabályok" (Democratic etiquette), *Magyar Hirlap*, Aug. 10, 1990; and László Búzás, "Szabad sajtó?" (Free press?), *Magyar Nemzet*, Aug. 21, 1990.
42. Ivan Szelényi, "Komprádorok, nomenklaturatőkések, kispolgárok" (Foreign facilitators, nomenklatura capitalists, and the petty bourgeois), *Népszabadság*, Aug. 21, 1990, p. 20.
43. See *Világgazdaság*, July 21, 1990; and *Népszabadság*, July 21, 1990.
44. Holders of VISA credit cards in Hungary must have a minimum bank balance of $3,000. As of mid-July 1990, there were 2,200 people with VISA cards in Hungary. *Magyar Vasárnap*, July 29, 1990. Eighteen months later, Hungary was inundated by other cards (Eurocard, American Express, Diners, etc.) issued to presumably equally creditworthy customers.

ary resources to support worthy causes—be these charitable foundations or political parties in need of discreet infusions of cash for campaign or operating expenses. It is known that many parties had borrowed, and have thus far failed to repay, substantial sums to meet campaign expenses in early 1990. The government is the principal stockholder in most commercial banks, and it is anybody's guess as to the amount each will be assessed to finance the ruling party's next campaign.

In sum, the outcome of current policy debates on the modalities of the transfer of the state's massive economic resources into private hands will have a decisive bearing on the future of Hungarian society and politics. It is certain that, by virtue of experience, professional qualifications, and being "in place," it will be the elites—new, old, and holdover—who will be the primary beneficiaries of the process of privatization in Hungary. As undisputed owners of property, rather than managers (which is what they are today, most often through default by the state), it will be this new bourgeoisie that will determine the shape of Hungary's politics in the years to come. Because it is the short-term outcome of the inter-elite competition for shares from the economic carcass of the old party-state that will decide the future balance of political power in Hungary, the stakes are extremely high; so is the intensity of behind-the-scenes struggles for the use, control, and ownership of the country's economic resources today.

"Moral Restoration"

The issue of moral restoration concerns the manner in which the ideological, moral, and ethical legacy of communist rule might be overcome by the new regime. In this policy arena, the prominent actors are the parliamentary parties, the intellectuals (liberal, Christian national, and socialist), and the leaders of organized religion, particularly the Roman Catholic Church.

According to the respondents of a June 1990 poll, the "transformation of moral-ethical norms" in Hungary is a low priority for the public. Only 8% of the national sample felt that the issue as "a government task" was worth mentioning.[45] However, unlike the lackadaisical (and remarkably secularized)

---

45. *Magyar Hirlap*, Aug. 24, 1990.

public, the government coalition is strongly committed to the restoration of Christian and national values in public life. The government's proposal to introduce religious instruction in public schools created a political storm in Hungary.

Although Cardinal László Páskai had no objection to allowing parents to decide whether or not to enroll their children in religion classes, he was critical of the AFD's opposition to the official appointment of priests to the school faculty, payment for religious instruction from school budgets, and the inclusion of grades earned in religion classes in the students' official transcripts.[46] When the AFD and LYD persisted, notorious HDF right-radical MP István Csurka escalated the dispute by equating what they called the liberal democrats' "materialistic philosophies" with those of the discredited communist party-state.[47]

Similar, though far more restrained, clashes between "pro-choice" and "right to life" advocates over proposed changes in government policies of underwriting the costs of abortion on demand helped focus public attention on the disintegration of family values in Hungary today.[48] Since the late 1960s, 4.5 million abortions have been performed in Hungary. In the last ten years, Hungary's population declined from 10.72 million to 10.37 million. The "moral arithmetic" of these astounding numbers has yet to reach the political conscience of the Hungarian public.

All elites seem to agree that society is in dire need of the restoration of civic virtues and the building of a new societal consensus for upholding high standards of moral rectitude. At issue is the historic precedent to which the nation ought to return in its search for new ethical guideposts. The alternatives are the prewar era and the mirage of a Western-style civil

---

46. László Páskai, "Válasz az SZDSZ törvényjavaslatára" (Reply to the legislative initiative of the AFD), *Uj Ember*, July 29, 1990. See also "Isten óvjon a kötelező hitoktatástól" (God save us from the compulsory study of religion), *Világ*, June 21, 1990, pp. 18-19.
47. "Hitler létrejöttében nem csak Hitler a bünös" (Hitler was not the only guilty party in becoming Hitler: Interview with István Csurka), *Pesti Kurir*, Aug. 8, 1990.
48. György Bánsági, "A nők védelmében" (In the defense of women), *Képes 7*, July 16, 1990. For the public's views on abortion on demand, see "A többség szerint: az abortusz emberi jog" (According to the majority, abortion is a human right), *Magyar Hirlap*, July 26, 1990. See also Leonora Mörk, "Inrauterin béke" (Intrauterine peace), *Világ*, June 14, 1990, p. 18.

society.[49] The latter may be a future option, therefore what seems feasible, at least as the government coalition sees it, is a selective resuscitation of such "traditional" values of public and private conduct that might be palatable to today's Hungarian middle class.

No one knows what the new Hungarian middle class is prepared to accept from the past. "Socialism," in whatever form, is out, and raw nationalism is unacceptable to the AFD, LYD, and socialist voters. On the other hand, the values of a yet-to-be-born "Central European civil society" are viewed with skepticism as alien, non-Hungarian, and, indeed, too materialistic by the coalition government's Christian national supporters. One side speaks of Béla Kun, Mátyás Rákosi, and Stalinist atheism (and really means the Jews), while the other side speaks of the Horthy era of great landowners, the ruthless rural gendarme, and mindless irredentism (but really means the people of rural Hungary, cultural nationalism, and traditionalist ambivalence toward the materialistic values of the West). To be sure, there is a very large, silent, and quite disoriented "middle" that is groping for a new kind of identity that is both "European" and "Hungarian." The voice of this "middle" has yet to be heard in Hungary.

In sum, the people and the elites are restless, and their tempers are frayed. From the rubbish heap of the old regime's lies, deceit, and severely eroded standards of decency, the new elites are trying to forge a consensus for new norms of public and private conduct—secular and religious alike. The process is treacherous, as it compels the elite actors in this policy arena to "ideologize" their concerns—at times with politically destabilizing results.

Political Justice

Four months after the free elections that brought the new regime to power, the people's sense of political justice was still dissatisfied. Indeed, the majority (51%) of the respondents to an August 1990 poll said that the change of the system had not yet occurred in their communities.[50] And the public still has yet to receive a full accounting from those who

49. See László Lengyel, "Vissza a harmincas évekbe?" (Back to the 1930s?), *Magyar Hirlap*, Aug. 11, 1990.
50. *Magyar Nemzet*, Sept. 22, 1990.

had been responsible for the humiliation, deprivation, and suffering that had been inflicted on the nation in the preceding four decades. In an earlier survey, the matter of calling to account those leaders responsible for "today's crisis" was mentioned by 44% of the public, although on further probing, only 5% thought that this was "the most important" task of the new government.[51]

A third survey found that the responsibility for Hungary's troubles belonged, on a six-point scale (1 = "most responsible"; 6 = "least responsible") to the former leaders of the HSWP (1.64), the USSR (2.93), the enterprise directors (3.03), former HSWP members (4.00), the "loafers and shirkers" (5.19), and the Western banks and credit institutions (5.65). However, as for the punishment of the culprits, only 17% demanded imprisonment and 65% the confiscation of ill-gotten gains.[52]

The policy arena of political justice may be likened to a mine field where all elites fear to tread. This suggests that all present elites are vulnerable to charges of having cooperated, or at least having gone along, with the old regime.[53] Indeed, to the extent that appointments to any mid- to upper-level white-collar position fell under the Communist Party's nomenklatura jurisdiction, 85% of the new parliamentary elites, including all but perhaps one or two members of the government, had held their pre-1989 positions with the approval of the old regime.[54]

Since the Hungarian people obviously have no wish to respond to past bloodletting in kind, nor do they seem particularly keen on locking up the old elites, what kind of justice are they demanding? The answer, much to the relief of all concerned, is symbolic justice and, when warranted by law, financial compensation. The list of grievances is long. The satisfaction of some, such as the full rehabilitation of military men executed in 1957 for their involvement in the 1956 revolution on the insurgents' side, was an honorable duty of the new government. Privates were posthumously promoted to majors, majors to generals, and the martyrs' surviving widows and children now receive full pensions. Tens of thousands imprisoned for their political beliefs are being credited for their prison years toward

51. *Magyar Hirlap,* June 18, 1990.
52. *Magyar Hirlap,* Aug. 31, 1990.
53. András Domány, "Három boriték" (Three envelopes), *Népszabadság,* Aug. 18, 1990.
54. See Tőkés, "Hungary's New Political Elites."

their retirement pensions. But what of the more than 1 million documentable cases of persecution, unlawful confiscation of property (including farm land from 500,000 small farmers), loss of jobs, official harassment, denial of children's admission to universities, and the rest of the repertoire of injustices visited on two generations of Hungarians since 1949?[55] The government's National Grievance Board, which opened for business in the fall of 1990, is likely to be busy for many years to come.

The Hungarian constitution defines the state as one of laws (*Rechtsstaat*), but the implementation of this principle is difficult. Whereas those officials who in the early 1980s sheltered the notorious terrorist Carlos may be indicted for their crime, the judge who on political instructions sent Imre Nagy and his codefendants to the gallows lives undisturbed.[56] So do the many scores of the Workers' Guards who in 1956–1957 hanged suspected revolutionaries without the benefit of a lawyer or a judge. And what of the several thousand clandestine officers of the old Ministry of Interior's Department III/III and the tens of thousands of informers signed up whose names are known to or are available to the authorities in closely guarded archives?[57] And what about the KGB's many Hungarian helpers throughout the government, army, police, and diplomatic service? Should they, as the Alliance of Free Democrats sensibly suggested, voluntarily make themselves known to the authorities, admit nothing, and, in return, be amnestied?[58]

However, what the new elites seem to be more than anxious to do is to satisfy the popular clamor for justice and strip the old elites of their luxurious villas, apartments, special benefits such as privileged access to the best-equipped hospitals, and extravagant pensions. Unlawful profits from the theft, embezzlement, dubious real estate transactions, privatization-linked kickbacks from Western investors, and similar economic gains by the old elites have yet to be investigated by the already overburdened public prosecutors.

The Hungarian Democratic Forum's "Justitia Plan" targets many of these issues and demands action on many new items

55. "És ön hol kap kárpotlást? Dokumentálhatatlan sérelmek" (And where will you get compensation? Undocumentable grievances), *168 Óra*, July 10, 1990, pp. 4–5.
56. See *Magyar Nemzet*, June 27, 1990.
57. "Nincs teljes lista" (There is no complete list), *Népszabadság*, Sept. 4, 1990.
58. *Magyar Nemzet*, Sept. 5, 1990.

that are controversial, to say the least.[59] For example, it is unclear that the proposed limits on top managerial salaries in the state sector would yield "justice" or merely drive the competent managers out of the state and into the private sector. On the other hand, the confiscation of the unlawfully acquired assets of the HSWP, the Young Communist League, the Trade Union Federation, the Patriotic People's Front, the Hungarian-Soviet Friendship Society, and the Workers' Guards, as well as the facilities abandoned by the Soviet army and air force and those of the Ministry of Defense's paramilitary organizations, and the redistribution of the same to local governments seems like a sensible idea to which only the politically discredited old elites might object.[60]

In any event, due to the deterioration of economic conditions and the outgoing Németh government's amnesty of many common criminals, there is a rising crime wave in Hungary. It is up to the government to decide whether to use the demoralized police to pursue the old or the new crooks, for there is not money and personnel to do both.

Social Justice

"Social market economy" (*soziale Marktwirtschaft*) is the economic policy concept the government has embraced to signal its commitment to private enterprise and the welfare of its citizens.[61] Given the scarcity of resources, the country's high foreign indebtedness and rate of inflation, the disastrous harvest of 1990 (and, ironically, the successful 1991 harvest, which drove milk, produce, and meat prices so low that the government was forced to intervene), and the unforeseen burden of doubled energy prices, the government can either "marketize" or see to the welfare of the people, but not both.

It is probably too early to produce a score card on the socioeconomic "winners" and "losers" in the change of political system in Hungary. According to the Hungarian sociologist Tamás Kolosi, the fall of the old regime helped undermine the

---

59. Text in *Népszabadság*, Aug. 28, 1990.
60. *Népszabadság*, Aug. 2, 1990. On the establishment of the Commission for the Investigation of Unlawful Advantages, see *Magyar Közlöny*, Aug. 30, 1990, p. 1767.
61. Péter Mihályi, "Szociális piacgazdaság . . . Hogy mit is jelent, azt senki sem tudja" (Social market economy: As to what it means, no one knows), *Figyelő*, May 17, 1990, p. 30.

economic security of approximately 300,000 families, but helped enhance the prospects of about 150,000 families.[62] One suspects that both sets of numbers pertain to the middle or lower middle class ("holdover sub-elites"?) rather than to the poor of Hungary. The latter, i.e., those who live below the minimum "existential" and "social" levels of poverty, number about 2 million, or 20% of the population.

The new elites are deeply concerned about the problem, but, much to their credit, they thus far have refrained from demagogic solutions such as hastily conceived crash programs to aid the poor by the massive expropriation of the old elites. In fact, even the parliamentary socialists, whom one would expect to try to profit politically from the situation, are on record as supporting a gradualist approach to this matter. As Imre Pozsgay, the former leader of the HSP's parliamentary caucus, put it in late March 1990, "The Hungarian Socialist Party is not going to be the party of the poor and the unemployed."[63]

Other than the Ministry of Welfare, the principal actors of this policy arena are the extraparliamentary parties of the left, the old trade unions (the new ones are mainly white-collar interest groups), the local governments, and the churches. Of these, the Trade Union Federation was the channel through which the party-state provided subsidized vacations, low-interest housing loans, and unstrenuous but well-paying jobs to all who merited such considerations. The unions also controlled vacation resorts, "Houses of Culture," and assorted recreational facilities. In other words, the TUF did many things except represent its members' interests at the workplace. With assets of over Ft 4 billion, and a pension fund of over Ft 10 billion that is still not fully accounted for, the TUF assets are fair game for all those who can do a better job for employees, pensioners, and the ill. The assets of the now-defunct Young Communist League and Young Pioneers are similarly vulnerable to claims of this sort.

Among the political actors, the local governments, voluntary organizations, and churches are the best equipped to address the burning welfare problems of Hungary today. Because the transfer of assets and other resources from the old and discredited organizations and from the state to these new enti-

---

62. *Heti Világgazdaság*, Sept. 6, 1990, p. 74.
63. Talk at the Kossuth Club, Budapest, March 30, 1990.

ties requires enabling legislation, the poor, the old, the ill, and the homeless have to wait their turn. Hunger marches are not in the cards, but the plight of the thousands of poor people with their electricity and heat turned off for nonpayment of utility bills, or on the brink of eviction for having fallen behind with the rent, awaits prompt action.[64]

The pity of it is that the poor are no longer news. Instead, the issue has become a low-denomination bargaining chip in Hungarian elite politics. For example, the Parliament appropriated a sum of Ft 22.4 million for the fourth quarter FY 1990 to support 27 "social associations." Of these, only 11 had anything to do with social welfare problems.[65] This sum is about one-hundredth of what would be needed for three months to make a dent in the problem.

Self-Government

The two-round September-October 1990 elections for local governments were important, albeit not decisive, milestones in Hungary's transition to democracy. At issue was what the new elites call the "recapturing" of local autonomy and powers of self-government for the citizens of Hungary. The disagreeable truth is that with the exception of the major municipalities prior to World War II, Hungary's villages, small towns, and cities have never had substantial fiscal or political autonomy.[66] Traditionally, it was Budapest and the administrative seats of the counties that controlled the purse strings and caused the appointment, or arranged for the election, of officeholders at all levels of public administration. The communist legacy of centralized decision making and the lengthy tenure of local party despots only further eroded local aspirations for self-government.

Against this background, we may now identify the actors and the stakes in this important policy arena. It is apparent from the lengthy parliamentary deliberations on this subject that the new elites are extremely anxious to escape their isolation at the

64. Zsuzsa Szemann, "Öregek és éhesek" (They are old and hungry), Figyelő, May 24, 1990, p. 5. See also Mrs. Sándor Szabó, "A lakossági jövedelmek várható alakulása" (Anticipated changes in incomes), Figyelő, June 14, 1990, p. 6.
65. Beszélő, Sept. 22, 1990, p. 9.
66. László Hovanyecz, "Beszélgetés Gombár Csabával" (Interview with Csaba Gombár), Népszabadság, June 6, 1990.

"top," i.e., at the national level, and set their political anchors in as many communities as possible.[67] The new elites' main adversaries (and possible potential partners) are the tens of thousands of holdover elites well embedded in local governments. Rural fears and suspicions of the changes that the new elites might introduce in the Hungarian villages represent another obstacle to rapid change. Indeed, according to pre-election polls, 54.6% of those living in villages would reelect the incumbent village councilors, while 48.5% would do the same for the current chairman (and future mayor) of the village government.[68] The story was somewhat different in Budapest and in the provincial cities, where 40.5% and 40.9%, respectively, of the respondents indicated their wish to replace the incumbent city councilors, while 35% and 38.7%, respectively, would retain them.[69]

When it comes to local politics, partisanship and party labels seem to be alien to the rural voters. In 2,758 villages where at least 40% of the eligible voters showed up at the ballot box for the first round, 82.9% of the elected village mayors were independents, followed by 3.8%(!) voted in on the Smallholders' slate.[70] Only in Budapest and in the major cities did the parties fare well and finish ahead of the independents. For the record, 42 parties, 647 social organizations, 12 ethnic minorities, and 447 ad hoc local alliances fielded a total of 69,000 candidates for 27,462 mayoral and councilor positions throughout Hungary.[71]

According to the official final results, the voting turnout was 40.16% in the first round and 28.94% in the second. The "independents" (at least 80% of whom were either old or holdover elites) made a clean sweep of the countryside in both rounds. This outcome was a stunning defeat for all new political parties—barely five months after the national elections, the old elites had made a partial political comeback. Of the new parties, the League of Young Democrats did extremely well, although

---

67. On this, see the record of parliamentary deliberations "on the modification of the Constitution and the Law on Local Governments" in Hungarian Parliament, Proceedings, extraordinary summer session, July 9, 1990, cols. 1355–1441; July 16, 1990, cols. 1625–1713; July 23, 1990, cols. 1888–1925; July 24, 1990, cols. 1939–1974; July 30, 1990, cols. 2100–2105, 2108–2122. See also "Helyhatóság '90" (Local Government, 1990), Special supplement to *Magyar Nemzet*, Sept. 24, 1990.
68. *Heti Világgazdaság*, Sept. 22, 1990, p. 5.
69. Ibid.
70. *Népszabadság*, Oct. 2, 1990.
71. *Népszabadság*, Sept. 21, 1990

the Alliance of Free Democrats strengthened its position throughout Hungary, particularly in the larger cities. Gábor Demszky, a youthful and popular member of the AFD executive, was chosen mayor as opposition parties "retook" Budapest—a stunning change from the previous April, when the Hungarian Democratic Forum took 18 of the 24 parliamentary seats of the capital city.

The outcome of local government elections was paradoxical, as it refuted the longstanding belief that local voters in Hungary tend to support party-endorsed candidates who are presumed to have access to national governmental decision makers and hence can do a better job of lobbying for local concerns. Whom will the "independent" AFD and LYD mayors approach in the Budapest ministries for paved roads, new schools, and hospitals? This, too, is one of the uncertainties of democracy.

At the municipal level, the stakes, and therefore the level of partisanship, are considerably higher than in the villages. In an average Hungarian city, there are scores of buildings formerly occupied by the HSWP or one of its front organizations, all kinds of state-owned facilities, including surplus military lands and buildings, and many other kinds of leftovers from the old regime.[72] The future disposition of municipal housing through privatization is another prize worth fighting for by the local elites. Next to the outcome of "who gets what and how?" of state assets, there are issues such as municipal services, schools, health, and cultural facilities that are subjects of fierce political contestation at the local level.

To put matters in perspective, it must be kept in mind that the real extent of local autonomy will be determined by the amounts of locally raised revenues that the community will be allowed to keep out of the hands of the Budapest government. Given the country's dire economic situation, the prospects for real local fiscal autonomy seem bleak for the foreseeable future. This may be particularly true in cities that have come under the control of "independents" or one of the opposition parties. The newly created, government-appointed "republican commissioners" will oversee the public administration of the eight

---

72. Zoltán Agg, "Hogyan lesz az állami tulajdonból önkormányzati tulajdon?" (How is state property going to become property of the local government?), *Magyar Közigazgatás*, May 1990, pp. 385–400.

regions of Hungary. This seems to be another safeguard for the protection of Budapest's prerogatives over the local communities.[73]

"Hungary's Place in the World"

In addition to that peaceful surrender of power, an early start on the development of an independent foreign policy was another "gift" of the old elites to the leaders of democratic Hungary. The search for a quasi-autonomous, or at least "national interest"-based, foreign policy had begun under Kádár. The HSWP Central Committee Foreign Affairs Secretary Mátyás Szűrös and former Prime Ministers Károly Grósz and Miklós Németh, each in his own way, sought to contribute to the realization of this policy.[74] The breakthrough came in August-September 1989, when Foreign Minister Gyula Horn and Prime Minister Miklós Németh broke with the GDR and authorized the exit of East German tourists through Hungary to the West.

The new elites' contribution to the future foreign policies of Hungary was threefold. The Hungarian Democratic Forum helped mobilize the nation to respond to the plight of Hungarian ethnic minorities in Ceauşescu's Romania and Jakeš' Czechoslovakia. The League of Young Democrats, particularly its leader Viktor Orbán, was the first to issue the demand "out with the Russians," and the Alliance of Free Democrats, especially its leader János Kis, was the first in Hungary to promote the idea of active cooperation among the human rights activists of Hungary, Czechoslovakia, Poland, and East Germany.

These background events to Hungary's independence in 1990 helped shape the foundations of an all-party consensus on foreign policy priorities, and defined the issues for this policy arena of elite politics. As far as can be reconstructed from official statements and parliamentary debates, the Antall government's

---

73. For the applicable laws on local self-government (Law LXV, 1990) and on the republican commissioners (Parliamentary decision no. 66/1990), see *Magyar Közlöny*, Aug. 14, 1990, pp. 1637–64.
74. Sándor Kopátsy, "Egy siker bukása" (The failure of success), *Népszabadság*, May 26, 1990; László Ablonczy, "Most is aggódom. Beszélgetés Szűrös Mátyással" (I am still worried: Interview with Mátyás Szűrös), *Tiszatáj* (June 1990), pp. 74–94. See also "A 2 + 2 monológ" (The two plus two monologue) [meeting of Károly Grósz with Nicolae Ceauşescu in Arad on August 25, 1988], *Tiszatáj* (June 1990), pp. 96–110.

foreign policies have three components: (a) a pronounced "European-Atlantic" orientation with emphasis on Hungary's special relationship with the Federal Republic of Germany; (b) a forceful assertion of Hungary's new identity in the region, with emphasis on its mission to promote and protect the human rights and linguistic and cultural autonomy of Hungarian ethnic minorities in Romania, Slovakia, Yugoslavia, and western Ukraine; and (c) a redefinition of Hungary's ties and a search for new patterns of partnership with the former Soviet Union and other former allies from the Warsaw Treaty Organization (WTO) and the Council for Mutual Economic Assistance (CMEA).

The old elites, except for a few slow learners (such as Gyula Thurmer of the Workers' Party, who until August 1991 used to run to Moscow to complain to the Soviet press about the Antall government), have few problems with adapting to these new foreign policy priorities. Although former Foreign Minister Horn (an HSP deputy and chairman of the Parliament's Foreign Affairs Committee) occasionally objects to Foreign Minister Géza Jeszenszky's foreign policy statements, he is on board as far as the essentials are concerned.

Substantial criticism of the government's foreign policies has come mainly from the Alliance of Free Democrats. Although the quality of AFD commentary is uncharacteristically amateurish, the leading opposition party has been concerned about three issues. The first is the government's, particularly Prime Minister Antall's, close ties with Germany and Chancellor Kohl. As the AFD's philosopher-geostrategist Gáspár Miklós Tamás sees it, Hungary's "German tilt" could jeopardize US confidence in Hungary. As Tamás put it, Germany's real interests lie in an alliance with the Soviet Union as co-landlords of the Central European parts of the common European house.[75]

The second issue of concern to the AFD is the manner of the Antall government's advocacy of Hungarian ethnic rights in the region. The AFD argues that the prime minister's policy statements may be interpreted by external critics as Hungary's relapse to prewar policies of irredentism. This concern, albeit in subdued form, is also shared by President Árpád Göncz. Although his position is presumably nonpartisan and his constitu-

---

75. Gáspár Miklós Tamás, "Csak száz nap a vilag . . . " (The first hundred days: On the Antall government's foreign policies), *Beszélő*, Sept. 15, 1990, pp. 4–6.

tional responsibilities do not include the right to advocate foreign policies of his own (or those of the AFD, of which he is a member), President Göncz is on record with foreign policy views that do not seem to accord with those of the government.[76]

The third issue of the AFD-HDF foreign policy dispute concerns military security and Hungary's position in the region after its departure from the WTO in late 1991. It all began in July 1990 in the journal *Beszélő*, the AFD weekly, when a military expert, now the principal military advisor to President Göncz, took on the HDF's military experts, criticizing the concept of "circular defense" that he attributed to the new government.[77] The dispute was ostensibly about the sufficiency of Hungary's military preparedness after the signing of the East-West conventional force reduction agreement, but the hidden agenda was that of contingency planning in case of a surprise attack by Romania. Though the issue is real enough, the arguments pro and con were strikingly uninformed of the broader international (particularly superpower) policy context in which potential regional conflicts might be addressed in the future.[78]

In sum, Hungary's new elites have had every reason to feel insecure in the uncharted waters of international relations in the postcommunist world. They must search for a secure place for Hungary in the former no-man's-land between Russia and Western Europe. The answer to Hungary's dilemmas might lie in a multifaceted policy that aims at linking up with Europe as well as maintaining "peaceful coexistence" with the Central European neighbors and establishing very correct ties with Moscow and the sovereign states of what used to be the Soviet Union.

■ *In Lieu of Conclusions: An Early Mid-Term Assessment*

In this chapter, I have sought to identify and discuss the key issues and policy dilemmas that confronted

---

76. In his speech of September 23, 1990, Prime Minister Antall reminded *all* concerned that "it is the government and the prime minister who speak for the foreign policies of Hungary." *Népszabadság*, Sept. 24, 1990.
77. Robert Pick, "Körkörös védtelenség" (Circular defenselessness), *Beszélő*, July 14, 1990, pp. 4–6.
78. The rest of the debate appeared in *Beszélő*, July 21 (pp. 22-23), July 28 (pp. 23–25), Aug. 4 (pp. 21–24), and Aug. 11, 1990 (pp. 23–26).

Hungary's freely elected government and the old and holdover elites in the first several months of that country's transition from authoritarianism to democracy. Within this context, I introduced the notion of a "second transition" to indicate the magnitude of the challenge facing the new government in endeavoring to implement its electoral mandate in eight "policy arenas" ranging from institutional transformation to foreign policies.

Fifteen months later, the government and the legislature were about midway between the last and the next (1994) national elections. When the overall record of the last 22 months is examined, it appears that by early 1992 more than enough had been accomplished to call the results evidence of not merely "transition" but of substantial progress toward the democratic consolidation of Hungary.

As Philippe C. Schmitter explains, "democratic consolidation of a political democracy involves the structuration of a particular type of regime." Specifically,

> regime consolidation consists in transforming the accidental arrangements, prudential norms, and contingent solutions that have emerged [in the transition period] into relationships that are reliably known, regularly practiced and habitually accepted by the participants of such structures.[79]

As discussed above, the Hungarian political actors' exclusive reliance on negotiations, "pacts," informal agreements, and understandings as instruments of choice for the resolution of ideological and personal differences was a necessary condition for a peaceful transition from one political system to another. However, even with the old regime's prominent representatives safely consigned either to the opposition benches of the legislature or to the extraparliamentary political wilderness, the potential for bruising confrontations was still present in Hungarian politics well into 1991.

The nationwide taxi and transportation strike of October 1990, though badly mishandled by both sides, was a useful reminder that the "rules of engagement" of political contestation between the ruling government coalition and its parliamentary opposition required rethinking, if not necessarily written clarification. Although the terms of the new modus vivendi were never spelled out, the outcome, to quote O'Donnell and

---

79. Philippe C. Schmitter, "The Consolidation of Political Democracies: Processes, Rhythms, Sequences and Types" (Unpublished, October 1991).

Schmitter, amounted to "a compromise under which actors agree[d] to forego or underutilize their capacity to harm each other by extending guarantees not to threaten each other's corporate autonomies or vital interests."[80]

The task of sorting out the operational details of a new kind of political coexistence among the main political actors took time and a great deal of both public and behind-the-scenes soul-searching by the new party elites. However, by the middle of 1991, even the ideological purists in the AFD executive realized that there was no political profit in trying to force a government with an ironclad parliamentary majority to accommodate frustrated liberals and call new elections. Thus, with the bulk of the government's legislative agenda for the institutional transformation of Hungary from postcommunism to liberal democracy enacted into law, the essential elements of the transition from authoritarianism to the threshold of a working democracy were completed in Hungary by the end of the year.

Disillusionment with democracy, declining levels of political participation, and mounting public criticism of the government are sure signs of "political transition in progress" in Eastern Europe, and Hungary is no exception. According to a mid-1991 Times-Mirror survey, 82% of the Hungarian respondents "completely" or "mostly" agreed with the statement that "generally speaking, elected officials lose touch with the people pretty quickly." On the other hand, 49% agreed either "completely" or "mostly" that voting gives people some say about how the government runs things.[81]

Survey results on popular attitudes toward politicians as officials and as prominent members of political parties display a dual tendency in Hungary. Over a period of 18 months, Prime Minister Antall slipped from the highest to the lowest quintile in the monthly popularity charts. On the other hand, the opposition politicians who could not be held responsible for tough government decisions, particularly the League of Young Democrats, the independents, and the President of the Republic Árpád Göncz, were at the top throughout. Indeed, answers to the question "if elections were held next Sunday, which party

---

80. O'Donnell and Schmitter, *Transitions From Authoritarian Rule*, p. 38.
81. Times Mirror Center for the People & The Press, "The Pulse of Europe: A Survey of Political and Social Values and Institutions" (Washington, DC, September 1991), p. 116.

would you support?" showed nearly as high voter approval for the LYD (25%) as for the three parties of the government coalition (27%).[82]

What may be at issue here is not merely the Hungarian voters' temporary disenchantment with seemingly unresponsive politicians, but possibly the drastic realignment of the six parliamentary parties' electoral support. By late 1991, one would wonder whether the March-April 1990 electoral outcome had been, in terms of party preferences, not a precedent-setting expression of the nation's political will, but rather a one-time collective anticommunist temper tantrum of the Hungarian people. The six parliamentary parties' legislative voting record since offers convincing evidence for the new elites' keen awareness of their fragile electoral mandate and of the measures they took to assure the irreversibility of the presumably unambiguous political-ideological mandate of the Hungarian "founding elections" of 1990.

Hungary's new and holdover reform communist elites proved to be farsighted politicians when the two struck the bargain in the summer of 1989 on the technical details of the first free elections in the following spring. By dividing the 386 parliamentary seats between 176 individual constituencies and those 210 MPs who came in on party slates, they assured that more than half of the Parliament would not be directly accountable to the Hungarian voters. By so "immunizing" the majority of MPs from constituency pressures, the legislature has been free to enact the government's transition agenda without much regard to the state of public opinion. Indeed, a study on the legislative history of the first 107 laws enacted by the Hungarian Parliament between May 1990 and the summer of 1991 shows that 80% of these laws were enacted by a majority of 70% to 100%.[83]

Given the ruling party coalition's share of 59% of seats in the Parliament, the achievement of more than 70% endorsement for the government's legislative program is clear evidence of an all-party consensus on the essential, albeit painful and unpopular, measures for the completion of Hungary's transition to a qualitatively new kind of political and economic system. How-

---

82. Ibid., p. 101.
83. Sándor Kurtán, *Pártok és törvények* (Parties and the laws), Budapest Papers on Democratic Transition, no. 5, (Budapest: Department of Political Science, Budapest University for Economics, 1991).

ever, near-unanimity on sensitive transition issues is also a manifestation, as well as the cause, of the growing distance between the "parties in Parliament" and the same parties as political movements. The latter are exposed and vulnerable to constituency demands and pressures from the extraparliamentary universe of political forces, such as the media, business groups, labor unions, and other self-appointed spokespersons for the social and economic victims of budget cuts and harsh economic reforms.

Hungary's six largest political parties were caught between, and became victims of, conflicting pressures for legislative progress and delivery on constituency expectations for a better life after communism. By the end of 1991, the Smallholders' Party and the Alliance of Free Democrats fell apart into feuding factions. Though personality conflicts played an important role in both cases, the party insurgents' claims concerning the parliamentary leadership's alleged unresponsiveness to grassroots demands proved convincing enough to cause both parties' disintegration into politically inconsequential ideological caucuses. Insofar as Hungary's political stability is derived from the viability of its multiparty system, the absence of the second and the third largest parties as competent actors in the political arena is a risk that the country can ill afford.[84]

The possession of government resources and the availability of political patronage to the national leadership are probably the only things that keep the Hungarian Democratic Forum together as a coherent political force. Similar to the AFD, the HDF has been a catch-all electoral party that attracted voter support for reasons that had little to do with the policy issues of the transition period. More than two years after the elections, it appears that both parties harbor up to a half-dozen "mini-parties"—each with a distinct agenda of its own.

The principal constraint on such intraparty policy factions' capacity for mischief is the party executives' control of the purse strings. Thanks to Hungarian party finance laws, each parliamentary party—and not the movement—receives a substantial budgetary allotment in accordance with the percentage of seats held in the legislature. Therefore, would-be party rebels had better

---

84. Attila Farkas and Pál Szombathy, "Parlamenti pártok a választási ciklus félidejében" (Parliamentary parties: A mid-term assessment), *Magyar Hirlap*, Jan. 23, 1992.

think twice before challenging the "iron laws" of the fledgling Hungarian party oligarchies—on either side of the legislative aisle.

Unlike the foregoing overview of recent developments in Hungarian party politics, a comprehensive update on the correlation of the old, new, and holdover elite forces and the respective postures of these amorphous clusters in each of the eight policy arenas is well beyond the scope of this study. However, a brief summary of the highlights might suffice as a way of registering the status of political contestation in five of Hungary's policy arenas in early 1992.

The most striking development in the area of institutional transformation has been the ascendance and, from the perspective of the opposition parties, the alarming growth in the powers of the office of the prime minister. Since late 1990, the office developed into a "super ministry" with vast budgetary resources and unlimited jurisdiction over the entire government bureaucracy. The prime minister's team of six ministers without portfolio, four secretaries of state, their deputies, and several nameless and faceless but highly influential advisory committees has acquired an image of a potentially menacing political monolith. Perhaps this is what it takes to run a small country in troubled times, but the apparent resuscitation of a functional equivalent of the old regime's "hands-on manager" party Central Committee Secretariat is of legitimate concern to the government's domestic critics and foreign well-wishers alike.

The battles of Hungary's economic transformation are being fought on several fronts. Thanks to tightfisted monetarist policies and the export industries' remarkably rapid reorientation from Soviet to Western markets, inflation has been kept in check at an annual rate of 34%. The process of privatization seems to be well in hand. In 1991, one-fifth of the state's assets, with a book value of about $5 billion, were privatized.[85] The flood of "business-friendly" legislation and the government's willingness not to look too closely into the details of privatization (particularly the origin of the Hungarian investors' assets) created an attractive environment for direct Western investment and the proliferation of joint ventures—mainly with German, Austrian, and US investors.

---

85. On this, see the 1991 annual report of the Hungarian State Property Agency. Excerpts in *Heti Világgazdaság*, Jan. 18, 1992.

Whereas the privatization of the state's industrial assets benefitted mainly the old and holdover elites, the new compensation laws for economic losses sustained by Hungarian citizens in the last 40 years offer "economic justice" to 800,000 people in the form of government bonds and coupons. Much of this, such as the receipt of vouchers worth about one-twentieth of losses sustained, is highly symbolic, but this is the best the government can do for the average Hungarian. Another round of legislation will seek to provide compensation to the 250,000 victims (or their surviving descendants) who suffered political imprisonment and internment in Hungary or were abducted by Soviet troops to perform forced labor in the USSR. The survivors of the Holocaust and of the 450,000 Hungarian soldiers killed in the war or starved to death in Soviet POW camps are also slated for compensation of some kind.

The lingering issue of political justice and punishment of those "criminally responsible" for wrongdoing under communist rule was revived by the HDF's parliamentary caucus in September 1991. The date was not accidental and should be seen in the context of the alarm (and the subsequent sense of relief) over the Moscow coup and the government elites' decision to stamp out the remaining vestiges of communism in Hungary. Thus, the Parliament labored and gave birth to a draft law that would lift the statute of limitations on such crimes as treason, murder, and the "inflicting of bodily injury that led to the victim's death" that had been committed in the preceding 45 years.[86]

The proposed law has been reviewed by the Constitutional Court and has been found unconstitutional in its original form. Whatever the outcome, the odds are very good that in the end no one will go to jail for past crimes. For one thing, a very high percentage of the public appears totally uninterested in exacting legal revenge at the expense of a few score of septuagenarian pensioners of the old regime.[87] More to the point, the private archives of these old apparatchiks have more than sufficient documentary evidence to incriminate many of the new regime's would-be inquisitors. In any event, because the (now invalid) draft law has sought to close the books on every other kind of

---

86. Hungarian Parliament, Proceedings, Stenographic Minutes, Fall 1991 session, Nov. 4, 1991, cols 11299–11301. See also *Népszabadság*, Nov. 6, 1991.
87. According to a report in *Heti Világgazdaság*, Jan. 11, 1992, 71% of the respondents had no idea what the law was about, and of the 29% who did, only 36% supported it.

old malfeasance, the proponents' real objective may have been to put pressure on the holdover elites to stand up and be counted as pillars of the new regime.

As discussed above, the September-October 1990 elections for Hungarian city, town, and village local governments yielded a clean sweep for the opposition parties at all levels. However, when it came to taking possession of their political prize and dividing the economic spoils, the result was political infighting, vicious personality conflicts, and chaos of epic proportions. The difficulty of managing bankrupt cities and towns has been further exacerbated by the appearance of the Budapest-appointed republican commissioners, with sweeping powers to invalidate local decrees on such critical matters as taxes and public service appointments. In a country where the national government, through the process of central budgetary allocations, controls 80% of the local governments' fiscal resources, local autonomy tends to be an illusory proposition.

"Hungary's place in the world" was an unresolved issue in the first six months of the Antall government. A year later, however, Hungary was no longer a member of the Warsaw Treaty Organization or the CMEA. The Soviet troops that had been "temporarily stationed" in Hungary for the preceding 45 years returned to their homeland in June 1991. Hungary and its Polish and Czechoslovak partners are now Associate Members of the European Community, as well as of NATO's new North Atlantic Cooperation Council.[88] These astounding developments have helped strengthen the government's domestic political prestige and have contributed to the birth of what appears to be an all-party parliamentary consensus on Hungarian foreign policy priorities—at least for the next year or two.

In sum, it appears that through a combination of hard work, patriotism, political chicanery, and a great deal of good luck, Hungary's new and holdover elites have laid the foundations for democracy, the rule of law, and a market economy. These changes seem irreversible. The Antall government and the parliamentary opposition may have found the navigational charts for the treacherous waters between dictatorship and consolidated democracy.

---

88. See Rudolf L. Tőkés, "From Visegrad to Cracow: Cooperation, Competition and Coexistence in Central Europe," *Problems of Communism* (November-December 1991), pp. 100–114.

6

Polish Elections, 1989–1991: Beyond the "Pospolite Ruszenie"

KRZYSZTOF JASIEWICZ

1

"Solidarity brought communism in Poland to its end. But with the end of communism comes the end of Solidarity." This bitter message came from Zbyszek Bujak, the legendary leader of Solidarity, a fugitive who for five years led the underground movement through its most difficult period: the times of martial law and subsequent "normalization." He spoke these words in July 1990, at the Fourth World Congress of Soviet and East European Studies in Harrogate, England. At the congress, scholars from East and West assembled to share their astonishment at what has been so senselessly called "The Autumn of the People."

Autumn means decline, decay, fall. But this was the fall of communism, not of the people! For the people of Eastern Europe, it is their new beginning, their spring—as the original Spring of the People in 1848. It was indeed the spring of the people, and only happened to occur in the fall; yet, spring also means joy, and in Eastern Europe, "the Party is over," but the joy is over as well.

New beginnings too often mean new troubles, or the old troubles multiplied several times: ethnic strife, inflation, unemployment, etc. But Bujak's bitterness comes, I suppose, not from the mere recognition of all these problems. He knows, as do most politically aware Poles, that our task must be to create a

This chapter is a substantially revised and updated version of my chapter in W. Connor, P. Płoszajski, eds., *The Polish Road From Socialism* (Armonk, NY: M.E. Sharpe, 1992); the book has been published simultaneously in Poland under the title *Escape from Socialism: The Polish Route* (Warsaw: IFiS Publishers, 1992).

new economy and a new society—in an international environment that is possibly friendly but not quite cooperative. But he—we—could have hoped that to build a new democratic political system would be the easiest of all our efforts.

From its very beginning in 1980, Solidarity has struggled for democracy, using democratic means. Even if there has been an authoritarian component—in the personalities of some leaders or, understandably, in actions of clandestine units—the people of Solidarity, and their "fellow travelers" as well, remained fundamentally democratic. This was proven in the June 1989 elections, when the people of Poland voted the Communists out of government. At that time, the threat to the young Polish democracy seemed to come from the remnants of the *ancien régime*: the postcommunist president (Gen. Wojciech Jaruzelski), the "old coalition" 65% majority in the Sejm, the Communist-controlled army and secret police, and the omnipotent nomenklatura. But after he became president, Jaruzelski did not make a single move to slow down the process of reform, and finally decided to give up his office; the old coalition fell apart, with the formerly puppet Peasant and Democratic Parties forming a new coalition with Solidarity; the Communist Party promptly dissolved itself, while the secret police was dismantled by the Mazowiecki government, the army eagerly depoliticized itself, and the nomenklatura holds only some of its old positions, on the lower and middle levels.

One could have hoped that the victory over the *ancien régime* would mean a smooth transition to a well-functioning democracy and a democratic political culture. One could have predicted, however, that from the victorious camp would emerge different opinions, plans, and programs for a free Poland. This was unavoidable—but did this differentiation, or, to put it bluntly, deep split within Solidarity, have to come before the establishment of a truly democratic political system? Did it have to precede fully free parliamentary elections? Did it have to come during a very deep economic crisis, when the Balcerowicz plan had only begun to work? Such doubts lie, I believe, at the bottom of Bujak's statement about the end of Solidarity.

Why did the end of the Solidarity movement come so abruptly? What will replace it? Addressing such questions in this chapter, I will try to show connections between the actions of political leaders and the attitudes of the people. In particular, I am interested in describing in political and sociological terms the constituencies of the most prominent leaders and orientations emerging from the Solidarity movement.

2

The British historian Norman Davies, in his excellent book *Heart of Europe: A Short History of Poland*, wrote that

> The first thing which Poles have to realize in recent years is that the agents of their oppression today are not weird-looking foreigners wearing a pickelhelm or a Tartar cap. The oppressors are Poles like themselves, instantly recognizable by their dress, their manner, and their jargon, but men and women in the main part from their own towns and villages, from their own families. The line which divides the oppressor from the oppressed runs through the blood and bone of Polish society, and often enough, in the event of divided loyalties, through the heart and soul of an individual person. One of the principal products of a generation of Communism is this division between the "power" (*władza*) and "society" (*społeczeństwo*), between the bosses and the people, between "them" and "us."[1]

In the mid-1980s, when Davies' book was first published, this opinion was shared not only by many scholars (one notable example being the late Polish historian Tadeusz Łepkowski),[2] but also, more importantly, by the majority of Poland's populace. Were they right? Was the mental and emotional gap between the people and a handful of oppressors really so deep? Careful analysis of various survey data gathered in Poland throughout the 1980s indicates that the reality was much more complex.

Lack of space prevents even a partial presentation here of such data,[3] but one could draw from them the conclusion that a

---

1. Norman Davies, *Heart of Europe: A Short History of Poland* (Oxford: Oxford University Press, 1984), p. 45.
2. See Tadeusz Łepkowski, *Uparte trwanie polskości* (Stubbornly being Polish) (London-Warsaw: Aneks, 1989).
3. They are, however, available from several sources (in Polish and in English). See, in particular, Władysław Adamski, Krzysztof Jasiewicz, and Andrzej Rychard, eds., *Polacy '84: Dynamika konfliktu i konsensusu* (Poles '84: Dynamics of conflict and consensus) (Warsaw: IFiS, 1986); idem, *Polacy '88: Dynamika konfliktu a szanse reform* (Poles '88: Dynamics of conflict and the chances for reform) (Warsaw: IFiS, 1989); *Sisyphus: Sociological Studies*, vol. 5; and Krzysztof Jasiewicz, "Kultura polityczna Polaków" (The political culture of Poles), *Aneks*, no. 48.

dichotomized vision of two—and only two—"nations," two classes with distinct systems of values, attitudes, and political views could hardly be sustained. Rather, there was a significant differentiation of those values, views, and attitudes. Moreover, one can find various dimensions to that differentiation, with the ends of the political continuum spread, literally, poles apart. At those ends one could find coherent syndromes of political thought: populist-authoritarian (those supporting the communist regime, "the oppressors"), and liberal-democratic (the opponents of the regime). One should stress, however, that individuals with consistent political profiles inside each of those two groups were in a minority, and each group may be perceived as a broad and loose political alliance. So, among supporters of the communist rule were not only authoritarian populists, but also quite liberal-minded people who believed, for instance, that geopolitical reality prevented Poland from attaining any other form of government. On the other hand, among those who opposed the established political order were not only convinced liberal democrats, but also individuals who sought authoritarian solutions and supported populist slogans while at the same time rejecting the communist version of authoritarianism because of, say, its Soviet provenance.

Between those two extremes there was an even less coherent "centrist" group, one that should not be perceived as a genuine political center. A true center would consist of persons and groups who consciously express cautious and moderate views, are inclined to search for a common language with extremist groups, and would be perceived by other groups as the center. Instead, the "centrists" of the mid-1980s were people with not fully crystallized views, inclined in certain matters to decide in favor of one side and in other matters in favor of the opposing side, avoiding—at least when surveyed—a firm stand in support of anything or anyone. On the sidelines there was also a sizable group, the "silent minority"—persons who were either too apathetic to hold any political views or who may have preferred to avoid an expression of their views in front of an interviewer.

In general, this was a picture of a society in which, in their daily lives, many people seemed to accept the established political order, while their values favored far-reaching changes in the model of public life. The views and attitudes of the people were polarized, with the axis of this polarization drawn by two opposed syndromes of political thought: liberal-democratic and populist-authoritarian.

Such a picture of the political differentiation of Polish society in the mid-1980s reflects the general political situation of those days ("normalization," the weakening of Solidarity's underground, crippling economic reforms), but it indicated that there was also a potential for change. And that change, a rapid one, indeed came. First, two waves of massive strikes in industrial centers (spring and summer 1988); then, the painful but successful process of negotiation between the communist power elite and the leaders of the opposition (the roundtable); finally, the elections of June 1989—the first elections ever in which a ruling Communist Party was defeated. The suddenness of this process is well illustrated in table 1 (at the end of this chapter), in which the coefficients of confidence in selected political personalities and institutions are presented.

All of a sudden, some time in 1988, many Poles gained (or regained) confidence in Wałęsa and Solidarity, while withdrawing or suspending such confidence in Jaruzelski, Prime Minister Mieczysław Rakowski, and the institutions of the *ancien régime* (note a very stable level of confidence in the Church). This meant first the creation of a real political center (those willing to support a compromise between the communists and Solidarity), and, ultimately, Solidarity's landslide electoral victory of June 4, 1989. The majority of voters—the notorious rebels along with the "hamletizing" conformists—when forced to the dichotomous choice between the ruling coalition or the opposition, dared to vote for the Solidarity candidates.

Throughout the 1980s, seeing no alternative to the established political order, many people fell into apathy or acted in a most opportunistic way. In 1988, when a real alternative emerged, the same people turned against the communist system—the system that they had never perceived as their own.

3

It is time to explain the mysterious Polish expression in this chapter's title. The use of this term in English is justified: one can find in *Webster's Third New International Dictionary* the following entry:

> Pospolite [Pol. *pospolite* (*ruszenie*) general levy, fr. *pospolite* (neutr. from *pospolity* general) + *ruszenie* movement, levy] a former Polish militia in Poland called out in case of invasion.

In aristocratic Poland there was no regular army, and the *pospolite ruszenie* played the role of armed forces composed of all citizens (noblemen) to defend the Commonwealth of Two Nations (as the Polish-Lithuanian union was called) against the enemy. Such a *pospolite ruszenie* won the parliamentary elections of June 1989. People of various political self-identifications—rightists, centrists, and leftists; cosmopolitans, nationalists, and chauvinists; liberals and populists; democrats and republicans; monarchists and anarchists; and those with no political identification whatsoever, were all united in one conviction—no more rule of the PUWP (Polish United Workers Party). And so they voted for the Civic Committee Solidarity candidates. To be precise: those voting for Solidarity were not the majority of the electorate, but only a plurality. Almost 40% of eligible voters stayed home (a silent minority?); almost 20% voted against Solidarity and for the "ruling coalition" candidates. To be even more precise: the majority of voters had no idea of the actual consequences of their vote. On the day of the elections, they did not dare think that the PUWP could be voted out of office. The Communist Party and its allies were guaranteed 65% of the seats in the Sejm, and—it seemed—the office of the president. But although Jaruzelski was elected (by only one vote in the National Assembly), the communists were not able to form a government, and from August 1989 the Polish government was led by Tadeusz Mazowiecki—the first noncommunist prime minister in Eastern Europe in 40 years.

The *pospolite ruszenie* won the battle—but was it able to conduct a war? For some time, the answer to this question might have seemed positive. The Mazowiecki government was welcomed enthusiastically; there was a widespread feeling that the state and its institutions had been revindicated by the people (see table 1 for the rapid rise of confidence in the Sejm, the government, and the army). Resistance, particularly by the old secret police and nomenklatura cliques on the lower and middle levels, kept the *pospolite* together and led it to another battle—the municipal elections of May 27, 1990. And the *pospolite ruszenie* won again.

It is not easy to analyze the results of these elections, due to the complexity of the electoral law (the "first-past-the-post" system in single-seat districts in rural areas; proportional representation in multi-seat districts in urban areas), and also due to the vagueness of the political arena. The party system has still not yet emerged from the swarm of groupings, cliques, and ambitious individuals; many such groupings formed ad hoc coalitions, hoping in this way to increase their odds; and many of those groupings and coalitions used misleading names rather than proper guidelines for the electorate (one could find former communists running as a Democratic Civic Committee or a Coalition for Free Enterprise!). Nevertheless, it is clear that the Civic Committees Solidarity won; they collected 38% of the seats in single-seat districts and 74% in multi-seat districts. In single-seat districts, 43% of the seats were won by independent candidates, most, one way or the other, coming out of the Solidarity movement. Detailed results are presented in table 2.

But this was, apparently, the last victory of the *pospolite ruszenie* (in this context one should also note a turnout of 42.1%—20 percentage points lower than on June 4, 1989). For the last time, the majority of politically aware Poles came out to vote, united by the common understanding of who the "enemy" was. But in these elections, beneath the cover of unity, future splits and divisions already simmered. In several areas, they even rose to the surface. Most noteworthy was the case of the city of Łódź, where two Civic Committees, Provincial Civic Committee (WKO) and Łódź Civic Alliance (ŁPO) fought against each other mercilessly. Both groups had sprung from the Solidarity movement; each included very prominent members of the old opposition. It would be difficult to say how they differed from each other as far as their programs (particularly municipal policies) were concerned. But, apart from personal animosities, there was also an ideological dimension to this split. The ŁPO accused its foes of being "leftists," "pinkos"; the WKO answered with labels of "nationalists"[4] and "populists." In May 1990 in Łódź, the ŁPO won; out of 80 seats it collected 50, while the WKO obtained 24, and the postcommunist SdRP only 6.

Shortly after the municipal elections, the Łódź split within Solidarity was duplicated on the national level. Before the presidential elections, two major political movements emerged: the Center Alliance (Polish acronym PC) and the Civic Movement-Democratic Action (known as ROAD). PC labeled ROAD leftist, but itself preferred to be identified as the center rather as the right. ROAD tried to escape the undesired label, saying that

---

4. This word has in Polish, unlike in English, quite a strongly negative connotation, though not so strong as the term "chauvinism."

it was not left of center, but west of the Center Alliance. Again, their respective programs and policies did not differ much. Differences were rather in the personalities of leaders, some general slogans (a very catchy "acceleration" by PC), and labels. The most spectacular distinction between the two was in their perception of Lech Wałęsa: PC orchestrated his bid for the presidency, while ROAD, fearing Wałęsa's alleged authoritarianism, persuaded Tadeusz Mazowiecki to run against him.

4

The first round of the presidential election—the first presidential election by popular vote in Poland's history—took place on November 25, 1990. Altogether six politicians managed to collect more than 100,000 signatures in support of their candidacy; they were:

- Roman Bartoszcze, the leader of the Polish Peasant Party;
- Włodzimierz Cimoszewicz, the leader of a major postcommunist faction in the Sejm;
- Tadeusz Mazowiecki, since August 1989 the prime minister of the Solidarity-led government;
- Leszek Moczulski, the leader of KPN—an anticommunist and anti-Soviet political party;
- Stanisław Tymiński, a previously unknown businessman from Toronto, Canada, and Iquitos, Peru, still holding his Polish citizenship;
- Lech Wałęsa, the chairman of Solidarity.

The election was preceded by a short, vigorous, and somewhat clumsy campaign. The abovementioned labels and stereotypes were often used and abused. Not only these labels: Stanisław Tymiński called Mazowiecki "a traitor of the nation," and himself was in turn labeled and libeled in various ways by Mazowiecki's and Wałęsa's supporters. The negative campaigning, used for the first time in Poland on such a massive scale, probably influenced substantially the outcome of the voting. The official results, as published by the State Electoral Commission are listed in table 3.[5]

---

5. *Wyniki wyborów prezydenta Rzeczypospolitej Polskiej* (Results of the elections for the president of the Republic of Poland) (Warsaw: National Electoral Commission, 1990).

The turnout was 60.6% of eligible voters. The same source shows the results broken down by place of residence, shown in table 4.

On election day, an exit poll was conducted in a joint effort by the German INFAS and Polish OBOP public opinion polling centers. From this (unpublished) source, the most representative of all available (10,494 respondents), came the data shown in tables 5, 6, and 7.

To sum up these tables, one may note that out of the three top finishers, Mazowiecki did particularly well among urban professionals, Tymiński among young people with vocational education living outside of big cities, and Wałęsa among the less educated and older. Similar conclusions may be drawn from primary results of various pre- and post-electoral surveys and studies. Many analyses focused on the so-called Tymiński phenomenon. The researchers tried to explain how it was possible that a "man from nowhere" gained enough support within a couple of months to collect almost one-fourth of the popular vote and, above all, to eliminate Tadeusz Mazowiecki, the prime minister of the first noncommunist government in Eastern Europe, from the presidential race. Leaving the full presentation of my views for another occasion, I would like to mention here only that the Tymiński phenomenon is not entirely new. Looking at the data aggregated on the voivodship (province) level, one may note that votes for Tymiński came from the same areas that were reluctant to boycott the quasi-elections of 1984 and 1985, that more often voted against the Solidarity candidates in the 1989 senate elections, and that more often voted for the National List (composed of communist and pro-communist candidates) in the 1989 Sejm elections.

Tymiński, who from a certain point on was perceived as the only serious challenger to the Solidarity candidates, Wałęsa and Mazowiecki, obviously collected many anti-Solidarity votes. These often came from milieus that were traditionally hostile to Solidarity. What is really new (and requires more elaborate analysis), is the overrepresentation in Tymiński's electorate of young manual and nonmanual workers.

A different kind of overrepresentation may be found in Mazowiecki's electorate. Well-educated urban dwellers were the core of his support. This seems to be a genuinely new phenomenon. Throughout the 1980s, as indicated earlier, one could not point out real political cleavages in terms of status groups or classes. Mazowiecki's electorate, on the other hand, can be very well defined in these terms.

Wałęsa's electorate, apart from overrepresentation of the less educated and older, in general reflected the heterogeneity of Polish society. One should stress at this point that the above generalizations oversimplify the reality; in fact, each of these groups (Wałęsa's, Tymiński's, and Mazowiecki's supporters) was heterogeneous, both sociologically and politically. Among Wałęsa's supporters are liberals seeking a quicker privatization and populists looking for a more protective state. Tymiński's electorate seems to be the most frustrated of all, but this frustration comes either from the belief that the political and economic change has been too fast or too slow. Mazowiecki's supporters were, among others, veterans of the Solidarity underground and ex-communists voting to stop Wałęsa. In short, a map showing electorates of all six candidates located in the socio-political space may be drawn as in table 8.

Mazowiecki's defeat and Tymiński's rise from a nobody to a major contender came as a shock. Also, Wałęsa's 40% of the popular vote, achieved out of a 60.6% turnout, was for many of his supporters—as well as for himself—a most unpleasant surprise. The people of Solidarity, divided into the Mazowiecki and Wałęsa camps, realized suddenly that in a democratic process there is room for outsiders, political gurus, and false prophets; that nobody gets popular support forever and unconditionally; that the winners of yesterday may become losers tomorrow. No wonder that the *pospolite ruszenie* struck again: in the runoff round, Wałęsa collected 74.3% of the vote and Tymiński 25.7%, with a turnout of 53.4%. This means that some 40% of Poland's population voted for Wałęsa in the runoff—almost exactly as much as had supported Solidarity's candidates in the 1989 parliamentary elections.

5

In the runoff round of the presidential election, the pro-Solidarity voters reunited, but there was no reconciliation of Solidarity elites. In fact, the presidential election marked the end of the Solidarity era and the beginning of a new, post-Solidarity chapter in Poland's history. Tadeusz Mazowiecki (who immediately after the election resigned from his prime minister's post) managed, not without difficulty, to unify two major supporting groupings: ROAD and the Forum of the Democratic Right (FPD) and his individual followers into a new political party—the Democratic Union (UD).

Similar progress did not occur in the other post-Solidarity camp, a loose coalition of Wałęsa's devoted followers, Mazowiecki's political opponents, ambitious politicians hoping to manipulate Wałęsa after the elections, and opportunists hoping to be awarded government positions for their loyalty to the newly elected president. Shortly after his inauguration, Wałęsa nominated Jarosław Kaczyński, the leader of the Center Alliance (PC), as his chief of staff (official term: chief of the president's chancellory). Along with Kaczyński, several other Center Alliance activists obtained positions in the president's office. But Wałęsa's choice for prime minister was Jan Krzysztof Bielecki, a leader of another pro-Wałęsa party, the tiny Liberal-Democratic Congress (KLD). He included in his cabinet only two members of the PC, and four of his own party. Moreover, he retained Mazowiecki's Foreign Minister, Krzysztof Skubiszewski, and Deputy Prime Minister/Minister of Finance Leszek Balcerowicz. Both had been objects of violent attacks, Balcerowicz in particular, by some of Wałęsa's supporters during the campaign, and Balcerowicz symbolized for the public all the negative aspects of the pro-free market policies. The government that many had expected to be one of "acceleration" would, in fact, continue the major policies of its predecessor. From early 1991 on, politics in Poland were marked by the ongoing rivalry of the president's chancellory staff and the cabinet. The former were hoping that the Center Alliance could become the presidential party, but Wałęsa preferred to present himself as (and honestly wanted to be) the president of all Poles.

The problem was, however, that all Poles were not happy with their president. As early as February 1991, public opinion polls indicated a significant decline in Wałęsa's popularity—the boomerang effect of undeliverable promises.[6] But there was somebody else to blame for preventing the acceleration from materializing: the relict of the *ancien régime*, the contractual Parliament, the Sejm, with its 65% majority of communist nominees. Wałęsa himself, once elected president, could have come

---

6. For instance, a poll co-authored by Krzysztof Jasiewicz, R. Markowski, and T. Żukowski, conducted by OBOP (unpublished).

to terms with this fossil, but his supporters, already divided and frustrated, pressed strongly for new parliamentary elections. There was some obstruction on the part of the postcommunist deputies, but everybody in Poland understood that the Parliament was, in fact, obsolete and the elections unavoidable.

The elections to both houses of the Polish Parliament, the Sejm and the Senate, took place on October 27, 1991, with a turnout of 43.2%. The Sejm was elected on the basis of a proportional representation voting system, with 391 seats awarded in 7- to 17-member districts, and 69 seats distributed on a nationwide basis to the parties with the strongest electoral showing. For the Senate, a strikingly different system was adopted, a version of the plurality system: first-past-the-post in two- (or three-) member constituencies (so a "first-two-or-three-past-the-post" variant). In the elections to the Sejm, 111 parties, groupings, and organizations participated; 27 of them managed to register their national lists. The results are presented in table 9; the results of the Senate elections are presented in table 10.

In October 1991, two opposite electoral systems produced the same results: deeply fragmented houses of Parliament. The current distribution of seats is slightly different, due to some mergers and secessions, but the major actors remain the same. Following are their characteristics in brief.

The post-Solidarity organizations consist of:

1. The Democratic Union (Unia Demokratyczna or UD). The party of Tadeusz Mazowiecki and several other very able and popular leaders: Jacek Kuroń (a veteran of the anticommunist opposition, the founder of KOR—Committee for the Defense of the Workers), Bronisław Geremek (a historian, in 1989–1990 the chairman of the OKP—Solidarity's parliamentary representation), Aleksander Hall, Zofia Kuratowska, Władysław Frasyniuk. Ideologically, the party represents a very broad spectrum: from modern, liberal right to West European-style social democracy. Its hopes of becoming the political representation of all pro-reform forces were not fulfilled; the party, a clear front-runner in the pre-election polls, barely accomplished a plurality of the popular vote (its 1.4 million votes equalled only 47% of the 3 million collected by Mazowiecki in the 1990 presidential race). This defeat was most likely due to the party's firm commitment to austerity policies. But some analysts suggest that the Democratic Union, being a coalition of moderate leftist, moderate rightist, and centrist groupings,

lacks a high ideological profile.[7] In public opinion polls, people speak of the Union favorably; in the election booth they may prefer a party with a clearer ideological stand.

2. Catholic Electoral Action (Wyborcza Akcja Katolicka, or WAK). This was the name used in these elections by the Christian-National Union (ZChN). The party represents Roman Catholic fundamentalism and a moderate version of traditional Polish nationalism. Its representation in the 1989–1991 Sejm (Stefan Niesiołowski, Jan Łopuszański, Marek Jurek) became notorious for advocacy of extreme anti-abortion legislation. The party was semi-officially endorsed by the Roman Catholic Church (there was intensive campaigning during services in the churches), which gave it relatively strong support in rural areas.

3. Civic Alliance "Center" (Porozumienie Obywatelskie Centrum, or POC). A structure composed of the Center Alliance and the remnants of the Civic Committees was hoping to lead a broader coalition of Solidarity forces and become a presidential party. It failed to gain Wałęsa's endorsement (and its leaders lost their jobs in the president's chancellory). Despite this setback and an unimpressive performance in the elections, Jarosław Kaczyński was a central figure of the coalition-building process, and another leader of the party, Jan Olszewski, overcame Wałęsa's resistance and eventually gained the post of prime minister in December 1991.

4. The Liberal-Democratic Congress (Kongres Liberalno-Demokratyczny, or KLD). The party of former Prime Minister Bielecki was—along with the Democratic Union—the only one to advocate continuation of anti-inflationary, free market-oriented policies.

5. The Agrarian Alliance (Porozumienie Ludowe, or PL). A loose coalition of post-Solidarity peasant groupings.

6. Solidarity. The trade union decided to acquire its own representation in the Parliament, declaring, however, that it would not join any coalition, but rather play a role of a pro-employee pressure group.

The postcommunist organizations are:

1. The Alliance of the Democratic Left (Sojusz Lewicy Demokratycznej, or SLD). The coalition of the post-Polish United Workers Party forces. Its main component is the Social Democracy of the Republic of Poland (Socjaldemokracja Rzeczypospolitej

---

7. See, for example, Maria Zakrzewski, a psychologist, in *Gazeta Wyborcza*, Nov. 29, 1991; and Jan Walc in *Życie Warszawy*, Dec. 5, 1991.

Polskiej, or SdRP), the direct successor of the PUWP (the leaders are Aleksander Kwaśniewski and Leszek Miller), joined by the postcommunist trade unions (OPZZ), and some independent former PUWP members (such as 1990 presidential candidate Włodzimierz Cimoszewicz). Finishing a strong second, the SLD created an impression of a successful communist resurgence and prompted considerable concern in Poland and abroad. But one should note that the postcommunists did not collect more votes in these election than Cimoszewicz did a year earlier (approximately 5% of eligible voters). Their constituency, composed of the former nomenklatura and other beneficiaries of the *ancien régime*, seems stable over time, at the abovementioned 5% level (no more than 1.5 million individuals).

2. The Polish Peasant Party (Polskie Stronnictwo Ludowe, or PSL). A reformed version of the United Peasant Party (ZSL), a loyal communist ally in the 1947–1989 period, now claiming the legacy of the 1944–1947 PSL, the only political opposition to the communists at that time.

Other organizations include:

1. The Confederation for an Independent Poland (Konfederacja Polski Niepodległej, or KPN). This non-Solidarity opposition party, organized in the late 1970s, scored a major electoral victory. Within a year, it more than doubled its constituency, from less than half a million (a mere 2.5% of the votes) collected by its leader, Leszek Moczulski, in the presidential race, to almost a million. The KPN organized its campaign along two seemingly mutually exclusive slogans: strong anticommunism and a call for protection of workers employed in state-owned enterprises facing bankruptcy due to privatization and free market policies.

2. The Beer Lovers Party (Polska Partia Przyjaciół Piwa, or PPPP). A joke that got out of hand—a party organized by a few comedians and journalists as an antidote to a grim economic situation and serious politicians apparently caught up with the anti-establishment mood of the public. The party's campaign was financed in part by a group of business people in exchange for placing them on the ballot. They also proved to be too serious and, once elected, formed a separate parliamentary faction, the Polish Economic Program (Polski Program Gospodarczy, or PPG).

3. One should also mention here Party X, organized by Tymiński after his defeat in the runoff of the presidential election. Party X was prevented from registering nationwide because in some

districts it allegedly presented forged signatures of supporters, and eventually competed in only four districts, winning three seats in the Sejm and none in the Senate.

Is there any way to make some sense of this swarm of parties, groupings, and organizations? The often-used traditional left-right dimension does not really seem relevant here, even in the parties' own perceptions. When they were asked where they actually wanted to sit in the house, the Alliance of the Democratic Left indicated the left side, the Christian-National Union the right—and all the others insisted on being seated in the center! Alliances in the Sejm are formed on an ad hoc basis, depending on the issue in question. This situation reflects the attitudes of parties' constituencies: they may be close to each other on one issue, and poles apart on another. Data collected in a recent study of electoral behavior[8] suggest that there are at least four major dimensions of the differentiation of political opinions and beliefs: nationalism vs. occidentalism (pro-Western or "cosmopolitan" orientation); authoritarianism vs. parliamentarian democracy; secularism vs. religiosity; and state protectionism vs. free market orientation. Where do the constituencies of the ten major parties stand on each of these dimensions?

Nationalism vs. occidentalism. This dimension represents opinions about the place of Poland in Europe; views of whether Western countries are a desirable model for Poland's political and economic systems; and attitudes toward other nations, foreign capital, and ethnic minorities. The nationalistic end of this continuum is occupied by the supporters of the Polish Peasant Party, the Christian-National Union, and the Confederation for an Independent Poland; the center by those voting for Solidarity and the Alliance of the Democratic Left; the pro-Western end by the supporters of the Democratic Union and the Liberal-Democratic Congress. The supporters of the Center Alliance, the Agrarian Alliance, and the Beer Lovers Party present fairly inconsistent views in this respect, with the former two leaning rather toward the nationalistic end, the latter toward the occidental one.

---

8. Unpublished panel study, conducted in October and December 1991 by the Division of Electoral Studies of the Polish Academy of Sciences' Institute of Political Studies.

Authoritarianism vs. parliamentary democracy. The question of whether Poland should adopt a presidential or a parliamentary model of democracy has been hotly debated, but the positions of the various parties reflect not only their general views on this issue but also their more fundamental pro- or anti-authoritarian sentiments on the one hand, and their attitudes toward the incumbent president, Lech Wałęsa, on the other. Constituencies of the parties that in the more or less recent past had opposed Wałęsa (the Democratic Union and the Alliance of the Democratic Left) tend to speak in favor of parliamentary democracy and a system of checks and balances; others are more willing to accept the rule of a strong leader, and even—in the case of the Christian-National Union and the Center Alliance—grant him the right to suspend civil rights when law and order are endangered.

Secularism vs. religiosity. The contribution of the Roman Catholic Church in Poland to the defeat of communism can hardly be overestimated, but presently many of its former allies and even scores of lay Catholics are critical of the Church for forcing its own political and social agenda in times of reform and reconstruction. The controversies concerning the right to abortion or religious instruction in public schools deeply divide the public. Even if the majority (up to 80%, depending on the specific issue) of Polish society speaks in favor of a secular and not a confessional state, and rejects Church intervention in private and public affairs, there is still a vocal and militant minority supporting the opposite point of view. On the continuum from religiosity to secularism, the extreme confessional position is occupied by the constituency of the Christian-National Union, followed by the moderate religiosity of the Agrarian Alliance; in the center one can find supporters of the trade union Solidarity, the Polish Peasant Party, the Center Alliance, and those who did not vote in the parliamentary elections. A moderate secularism is represented by constituencies of the Confederation for an Independent Poland, the Democratic Union, and the Liberal-Democratic Congress; at the secular end of this continuum are those who voted for the Alliance of the Democratic Left and the Beer Lovers Party.

State protectionism vs. free market orientation. In the cited study, 66% of respondents expressed a negative opinion about the economic dimension of the changes occurring in Poland since 1989. Almost exactly the same number—62%—said they prefer high prices and shops full of goods (the present situation) to low prices accompanied by short supplies and long lines (the pre-1989 condition). This ambivalence was reflected in the electoral campaign and voting behavior: the parties promising easy and quick solutions and critical of the Balcerowicz plan lured more voters. When asked to indicate a desired general model of the economy—free market/free enterprise, allowing for both great fortunes and unemployment, with the state playing only the role of the guardian of law, or a centrally run economy, with the state preventing the emergence of overly rich and overly poor people—the respondents were divided almost exactly fifty-fifty. As far as the constituencies of the major parties are concerned, none represents a genuinely centrist (close to the mean or median in the whole sample) point of view; also none could be described as extremely pro-protectionist. Parties' constituencies are clustered in three groups, moderate pro-protectionists (the Polish Peasant Party, the Alliance of the Democratic Left, the Christian-National Union, and those who did not vote), moderate proponents of a free market (Solidarity, the Confederation for an Independent Poland, the Agrarian Alliance, and the Democratic Union), and extreme supporters of a neo-liberal, free market/free enterprise model (the Liberal Democratic Congress and the Beer Lovers—the latter perhaps inspired by permanent shortages of beer in Polish shops under the communist command economy). Noteworthy is the anti-free market position of nonvoters (almost 60% of the adult population). Their apathetic behavior should be perceived by the advocates of capitalism in Poland as a blessing: had they decided to vote, the protectionist faction in the Parliament could have been much stronger.

There are practically no correlations between the above-described four dimensions; knowing a given party constituency's position on one hardly helps us predict its location on another. To reduce this complex picture to a single-dimensional one (left-right, or along any other lines) would be an oversimplification. For the present fragmentation of the Polish Parliament, neither a bad electoral law (which could have been better) nor inexperienced party leaders (who could have acted more wisely) should be blamed. This fragmentation reflects the state of mind of the public: lost and confused, facing so many choices and so few constants. After its most spectacular victory, the time of the *pospolite ruszenie* is over—no more is there an alien enemy within the borders of the Commonwealth. The old Commonwealth of Two Nations experienced times of glory and times of shame, times of unity and times of anarchy. It is still a new beginning now; whether it leads to glory or to shame, to unity or to anarchy, remains to be seen.

Table 1
Confidence in Political Personalities and Institutions[1]

Person/ Institution	1984	1985	1987	Spring 1988	Spring 1989	Autumn 1989	Summer 1990
W. Jaruzelski	.21	.51	.39	.39	−.01	.25	−.09
L. Wałęsa	.04	−.03	−.09	−.01	.68	.67	.49
M. Rakowski	−.27	−.07	−.28	−.28	−.03	−.64	—
T. Mazowiecki	—	—	—	—	—	.78	.64
Church	.65	.72	.65	.74	.66	.58	.59
Sejm	.31	.49	.45	.37	.13	.58	.45
Army	.39	.46	.42	.44	.19	.16	.41
Government	.17	.39	.26	.26	−.12	.61	.47
PUWP[2]	−.08	.12	−.08	−.17	−.48	−.76	—
OPZZ[3]	−.19	.22	−.02	.00	−.20	−.29	−.26
Solidarity	−.52	−.55	−.23	−.46	.58	.61	.45

[1]Coefficients vary from −1 to +1. For details see *Polacy '88.*
[2]Polish United Workers Party.
[3]Pro-Communist trade unions.

Sources: Władysław Adamski, Krzysztof Jasiewicz, and Andrzej Rychard, eds., *Polacy '84: Dynamika konfliktu i konsensusu* (Poles '84: Dynamics of conflict and consensus) (Warsaw: IFiS, 1986); idem, *Polacy '88: Dynamika konfliktu a szanse reform* (Poles '88: Dynamics of conflict and the chances for reform) (Warsaw: IFiS, 1989); and unpublished data from the author's 1989 and 1990 surveys.

Table 2
Results of May 27, 1990 Municipal Elections

Organization/ Coalition	Percent of Seats Won in Districts:		
	Single-Seat	Multi-Seat	Total
PSL (Polish Peasant Party)	6.3	.7	5.8
Tenants' committees	1.0	2.1	1.1
Civic Committees Solidarity	38.2	74.0	41.5
Solidarity of private farmers	3.6	0.2	3.2
Independent candidates	43.2	2.2	39.5
Solidarity (the trade union)	1.2	4.0	1.4

Source: Election Commissioner-General's Computer Service; organizations and coalitions that won less than 1% of total of seats omitted.

Table 3
Official Results of the 1990 Presidential Elections, Round I

Roman Bartoszcze	7.2%
Włodzimierz Cimoszewicz	9.2%
Tadeusz Mazowiecki	18.1%
Leszek Moczulski	2.5%
Stanisław Tymiński	23.1%
Lech Wałęsa	40.0%

Table 4
Results of 1990 Presidential Election, Round I, by Place of Residence of Voters (Percent)

	Bartoszcze	Cimoszewicz	Mazowiecki	Moczulski	Tymiński	Wałęsa	Total
Rural communes	17.1	7.4	7.4	2.3	24.2	41.7	100.0
Integrated communes (town + rural area)	8.9	9.3	15.2	2.6	27.3	36.8	100.0
Towns to 10,000 inhabitants	2.6	9.4	21.8	2.8	26.8	36.7	100.0
Towns of 10,000–20,000 inhabitants	3.1	10.8	18.0	2.5	25.3	40.3	100.0
Towns of 20,000–50,000 inhabitants	2.1	11.3	20.0	2.5	25.9	38.1	100.0
Cities of 50,000–100,000 inhabitants	1.8	11.1	20.5	2.9	26.1	37.6	100.0
Warsaw	1.1	10.0	27.8	1.5	10.7	48.9	100.0
Voters from abroad	1.7	3.8	36.6	2.5	10.7	44.9	100.0

Table 5
Results of 1990 Presidential Election, Round I, by Gender of Voters (Percent)

	Bartoszcze	Cimoszewicz	Mazowiecki	Moczulski	Tymiński	Wałęsa	Total
Men	7.6	7.1	18.6	3.0	23.5	39.8	100.0
Women	5.0	9.7	23.3	2.1	23.1	36.5	100.0

Table 6
Results of 1990 Presidential Election, Round I,
by Age of Voters (Percent)

	Bartoszcze	Cimoszewicz	Mazowiecki	Moczulski	Tymiński	Wałęsa	Total
18–25 years	5.9	7.5	20.8	3.2	31.2	31.2	100.0
26–45 years	5.6	8.7	20.1	2.9	27.0	34.4	100.0
46–60 years	5.8	8.8	21.9	2.0	16.5	44.8	100.0
61 years and older	7.5	6.8	21.6	1.7	7.4	54.7	100.0

Table 7
Results of 1990 Presidential Election, Round I,
by Education Level of Voters (Percent)

	Bartoszcze	Cimoszewicz	Mazowiecki	Moczulski	Tymiński	Wałęsa	Total
Primary	12.5	5.6	10.5	3.2	20.3	47.6	100.0
Vocational	7.2	6.0	12.2	2.6	31.3	40.5	100.0
Secondary	4.5	9.5	22.7	2.4	24.3	36.4	100.0
College	2.8	12.4	39.7	2.4	13.2	29.4	100.0

Table 8
Affiliations of Polish Electorate

```
                         Mazowiecki
                          (high)
            Moczulski       U
                            R
                            B
                            A
                            N
   Wałęsa (pro)-----S O L I D A R I T Y------(anti) Tymiński
                            Z
                            A
                            T        Cimoszewicz
                            I
                            O
                            N
                          (low)
                        Bartoszcze
```

Table 9
Results of October 27, 1991 Elections to the Sejm

Party	Votes Number	Percent of:		Seats	
		Valid Votes	Eligible Voters	Number	Percent
UD	1,382,051	12.32	5.02	62	13.48
SLD	1,344,820	11.99	4.89	60	13.04
KPN	996,182	8.88	3.62	51	11.09
PSL	1,033,885	9.22	3.76	50	10.87
WAK	1,007,890	8.98	3.66	50	10.87
POC	977,344	8.71	3.55	44	9.57
KLD	839,978	7.49	3.05	37	8.04
PL	613,626	5.47	2.23	28	6.09
Solidarity	566,553	5.05	2.06	27	5.87
PPPP	367,106	3.27	1.33	16	3.48
Other				35	7.61

Table 10
Results of October 27, 1991 Elections to the Senate

Party	Number of Seats*
Democratic Union (UD)	21
Solidarity	11
Civic Alliance "Center" (POC)	9
Catholic Electoral Action (WAK)	9
Polish Peasant Party (PSL)	7
Liberal-Democratic Congress (KLD)	6
Agrarian Alliance (PL)	5
Alliance of the Democratic Left (SLD)	4
Confederation for an Independent Poland (KPN)	4
Other parties and independents	24

*Since the districts in the Senate elections were based on geography (provinces), not population, the distribution of votes is omitted as not relevant.

7

Privatization Versus Group Interests of the Working Class and Bureaucracy: The Case of Poland
WŁADYSŁAW ADAMSKI

■ *The Problem*

The issue of privatization as a remedy for the inefficiency of the state-run economy was analyzed in 1988, and then reanalyzed in 1991, in a research project on social conflict and systemic change conducted by the Institute of Philosophy and Sociology.[1] Three factors in particular that are important characteristics of the periods under research and that may have influenced Poles' attitudes towards privatization are (1) the collapse of the political structure of the one-party system and the consequent emergence of unrestricted possibilities of group interest articulation; (2) the stagnation or decrease in the level of consumption (affecting the majority of households), accompanied by increased feelings of social insecurity, connected mainly with the prospect of mass unemployment; and (3) the persistence of the old economic structures in which the state still preserves its position as the super owner, unable to surrender its responsibility for the employees' living standards.

We have assumed that these features of the transition period should have affected the attitudes of employees in the state-run sector as well as their awareness of their group inter-

---

1. The following research reports constitute the empirical background of this paper: Władysław Adamski, Krzysztof Jasiewicz, Lena Kolarska-Bobińska, Andrzej Rychard, and Edmund Wnuk-Lipiński, *Polacy '88: Dynamika konfliktu a szanse reform* (Poles '88: Dynamics of conflict and the chances for reform) (Warsaw: Warsaw University Political Science Department, 1989); Władysław Adamski, Andrzej Rychard, and Edmund Wnuk-Lipiński, eds., *Polacy '90: Konflikty i zmiana* (Poles '90: Conflicts and change) (Warsaw: Institute of Philosophy and Sociology, Institute of Political Studies, Polish Academy of Sciences, 1991).

ests. Such an effect might be observed not only in the level of approval of the market economy, but also in opinions as to how this goal should be achieved. The essential differences in interests and preferences in this respect would come to light, we assumed, when the necessity and real possibility of finding a proprietor for the formerly "socialized" enterprises became obvious; the awareness of this necessity of choice has been quite widespread among Poles. The true dilemma facing employees in the state-run sector concerns mainly the forms and scope of the envisaged privatization. The crucial question is whether state property should be replaced by exclusively private or mixed ownership, or whether it should be protected from any kind of privatization at all.

The research results allow us to indicate the vectors of the prevailing preferences in this field, as well as the social differentiation of these preferences. A working hypothesis of the analysis presented here posits that under the pressure of a prolonged economic crisis, the level of approval or disapproval of privatization revealed by individuals or social groups depends mainly on how the privatization process is perceived: either it is an existential threat to a particular social group's interests or it is a chance to improve the group's living standards and social status.

■ Continuity and Change in Societal Attitudes from 1988 to 1990

Our 1990 research results point to a strong differentiation in attitudes towards privatization, which is especially pronounced on the issue of which sections of the economy should be privatized. The most important fact about attitudes toward privatization revealed by the research seems to be that the extreme solutions, i.e., both unrestricted privatization and maintenance of state-controlled property intact, gain the least support. Thus, a mixed model of ownership that allows access to private property within a certain range gains the strongest support.

The expansion of private property receives unconditional societal consent only when it applies to commerce and state farms. In the case of farm service and ownership of press and publishing firms, societal preferences concerning limited and unlimited privatization are balanced. As for the remaining sections of the economy, the majority of Poles are in favor of limited privatization. This refers not only to these kinds of service whose "welfare" status is clearly established, such as hospitals, building maintenance, and municipal transportation, but also primarily to, the basic productive structure—large industrial enterprises. What deserves special attention is that, statistically speaking, one out of every two Poles declares his/her support for the limited privatization (under social control) of large industry, while only every eighth one supports its unlimited privatization.

Opposition to any kind of privatization, or, in other words, support for preserving the monopoly of the state, is strongest in the case of hospital health services (nearly 50% of the answers) and city transportation. The number of defenders of state-owned property in the sphere of material production is also considerable: nearly one-fourth of all respondents were definitely opposed to the privatization of large factories.

New ways of interpreting the results from 1990 become apparent when we try to compare them with corresponding data from 1988. The percentage of adherents of unlimited privatization doubled in reference to such institutions of public life as the press, publishing firms, and banks. A certain growth of support for unrestricted expansion of private property was also marked in the sphere of farm service and municipal transportation. But support for unlimited privatization in industry, housing construction, and hospital health service remained almost unchanged. Moreover, between 1988 and 1990, the consent to unrestricted privatization of residential buildings owned by the state, cooperatives, or municipal authorities decreased considerably.

However, approval for limited privatization, as opposed to its unrestricted form, shows more impressive dynamics of growth. Such growth was strongest in regard to banking and large industrial enterprises, but also, to a lesser extent, in regard to hospital management, the press, publishing firms, building maintenance, and farm service. As these data show, the prevailing tendency is a growing social approval of limited rather than extreme privatization in the Polish economy.

In spite of still remarkable levels of opposition toward any privatization, the level of social disapproval of any form of privatization has become weaker in reference to sections of the economy discussed above. It is also important that the relatively sharpest decrease in the disapproval of privatization concerns such important sectors as banking (26% decrease) and large industrial plants (16.8%).

■ Social Background and Attitudes Toward Privatization

The social status of our respondents usually reveals strong links with their perceptions of privatization. These links are illustrated by coefficients of correlation mentioned in table 1 (at the end of this chapter). The correlations found in 1990 differ radically from those of 1988. While in 1988, favorable or negative attitudes towards privatization were associated first of all with union affiliation (Solidarity as opposed to branch trade unions) and party membership, now they depend mostly on socio-demographic characteristics and income. The approval of privatization goes up quite clearly together with the level of education and the family's monthly income and positive perception of change in material standard within the last two years. Support for privatization is more often expressed by men than women and, independently of sex, by young rather than old people.

Although the preferences under discussion are weakly influenced by union membership, it should not be overlooked that affiliation with Solidarity usually inclines one toward privatization, while membership in the branch trade unions (OPZZ) is concurrent with the opposite orientation. Yet it seems also worth noting that a declared membership in the former Communist Party or other parties subordinated to it, or lack of links with any party, does not reveal statistically important interdependence with any particular preference towards privatization. These findings may be associated with the difference in background between Solidarity members (who as a rule are younger, more educated and not linked with positions of bureaucratic power at the enterprise level) and branch trade union members. The lack of correlation between privatization preferences and former PC membership could be explained mostly by the relatively higher education of the former Communists.

It should be underlined that the influence of a respondent's educational level is visible mainly in the case of extreme orientations, less so in the case of moderate ones. Let us see how this regularity is revealed through the attitude towards privatization of the press and publishing firms. Forty-eight percent of college-educated respondents and 22% of those with elementary education are in favor of unlimited privatization of this sector: 6.6% and 20.6%, respectively, are against any form of privatization. However, the moderate variant of privatization of the press is considerably supported by both groups: 28.9% and 42.1% respectively.

The differentiation of preferences regarding private versus state ownership in industry is also important. Here there are more significant conclusions: only 6.9% of persons with elementary education are in favor of unlimited privatization, while among college graduates the level is 19.7%. The opponents of any privatization in industry total 27.7% of the lowest educational category and 18.4% of the highest one. The preferences for limited privatization in industry reveal the same regularity: 40% of the people with elementary education and 59.2% of college graduates are in favor of limited privatization in this case.

Educational level differentiates Poles' attitudes towards privatization most strongly in the case of state farms. In comparison with the press and, especially, industry, the possibility of privatization of state farm gains the relatively strongest societal support and faces the weakest opposition. However, the adherents as well as opponents of extreme variants of privatization of state farms are highly differentiated. Exactly two-thirds of the most highly educated group fully approve of unlimited privatization of state farms, while only 32% in the group with elementary education do so. Only 5% of the former group and 18% of the latter are against privatization of land property. The middle-of-the-road solution, i.e., limited privatization, is chosen by 22% of college graduate respondents and 27% of those with elementary education.

In comparison, the attitudes towards privatization of industry, especially large industrial enterprises, are less dependent on the level of education. The scale of opposition to unlimited privatization of large industry seems to be a problem of great social importance that requires deeper analysis.

■ Social and Occupational Status and Union Membership

In considering societal consent to privatization of industry, we assign a special role to skilled workers and college-educated specialists. Against a background of other large social groups, blue-collar workers and specialists are conspicuous for their relatively stronger support for the idea of privatization of large factories. It should not be ignored, however, that this support concerns mainly the limited form of privatization. It is worth recalling here that these categories of blue-collar workers and specialists were most active during the campaigns of social protest in the 1980s. Maybe now their attitude will also determine the success or failure of the new economic structure. Workers and specialists deserve special attention not only for the reasons that make them favor the moderate variant of privatization in state-controlled industry, but also for the essential differences between them and other occupational groups in their preferences for the future model of Polish industry.

Workers differ from specialists not only in their weaker support for extremely liberal solutions (unlimited privatization), but also in a much stronger attachment to the status quo that can result in the rejection of any kind of privatization at all (see table 2). Workers' attitudes and preferences turn out to be also less liable to change. Whereas in the group of specialists, the approval of unlimited privatization doubled between 1988 and 1990, among workers it weakened slightly within the same period. On the other hand, however, 25.2% of the workers are among the opponents of any privatization, while specialists register less than 20%.

Workers' relatively stronger attachment to socialized property in industry and at the same time their weaker support than among specialists for extremely liberal solutions lead to the hypothesis that this particular social category, unlike specialists, considers this kind of property change as a source of menace rather than a chance to further its social and occupational interests. However, workers' reserve towards the extremely liberal model of privatization ceases to be shocking when compared to the preferences of the peasantry and employees in the nonagricultural private sector.

Contrary to common opinion, Polish peasants turn out to be the most averse to the privatization of industry. Employees in the nonagricultural private sector are not free from this aversion, either. In spite of their relatively strong approval of unlimited privatization, they are more often than others opposed to the introduction of private ownership into socialized factories. What is the origin of such attitudes in the groups in which one should expect the contrary? As far as peasants are concerned, it seems that their attitudes may be caused in part by not unfounded fears that privatization will affect part-time peasants who are full-time workers in state industry and who would be fired first. But the peasants' fears can be also linked with their perception that privatization will result in a rise in prices of industrial products that will directly threaten the very existence of their farms. A similar reserve towards free-market competition in the economy and fear of competition of new economic subjects seem to be felt by quite a number of small business people and employees in the nonagricultural private sector. They have contributed strongly to the appearance of a peculiar "ethos of entrepreneurship" under the influence of both the long-lasting symbiosis with the inefficient state-controlled economy and a kind of protection received through state policy.

The fears and hopes that social and occupational groups tend to attach to the prospect of privatization of large industry reveal new differentiations when examined from the point of view of the employee's part in control over the enterprise. A comparison of those who are in supervisory positions with those who are not (table 3) shows that access to authority substantially affects the preferences under consideration. In general, the managers display a much higher level of fear of privatization in industry than their colleagues in nonmanagerial posts. This regularity occurs most often among white-collar and intermediate workers. Every third manager from these categories is firmly against any kind of privatization. These fears, and most probably also the feeling that their interests are being threatened, are relatively weaker among nonsupervisors. On the other hand, among skilled workers in positions of lower-level supervisors or foremen, the opposition to privatization of large factories is much weaker than among other workers.

Being in a position of authority is also associated with weaker support for the extremely liberal form of privatization. This especially concerns white-collar and intermediate workers (mainly employed in the service sector) and also specialists—the most influential personnel in the structure of authority of an enterprise. The latter, mainly managing directors and other managers, differ from their colleagues in other posts by definitely weaker support for unlimited privatization, as well as by their strongest support for the idea of building a new structure of state-controlled industry that allows private property only within a certain range.

The conclusion of the analysis is that the privileged position of an employee in the authority structure of a socialized enterprise is usually connected with relatively stronger opposition to any changes in ownership of industry and the least readiness to accept unlimited privatization. The opposite regularity is revealed in the category of skilled workers. Those occupying nonsupervisory posts manifest much more unfavorable attitudes towards privatization than those in supervisory posts. With a view to the structure of preferences concerning privatization, the nonmanagerial workers are closer to managers in the category of technicians and specialists than to those who are not in such posts. What these categories have predominantly in common is support for limited privatization.

Another differentiation in the preferences under discussion reflects trade union membership (table 4). What is important here is the uneven influence of union affiliation on attitudes towards privatization. We see for example, a general tendency that, from 1988 on, points to stronger approval of privatization by Solidarity member than by other union members. However, this regularity covers sometimes contrasting patterns of differentiation: (1) among specialists, membership in one or another union only slightly influences the preferences under discussion, while the division between opposition and support for privatization of large industry is sharper between members of any union and those who are not affiliated at all than between members of Solidarity and the branch unions; (2) in both categories of blue-collar workers (skilled and unskilled), and, also to a high degree in the category of intermediate and white-collar workers, Solidarity members and the nonaffiliated show almost the same strength of opposition to privatization, as well much stronger support for its extremely liberal variant than members of the branch unions; (3) a quite opposite pattern is represented by technicians, whose attitudes are strikingly differentiated if we compare Solidarity members with members of other unions and the nonaffiliated. In the former group, almost 9 of every 10 members supported limited privatization, while in the latter only half did.

■ *Public Approval of the State Policy of Privatization*

How deeply rooted are the abovementioned social preferences, especially those concerning privatization of large factories?

Table 5 contains coefficients of convergence between attitudes toward private ownership and the evaluation of the state policy of privatization. These indices show a rather high coherence of the attitudes and preferences under consideration. This coherence is most distinct among those who are definitely against the current policy of privatization and against any possibility of introducing private ownership into state-controlled industry. On the other hand, the correlation between extremely favorable attitudes toward private ownership and strong support for the state policy of privatization is weaker. Bearing this in mind, and also given the fact that the state policy of privatization is opposed by a great number of adherents of limited privatization, it may be assumed that societal support for an extremely liberal strategy of structural changes in Polish industry will be too weak to balance the opposition on the part of firm supporters of socialized property. However, such a prospect may seem rather unlikely if we take into account the fact that on average fewer than one in five Poles is against the state policy of privatization, while the majority support it more or less strongly. This support is particularly strong among specialists and among employees in the nonagricultural private sector. On the other hand, abandonment of the policy of privatization is most often postulated by the peasantry, and next by intermediate workers and by both categories of blue-collar workers.

However, the question of the sphere of authority in the enterprise reveals stronger differentiations of opposition and support in this respect (table 6). Among all employees in the state-controlled economy, the category of specialists in nonsupervisory posts is distinct. Their support for the state policy is similar to that of managers in the nonagricultural private sector. On the other hand, specialists in supervisory posts are clearly more reserved in their support for the policy of privatization, which may be connected with their relatively stronger fears of losing their positions. The strongest opposition to and the weakest support for the policy of privatization turn out to be most characteristic of employees from the lower levels of the bureaucracy, especially managers from the category of intermediate workers employed in state service. Skilled workers as well as technicians and white-collar workers are usually on the middle level of support for privatization. In contrast to the case of specialists, however, being in a position of authority in these categories clearly strengthens this support.

■ Policy Relevance of Attitudes Toward Privatization

In the picture presented above of Poles' attitudes towards privatization, what is of particular relevance in making a prognosis concerning the course of the postsocialist economy?

The following research conclusions are, in the author's opinion, the most important:

1. The liberal orientation, which aims at unrestricted privatization, gains the prevailing support in relation to commerce and state farms. In contrast, support for keeping state property intact prevails only in the case of hospital services. On the other hand, support for limited privatization is predominantly connected to large industry and building maintenance.

2. In spite of a minority base of social support, the liberal orientation (support for unlimited privatization) is losing its opponents and gaining adherents, mainly where the press and the publishing business as well as banking are concerned. However, the number of supporters of unlimited privatization of large enterprises remains at the same low level, although the fraction of those who are against any privatization in this sphere is getting smaller.

3. Such socio-demographic factors as the level of education (the higher the level, the stronger the support) and the age of respondents (the reverse dependence) positively correlate with liberal and moderate attitudes toward privatization. On the other hand, lower than average income and, especially, a respondent's negative estimation of his or her family's material standard during the last two years turn out to be important reasons for reservation or opposition toward privatization.

4. Support for or opposition to privatization of large industrial enterprises on the part of employees in the state-controlled sector turns out to be interdependent mainly with social and occupational status as well as access to positions of authority, and to a lesser degree with membership in Solidarity or other unions. The relatively strongest support for privatization of industry, especially its moderate variant, comes from university graduate specialists and skilled workers. Opposition to any kind of privatization, however, is clearly stronger among those who held positions of authority, i.e., the higher and mid-level bureaucracy.

5. The differentiations of attitudes towards privatization in the Polish economy are of a structural character, meaning that support for or opposition to each of the three orientations— liberal, moderate, and conservative—is determined by existential and statutory group interests rather than by these groups' fundamental ideals and guiding values, which are reflected, for example, in the attitude towards Solidarity or other unions. However, the primacy of group interests must not overshadow the fact that in a situation of stagnation or regression of living standards, these interests in relation to privatization tend to be perceived by state employees in terms of threats rather than opportunities.

Given the picture of preferences presented above, one must look carefully for those social actors who might emerge from the inherited social structure as supporters or rebels vis-à-vis the government strategy of economic restructuring and democratic institution-building.[2] What is, in this respect, specific to the Polish situation is a deep-rooted social conflict that paved the way for the emergence of the Solidarity movement. One can observe in this conflict the social deprivations as well as the aggression of state employees. Their destructive feelings derive mostly from their perception that they are being deprived of privileges and exploited in comparison to the representatives of power. The people in power became the main target for the majority of deprived employees, who transformed their feeling of individual deprivation into the awareness of endangered group interests. What made this process of transformation work was, among other things, the violation of the system's supreme ideological principle, which promised that all goods and desired values would be distributed according to "work and social usefulness." As a result, the Polish working class, embodying in the Solidarity movement its aspirations, demands, and interests, and acting in close alliance with the proletarianized intelligentsia, for the first time revealed the basic contradiction of the totalitarian system.[3]

This alliance was strong enough to effectively prevent the

2. Władysław Adamski, "Aspirations, Interests, Conflicts," in *Sisyphus: Sociological Studies*, vol. 5 (Warsaw: Polish Scientific Publishers, 1989).
3. Stefan Nowak, "Dylematy i antynomie świadomości społecznej drugiej połowy lat osiemdziesiątych" (The dilemmas and antinomies of the social consciousness in the mid- and late-1980s), in *Zaspokajanie potrzeb w warunkach kryzysu* (The satisfying of needs in crisis), ed. Jerzy J. Wiatr (Warsaw: Institute of Sociology, 1986).

Communist Party from exercising its monopoly of power through the 1980s. At the same time, the strength of this alliance disclosed its limits. The ability of the two partners to act as independent agents was mostly practiced in a destructive or negative way. They proved to be effective mostly in boycotting the government's decisions and forcing it to make concessions.[4]

But is there a chance for transforming the alliance into a vehicle for positive action in democratic institutions? What lessons should we draw from this past development of contentious forms of social participation? The best way of approaching this is to look at the strategies of privatization. What we have observed in the policies offered by the postcommunist governments in Poland does not provide a clear picture yet of a strategy for the systemic restructuring of the economy. What is particularly unclear is not only how much privatization we really need in this country, but also at what speed this process should be implemented. The most relevant unanswered question regards the role in this process of those social actors who have contributed to the breakdown of the "really existing" socialism.

It seems that any attempt to solve these problems would require that they be studied in the context of their structural background.[5] In this case, social structure should be defined in the broadest sense, i.e., incorporating both the class divisions and the dominant value orientations as a powerful legacy of state socialism.[6] The prospects for systemic transformation in Poland strongly depend on our diagnosis of the type of social conflict that emerged between Solidarity and the former party-state apparatus. It should not, however, be overlooked that this historical conflict, defined as a clear-cut dichotomy between "us" and "them," tends to be extended to the postcommunist governments.

The main reason for this seems to be the failure of the new governments to absorb the contentious workers into the process of reform. The Polish roundtable negotiations of February-April

---

4. Andrzej Rychard, *Władza i interesy w gospodarce* (Power and interests in the economy) (Warsaw: Warsaw University, 1987).
5. Włodzimierz Wesołowski, and Bohdan Mach, *Systemowe funkcje ruchliwości społecznej* (Systemic functions of social mobility) (Wrocław: Ossolineum, 1989).
6. Edmund Wnuk-Lipiński, "Visions of Society: Differentiations and Inequalities in the Collective Consciousness," in *Sisyphus: Sociological Studies*, vol. 5.

1989, and first and foremost the Solidarity victory of the June 1989 election, definitely seemed to open the door for the further development of these processes. However, the early experience of the new governments brings sufficient evidence that this transition period will involve not only support, but also apathy or even resistance. The latter seems to apply even more strongly to state employees than to the former nomenklatura class.

Another problem in choosing a proper strategy for systemic change arises when we ask ourselves about the role of spontaneous movements as opposed to political action undertaken by those in power.[7] Should we expect this transformation to take place from below or from above? Relying on the Polish experience, one should conclude that the most likely way to achieve effective systemic change is neither from above or below, but rather when both strategies are used.

A real revolution from below took place in Poland in the 1980s. What has happened since? Have the spontaneous movements exhausted their potential? Is it true that these contentious workers should now be considered ridiculous or uncivilized? Should they be disregarded and ignored? We are not entitled to agree with such assessments, even if the alliance between workers and intellectuals has weakened considerably since many Solidarity leaders entered the new emerging political elites. The workers, i.e., those who accomplished the successful revolution in Poland, should not be ignored as a potential force for democratic change. The only problem is how to transform their experience in a protest movement into constructive participation in the process of restructuring basic social institutions. Otherwise, these powerful social forces will either openly oppose or, at the very least, boycott the programs of systemic restructuring.

---

7. See James S. Coleman, Władysław Adamski, Victor Azaria, David L. Featherman, Ettore Gelpi, Melvin L. Kohn, Jadwiga Staniszkis, and Edmund Wnuk-Lipiński, "Challenges to Pluralism and Democracy in Eastern Europe," in *Sisyphus: Sociological Studies*, vol. 7 (Warsaw: IFiS Publishers, 1991).

Table 1
Correlation of Preferences Towards Privatization in Poland and Characteristics of the Respondents' Social Position, 1990
(Pearson r for N = 1862)

Characteristics of Social Position	Approval of Privatization of			
	Large Industrial Enterprises	Trade	Press	State Farms
Education (1 = primary, 5 = higher)	.249	.287	.315	.240
Year of birth	.203	.193	.176	.126
Sex (1 = male 0 = female)	.157	.175	.138	.128
Family's monthly income per number of family members	.154	.169	.158	.141
Estimation of family's economic standard within the last two years (1 = decreased, 2 = not changed, 3 = increased)	.123	.104	.078	.091
Religiousness (1 = believing and church-going, 2 = believing but not going to church, 3 = unbelieving, 4 = other qualification)	.101	.095	.127	.062
Trade union affiliation (1 = Solidarity, 2 = branch)	.074	.039	.075	.083
Party membership in the past (1 = Polish United Workers Party, 2 = United Peasant Party, 3 = Democratic Party, 4 = no party affiliation)	.010	.029	.020	.021

Table 2
Dynamics of Extreme Preferences Towards Privatization in Industry: 1988 in Comparison with 1990

Socio-occupational Categories	Attitude Towards Privatization in Industry	Percentage of Answers in the Research of:		
		1988	1990	Disparity
Specialists	For unrestricted privatization	8.9	18.9	10.1
	Against privatization	43.8	19.6	−24.2
Skilled workers	For unrestricted privatization	15.5	13.6	−1.9
	Against privatization	40.0	25.2	−14.8
Peasantry	For unrestricted privatization	11.0	7.0	−4.0
	Against privatization	34.1	26.4	−7.7
Private, nonagricultural sector employees	For unrestricted privatization	—	24.1	—
	Against privatization	—	20.7	—

Table 3
Attitude Towards Privatization in Industry According to
Socio-occupational Position and Position of Authority

Socio-occupational Categories and Positions		Percentage of Answers			
		For Unrestricted Privatization	For Limited Privatization	Against Privatization	
Specialists	Nonsupervisors	21.7	56.0	17.9	V = 0.188
	Supervisors	12.5	66.1	21.4	
Technicians	Nonsupervisors	15.9	62.3	15.9	V = 0.112
	Supervisors	15.7	53.0	24.1	
White-collar workers	Nonsupervisors	14.6	55.4	15.9	V = 0.210
	Supervisors	0.0	33.3	33.3	
Intermediate workers	Nonsupervisors	13.2	48.2	25.4	V = 0.146
	Supervisors	3.8	42.3	34.6	
Skilled workers	Nonsupervisors	13.0	52.4	25.8	V = 0.079
	Supervisors	18.8	43.8	21.9	

Table 4
Attitude Towards Privatization of Big Industrial Enterprises
According to Socio-occupational Category and Trade Union
Affiliation (N = 1862)

Socio-occupational Categories	Trade-union Affiliation	Percentage of Answers			
		For Unrestricted Privatization	For Limited Privatization	Against Privatization	
Specialists	Solidarity	16.7	70.8	12.5	V = 0.124
	Branch	67.9	64.3	17.9	
	Nonaffiliated	19.8	53.8	22.0	
Technicians	Solidarity	4.3	87.0	4.3	V = 0.195
	Branch	16.7	45.8	33.3	
	Nonaffiliated	17.9	51.2	23.2	
White-collar workers	Solidarity	13.6	63.6	18.2	V = 0.203
	Branch	0.0	66.7	29.6	
	Nonaffiliated	16.0	48.8	15.2	
Intermediate workers	Solidarity	14.3	42.9	21.4	V = 0.094
	Branch	5.6	50.0	22.2	
	Nonaffiliated	11.5	48.7	27.4	
Skilled workers	Solidarity	23.8	48.8	21.4	V = 0.130
	Branch	6.5	62.3	20.8	
	Nonaffiliated	12.5	49.2	27.4	
Unskilled workers	Solidarity	17.2	51.7	24.1	V = 0.136
	Branch	0.0	46.7	20.0	
	Nonaffiliated	10.4	50.6	23.2	

Table 5
Correlation of Preferences Towards Ownership in Industry and the Postulate to Abandon Privatization (in Percent)

Should the Government Abandon Privatization in Industry?	Attitude Towards Private Ownership in Big Industrial Enterprises			
	Not to Allow	Allow, but Within Certain Limits	Allow, Without Any Restrictions	N*
Definitely no	15.1	54.8	25.2	449
Rather no	18.3	59.3	11.8	617
Rather yes	40.2	42.9	4.6	219
Definitely yes	50.4	34.3	5.8	137

Cramer V = 0.259
*Percentages do not total 100; the table does not include the answer "It is difficult to say."

Table 6
Attitude Towards the Government's Privatization Policy vs. the Socio-Occupational Position and Participation in Authority

Socio-occupational Categories and Posts		Percentage of Answers to: Should the Government Abandon Privatization in Industry?			
		Definitely Yes and Rather Yes	Rather No	Definitely No	
Specialists	Nonsupervisors	12.4	27.4	51.2	0.197
	Supervisors	16.3	40.0	40.0	
Technicians	Nonsupervisors	13.7	51.5	16.2	0.215
	Supervisors	16.9	31.3	39.8	
White-collar workers	Nonsupervisors	16.1	36.8	31.0	0.118
	Supervisors	16.7	16.7	41.7	
Intermediate workers	Nonsupervisors	21.2	29.2	28.3	0.136
	Supervisors	31.5	34.6	31.5	
Skilled workers	Nonsupervisors	21.4	37.3	24.9	0.095
	Supervisors	18.7	28.1	28.1	
Private, non-agricultural sector	Nonsupervisors	12.5	34.4	40.6	0.208
	Supervisors	8.0	28.0	52.0	

8

Nationalism, Democracy, and Economic Reform in Czechoslovakia: 1990–1992

MAREK BOGUSZAK

This chapter focuses on the nationalistic tendencies and tensions that occurred in Czechoslovakia from 1990 to 1992, taking into account the associated political, economic, and social correlates and consequences, with particular attention paid to the attitudes of the Czech and Slovak populations. The results presented are based on fully representative empirical surveys and analyses of data compiled by the Association for Independent Social Analysis (AISA) from the beginning of 1990. The aim of this chapter is to bring to light empirical evidence that could serve as a basis for the development of more theoretically well-founded hypotheses concerning the problem of nationalism in the newly emerging democracies in the so-called postcommunist countries of Eastern Europe.

The first section of this chapter gives a brief description of political, social, and economic development in terms of public attitudes. The second section deals with nationalistic attitudes and behaviors themselves and their relation to other political and socioeconomic dispositions. Finally, the third section offers ideas concerning the relation between nationalism and further democratic development in Czechoslovakia.

If the chapter appears to be somewhat open-ended, this stems from the fact that it was written three weeks after the June 5–6, 1992 election, an election that gave rise to a considerably complicated situation in Czechoslovakia in terms of Czech-Slovak relations. At the time the text was completed, the future development in Czechoslovakia was itself very unclear and open-ended as well.

■ Political and Economic Attitudes

The spring of 1990 in Czechoslovakia ended in euphoria as a result of the fall of the totalitarian regime. The election of 1990 was, to a considerable extent, a referendum repudiating the communist past. At the same time, however, it was also a resolute declaration by the majority of the people in favor of the start of a radical economic reform that they thought would bring Czechoslovakia into the community of countries with market economies, that is to say, countries with high living standards and prosperity levels.

Substantially, at this time, support for economic reform was universal, manifested by a political rejection of the communist regime on the one hand and a vision of prosperity on the other. The autumn of 1990, however, had already brought with it the first noteworthy differentiation of opinion regarding economic reform. The inconsistency between the general support for the reform and the readiness of the individual to accept the reform's negative consequences began to become manifest. The fear of negative reform consequences, resulting from declines in living standards, played a marked role. Passive, adaptive strategies prevailed as a segment of the population became characterized by resignation and a loss of perspective.

Congruently, there began to appear signs of socially differentiated political and economic attitudes among the population. A more noticeable support for political and particularly economic transformations began to be linked to higher educational and occupational status, more typically among the somewhat younger generation. Approximately at the same time, the period of extensive social consensus ended, and the interests of various social groups started to become differentiated.

Fundamental changes were begun and radical economic reform started by the beginning of 1991. The liberalization of prices was felt most strongly in the lives of the people, bringing price increases of nearly 50% within a four-month period. The first third of 1991 brought appreciable declines in the standard of living as well (falling by approximately one quarter in 1991, with the most extensive drop occurring in the first third of the year); for the first time in many years, unemployment was present in Czechoslovakia on a relatively wide scale.

These changes were soon reflected in the attitudes of the population. Support for radical economic reform, trust in politics as a proper form of management of public affairs, trust in the effectiveness of parliamentary democracy, and trust in the credibility and sincerity of politicians and their ability to solve the society's prominent problems—mostly economic—declined slowly but steadily from the beginning of 1991 to the election in 1992.

Two main political forces that won the election in 1990—Civic Forum in the Czech republic and Public Against Violence in the Slovak republic—found themselves disintegrating in 1991. The majority of the public were unable to find an institution within the new political system with which they felt comfortable placing their trust, one that satisfactorily represented and protected their interests. Most began to realize that the anticipated social changes would be more painful and longer in coming than they had previously expected.

Uncertainty and anxiety, as well as feelings of precariousness and loss of perspective, notably increased. In conjunction with this, the latent tendency to support authoritarian structures led to an increase in authoritarian leaders with a preference for unmodified, "direct" rather than parliamentary democracy. Nevertheless, the stabilization of support in favor of economic reform was a positive phenomenon.

The principal components of the pervasive public attitudes prior to the spring 1992 electoral campaigns took several shapes. Dominating the public's attention were the issue of economic reform and the worries and difficulties of everyday life, as well as the social decline resulting from the increase of unemployment and the loss of social certainty. Another prominent issue was the question posed by relations between the national republics and the problems arising over state legislation.

Support for post-November 1989 progress was manifested on three levels: attitudes toward economic reform, attitudes toward political reform, and preference of the current system over the previous one. Relatively speaking, economic reform receives the least support, although considerable advocacy may be found among a third of the population, while half of the population favors political reform in general. When asked to choose between the former communist system and the present system, with all of the problems and difficulties it has brought to the people, more than 70% voted in favor of the latter.

The second half of 1991, meanwhile, also brought the beginning of progress, which accelerated markedly through the first half of 1992. Overall, attitudes started to simplify, becoming more polarized and radical. Factor analysis distinctly identified a basic, differentiating axis for public attitudes, an axis that may be simply defined as "for" and "against" the situation following the November 1989 turnover. What this implies is that all three previously named levels—support for economic progress, support for political progress, and the choice between the former and the present system—are closely connected. The correlation between public support of economic and political progress increased from 0.42 (at the end of 1990) to an extremely high value of 0.68.

Attitudes toward economic reform are by far the most important, even determining, factor to take into account in an analysis of public opinion. The results of multivariate analysis show that the variance explained by economic attitudes is three times higher than that explained by any other bloc of attitudes. In addition, the crystallization of public attitudes halted—the association of attitudes with demographic and social variables stabilized and in the end started to weaken.

In contrast, emotional and irrational issues more noticeably began to surface as determining factors of opinion formation. On certain issues, at least half the public is characterized by rather inconsistent attitudes. The share of individuals possessing inconsistent opinions is even higher with regard to several controversial problems that have yet to be given even a temporary solution, such as the issue of a settlement with the communist past. In full, this attitude inconsistency relates to nationalistic points of view as well.

One of the most marked features of the situation in Czechoslovakia was and still is the large variance between attitudes within the Czech and Slovak public. For most fundamental dispositions, as well as for satisfaction with economic reform, support for political progress, trust in political institutions and their representatives, and so on, the differences range between 20% and 25%. The Slovak public varies from the Czech public in its more resounding refusal of economic reform, substantially lower support for political progress, and a greater feeling of nostalgia following the loss of many social certainties. The Slovak population desires more of a state role in the economy and social welfare, and is less willing to take responsibility for its own success and existence.

We will now leave the unreliably identified causes of the

striking differences between the republics and focus our attention on the 1992 election, its outcomes, and its main issues, which involve the main points of this discussion, namely, nationalism and democracy.

For both republics, the elections dealt primarily with economic reform and the continuity of the country's transformation. In the Czech republic, of course, a substantial majority favored a continuation along the present course of social progress. Conversely, in the Slovak republic, the majority markedly voted for those political parties and politicians promising to realize basic changes and modifications to the current development, placing particular emphasis on economic reform and the current ordering of relations between the national republics. The election in the Czech republic was, above all, about a fundamental choice between the past and present systems. The unambiguous rejection of the previous system and the fear of a return of the recently abandoned structure were taken into account by the voters in their decisions. In Slovakia, the election was distilled down to the choice of an alternative future development that would bring, sooner than expected, prosperity secured by a market system yet latticed with the economic and especially social advantages afforded the people within the old system.

The differentiation of attitudes between the Czech and Slovak republics, as well as the election results, allows for a basic understanding of the issues surrounding the problem of nationalism in Czechoslovakia.

■ Nationalistic Attitudes and Their Link to Political and Socioeconomic Views

The communist totalitarian system was recognized not only for the creation of centralization, but also for a basic ideology founded in the erosion of all social, demographic, and nationalistic differences. The opportunity for people to form their own interests and make their own decisions within their lives was removed. The application of this form of power and suppression resulted in the legalization of a socially homogenizing system and a centralized decision-making process, which left lasting consequences. The majority of people lost their "old" identities and were prevailed upon to painfully search for new ones. The sudden disappearance of these restrictions on political, economic, and cultural activity and the flow of information brought, for many people, disorientation and a loss of "old" certitudes, dramatically increasing anxiety and uncertainty and creating a vague "lost feeling." One feature of postcommunist Czechoslovakia has been a marked intolerance towards different attitudes, groups, and individuals distinguished from the rest by social or national demographics.

While engaged in the process of seeking a new identity, many people took recourse in "substitutes" that were easiest and closest at hand: they searched, in other words, for the enemy, the culprit responsible for the present difficulties. In this process, in this search for an identity, the nation becomes an easily procurable and reliable source at two fundamental levels: one's own nation is the foundation for the formation of a new identity, while another nation may easily be branded as the enemy and scapegoat for the people's difficulties.

If we examine the forms of nationalism in Czechoslovakia more closely, we can distinguish different levels. On the surface, relations between Czechs and Slovaks are relatively good—they do not feel strong intolerance, hatred, or animosity towards each other. The majority of Czech and Slovak people consider the two nations to have no reason for quarrels. There is still no strong ethnic grudge in the present Czechoslovakia that could grow and culminate in a situation of conflict.

Exploring the other levels is not so encouraging. The key dimension of the dispute is the problem of economic inequality in the republics. Coincidentally, the same opinion dominates in both republics that the common life of the republics is unprofitable—of course, those in the Czech republic think that the Czech republic pays for Slovakia (55%), and people in Slovakia consider the Czech republic to be at an advantage in the current system (73%).

The tight centralization of the past has led to strong opposition to it. It is no wonder that people in Slovakia gravitate toward the explanation that the root of all economic problems and difficulties is central economic reform. If we add to this the fact that the social disadvantages of economic reform are, in the Slovak republic, strikingly large, and that in the Czech republic the majority of the population is in favor of continuing fundamental economic transformation while the majority in Slovakia is in favor of fundamental modification of that transformation, we will necessarily come to the conclusion that there is great tension due to inequality in economic position and "unfair" economic distribution in Czechoslovakia.

If we, of course, look at the correlation between these attitudes, we find that empirical data support the hypothesis about their connection with general intolerance, the attempt to find personal identity in the nation, and the attempt to find the enemy in another ethnic group, but also with the general rejection of transformation in the postcommunist era. Among those inhabitants of the Slovak republic who consider the Czech republic to have the advantage in the present system, 66% disagree that Hungarians living in Czechoslovakia should have the same right to use their own language as Czechs and Slovaks, while among others it is 46%. More specifically, 63% of supporters of the opinion that the current system favors the Czech republic (in contrast to 43% among the others) believe that Jews have too much influence on political life in Czechoslovakia, 16% (as opposed to 38% of the others) are satisfied with the political progress, and 42% (as opposed to 58% of the others) support a market economy.

A natural consequence of the feeling of economic injustice is a tendency toward separatism. Among the inhabitants of the Slovak republic who believe the present system favors the Czech republic, 37% support separation, while only 14% of the others share that opinion.

The feelings of economic inequality between the republics can, of course, also be identified in other areas, though with less intensity. And so the question of the actual position of each of the two nations in the one state regarding equal rights has become one of the most important and sensitive issues. Both nations, but more strongly the Slovaks, share the opinion that the current form of common life is unequal and unfair and does not allow for the full progress of the nation.

On the Slovak side, there is an extremely extensive feeling of oppression by the Czech republic, a feeling that the Czechs do not allow the Slovaks to occupy an equal position in the common state. More than two-thirds of Slovaks feel that Slovakia is patronized as if it were an immature nation. The fact that only 9% of the population of the Czech republic shares this opinion is significant—there is no perception of the Slovak attitude on the Czech side, despite the fact that it has a concrete foundation in history and reflects real relations between the Czech and Slovak republics.

The Czech side is characterized by a certain feeling of superiority toward the Slovak side. Almost one-half of Czechs think that the Slovaks owe them much. The fact that Slovakia was in the past less developed and, unlike the industrialized Czech lands, was mostly agricultural country, along with the process of extensive industrialization and increase in the standard of living that has been realized through extensive redistribution to the benefit of Slovakia, has led the Czechs to think of Slovakia as "property." It is not surprising that the Slovak public is extremely sensitive to these Czech attitudes.

The Slovaks, in turn, tend to look for an enemy in the federation, in the Czech republic, and in economic reform, which is exported by the Czech lands into Slovakia, and which subjects Slovakia to further negative influence. Their struggle for emancipation, equality in the absolute sense, and a perfectly equal position in the context of the common state is predominant and does not take into account that many of the problems do not stem from an unequal status between the republics, but from a still underdeveloped social system marked by former centralism. This means that with a successful transformation to a system that will build a democratic civic society and market economy, many debates over which authority and competence should be on a federal or republican level will become unreasonable—the state will loosen this authority by devolving it onto lower levels—regional, municipal, or private. On the Czech side, there is a very widespread lack of understanding of the Slovak efforts to achieve equal status.

The nationalistic tensions that find recourse in separatism are still in the minority in Czechoslovakia. In April 1992, 16% were in favor of separation in the Czech republic and 30% in the Slovak republic. Nevertheless, a significant increase in separatism could be noted in the first half of 1992, and the analyses cannot deny its further increase.

Separatism is a part of a wider spectrum of attitudes of racial and ethnic intolerance, ethnocentrism, and xenophobia, which are relatively widespread in Czechoslovakia. This is illustrated in the connection of separatism with the classical, historically well-known image about Jews and the conspiracy of foreign capital, which remains in the background and has a powerful influence. It is naturally one of many variants of the search for an enemy and offender to blame for current difficulties. Among those who are in favor of the separation of Czechoslovakia into two independent states, 21% in the Czech republic and 80% in Slovakia think that Jews have too much influence on political or economic life in Czechoslovakia.

Separatist tendencies in Slovakia are tied as well to a rejection of the basic principles of all post-November 1989 development. In the Czech republic, these tendencies are on the contrary associated with impatience and with desire for faster and more radical changes. However, it is evident that the relation of separatism to other public attitudes toward the principal components of social development is generally rather weak. Regression analysis, in which separatism stands as a dependent variable with independent variables being attitudes toward political, economic, and social development, support of authoritarian trends, radicalism in solving the problems of the communist past, and also indicators of racial and ethnic intolerance, fears about the influence of foreign capital, and so on, explains only 5% of the variance of the dependent variable.

By contrast, if attitudes toward equality in the rank of nations or republics, and namely attitudes toward economic correlations of the separation of Czechoslovakia, enter as independent variables in the regression analysis, regression analysis explains 35% in the Czech republic and even 52% of the variance of the dependent variable in the Slovak republic.

It is evident that by far the strongest rein on separatism is the fear of the economic consequences in the event of separation. Of the Czech population, 82% are convinced that separation of the state would bring great economic difficulties to both republics, while in Slovakia 78% of the respondents share this opinion. Among those who are afraid of economic difficulties, 12% in the Czech republic and 20% in Slovakia express the wish to be separated. In contrast, 40% of Czechs and 59% of Slovaks who do not fear the economic consequences are in favor of separation.

The conviction of economic inequality between the two republics is one factor for separation. But the strongest factor in support of separation is the belief that the event of separation will enable one's respective republic to overcome its economic difficulties more quickly. If the majority of people, whether in the Czech or the Slovak republic, would form the opinion that separation would bring the consequence of economic prosperity, then the majority would prefer separation.

■ Nationalism and Democracy

The results of the 1992 election in Czechoslovakia have complicated the situation a great deal. In the Czech republic a majority was gained by political parties advocating continued radical economic reform and refusing arrangements of the common state that would hinder their reform plans. In Slovakia the clear victors were the parties that advocated fundamental changes not only in economic reform but also in the federative arrangement—the confederative principle is the most strongly advocated. That form of government is rejected by the victorious Czech political parties, which call for a sound or functional federation or else two independent states.

The entire situation is complicated by the reality that most of the public is not oriented toward the problem of determining the basic necessary attributes of the common state. The majority of the Slovak population rejects the current state of the federation and prefers the form that allows Slovakia full economic independence through essential changes in economic reform, but at the same time preserves the common state. On the other hand, the Czech public generally prefers the current form of the common state and the furthering of economic reform without fundamental changes to that state.

Now that the elections are over, the different attitudes toward economic reform and the strong nationalistic and dividing tendencies therein have become the greatest burden to the common state and one of the greatest obstacles to its preservation. In addition to this problem, parties of the left have a majority in the federal Parliament, and the image of a left federal government and its political course seems to be extremely hard to accept for a majority of the Czech population. Signals that the dominant Slovak powers will not behave in accordance with the principles of democracy are creating a striking increase in rejection of the Slovak leftist course by the Czech side. On the Czech side there is a growing feeling that further coexistence with Slovakia will jeopardize all the changes since November 1989. In turn, the Slovak side is characterized by the feeling that its political voice, though constituting the majority voice regarding the principal change of economic course in the elections, is becoming increasingly endangered by alliance with the Czech republic, and it believes that further alliance will tend not to lead to desirable change.

There is no doubt that the nationalistic and divisive trends are rooted in undemocratic public attitudes. If the public is concentrated on enemies or offenders, it can easily develop undemocratic attitudes toward racial and ethnic minorities, or if it is not willing to accept the results of the recent elections, fundamental changes in economic development could occur that would be refused by most of the Czech population. It is evident that the current stalemate does not enhance the development of democracy in Czechoslovakia.

There seems to be a great inability on both sides to accept different attitudes and opinions. This intolerance heightens the nationalistic and separatist tendencies. For most of the people in Czechoslovakia, plurality and democracy are unusual and unpleasant when they get to the situation in which their conceptions of further development are not realized in the elections and they have to live in a state where the government has different notions than they. The course of this situation, in many ways a stalemate, which arose in Czechoslovakia through the rise of different powers in the Czech and Slovak republics and which does not allow for the federal government to be built from the victorious majority of both republics, will lead to a basic reexamination of democracy. Not one of the parties evidently intends to retreat from its own convictions, and there is a great likelihood that they will vote for the state's separation rather than search for another solution. Preserving the democratic character of future development in Czechoslovakia will clash with nationalistic and separatist tendencies for a long time if the common state is maintained.

In the case of Czechoslovak disintegration, it will be very hard to avoid an increase of nationalistic tension and passions. If there are today different views on economic development connected with nationalistic and separatist tendencies that will end up distributing the federation in such a way that both parties feel they are being robbed by the other party, there will be an increase in mutual accusations and tensions between the two nations. It seems that the primary responsibility for ensuring the civilized and democratic character of the separation of the common state and further development in both republics is in the hands of the leading political powers in both national republics.

ABOUT THE AUTHORS

Władysław Adamski is a professor at the Institute of Philosophy and Sociology of the Polish Academy of Sciences in Warsaw. He specializes in structural dynamics, generational relations, and industrial conflicts in state socialist and postcommunist societies. His most recent publications include *Societal Conflicts and System Change: The Case of Poland, 1980-1990* (forthcoming); *Challenges to Pluralism in Eastern Europe*, vol. 7 of *Sisyphus:Sociological Studies* (1991) (co-editor); and *Interests and Conflicts: The Dynamics of Social Structure in Poland* (1990).

Marek Boguszak is the Managing Director of the Association for Independent Social Analysis (AISA), a private market research and opinion polling firm in Prague. Previously he was at the Institute of Philosophy and Sociology, where he conducted research on social stratification and mobility. The results of his surveys and public opinion polls are published regularly in the media.

Tamas L. Fellegi is a Wallis Postdoctoral Fellow in Political Economy at the Department of Political Science in the University of Rochester, in Rochester, New York.

Germaine A. Hoston is professor of political science at the University of California, San Diego. Previously she taught at Johns Hopkins University. Her recent publications include *The State, Identity, and the National Question* (forthcoming); and *Marxism and the Crisis of Development in Prewar Japan* (1986). Prof. Hoston is currently studying the nurturance of civil society and the quest for democratization in China and Japan.

Krzysztof Jasiewicz directs electoral studies at the Institute of Political Studies of the Polish Academy of Sciences in Warsaw. In the 1980s he was the co-author of a series of political attitude surveys, starting with *Polacy '80* (The Poles of 1980). He is currently a visiting professor of sociology at Washington and Lee University in Lexington, Virginia.

Terry Lynn Karl is the Director of the Center for Latin American Studies, associate professor of political science, and Senior Fellow at the Institute for International Studies at Stanford University. Her most recent works include *The Paradox of Plenty: Oil Booms and Petro-States* (1992) and "Negotiating Revolution in El Salvador," *Foreign Affairs* (Spring 1992).

Philippe C. Schmitter is professor of political science and Director of the Center for European Studies at Stanford University. Previously he taught at the European University Institute in Florence and the University of Chicago. He is the co-author of *The Organization of Business Interests* (forthcoming); and *Transitions from Authoritarian Rule: Prospects for Democracy*, 4 vols. (1986).

George Schöpflin is Lecturer in East European politics at the London School of Economics and Political Science.

Rudolf L. Tőkés is professor of political science at the University of Connecticut, Storrs.

Peter M.E. Volten is Senior Vice President of the Institute for EastWest Studies. Previously he was professor of the history of war at the University of Utrecht and Director of Studies and Strategic Planning at the Ministry of Defense of the Netherlands. He is the editor of *Uncertain Futures: Eastern Europe and Democracy* (1990) and co-editor of *The Guns Fall Silent: The End of the Cold War and the Future of Conventional Disarmament* (1990).